The Other Side of Despair

Previous Books by Daniel Gavron

Nonfiction
Israel after Begin: Israel's Options in the Aftermath of the Lebanon War
The Kibbutz: Awakening from Utopia
Peace Pays (with Samir Huleileh and Simcha Bahiri)
Saul Adler, Pioneer of Tropical Medicine: A Biography
Walking through Israel

Fiction
The End of Days
Pilgrims'

The Other Side of Despair

Jews and Arabs in the Promised Land

D ANIEL G AVRON

ROWMAN & LITTLEFIELD PUBLISHERS, INC.
Lanham • *Boulder* • *New York* • *Toronto* • *Oxford*

ROWMAN & LITTLEFIELD PUBLISHERS, INC.

Published in the United States of America
by Rowman & Littlefield Publishers, Inc.
A wholly owned subsidiary of The Rowman & Littlefield Publishing Group, Inc.
4501 Forbes Boulevard, Suite 200, Lanham, MD 20706
www.rowmanlittlefield.com

P.O. Box 317, Oxford OX2 9RU, UK

British Library Cataloguing in Publication Information Available

Library of Congress Cataloging-in-Publication Data

Gavron, Daniel.
  The other side of despair : Jews and Arabs in the promised land /
Daniel Gavron.
     p. cm.
Includes bibliographical references and index.
  ISBN 0-7425-1751-9 (cloth : alk. paper) — ISBN 0-7425-1752-7 (pbk. : alk. paper)
1. Arab-Israeli conflict. 2. Jewish-Arab relations—History—1917–1948. I. Title.

DS119.7 .G3825 2004
956.9405—dc21
                                                                2003011858

Printed in the United States of America

♾™ The paper used in this publication meets the minimum requirements of American
National Standard for Information Sciences—Permanence of Paper for Printed Library
Materials, ANSI/NISO Z39.48-1992.

To the memory of Howard Fast,
valiant fighter for human freedom and dignity

You are never stronger, thought Samad as he approached the Doctor, than when you land on the other side of despair.

—Zadie Smith, in *White Teeth*

CONTENTS

CHRONOLOGY

1000 B.C.E. (approx.)	An Israelite entity emerges in the hills of Canaan. King David conquers Jerusalem and makes it the Israelite capital. Solomon, his successor, starts construction of the First Temple.
586	Destruction of the First Temple by Babylonians. Many Jews exiled.
538	Jews return to Judaea. Construction of the Second Temple started.
76 C.E.	Destruction of the Second Temple by the Romans. Start of Jewish diaspora (dispersion; also called *galut*, or exile).
630	Muhammad, the founder of Islam, conquers Mecca.
638	Muslims conquer Jerusalem.
1099	Crusaders conquer Jerusalem.
1187	Muslims recapture Jerusalem.
1516	Palestine becomes a province of the (Turkish) Ottoman Empire.
1868	Ottoman land ordinances change, enabling foreigners to buy land in Palestine. Britain, France, Russia, Germany, and the United States build new churches and monasteries.
1881	Wide-scale pogroms (organized violence) against two hundred Jewish communities in Russia.
1882	Start of modern organized Jewish immigration to Palestine.
1896	Theodor Herzl publishes *The Jewish State*.
1897	First Zionist Congress. Establishment of Zionist Organization.

1909	Formation of Hashomer, a unit of Jewish guards for Jewish villages in Palestine.
1914	Outbreak of World War I.
1917	British army invades Palestine and takes Jerusalem. Britain issues Balfour Declaration.
1918	End of World War I.
1920	First serious attacks against Jews by Arabs of Palestine. Establishment of Hagana, the Jewish defense organization (incorporating Hashomer).
1921	Britain awarded League of Nations Mandate for Palestine. Haj Amin Husseini appointed mufti of Jerusalem.
1929	Wide-scale Arab attacks on Jewish settlements throughout Palestine.
1933	Adolf Hitler becomes chancellor of Germany. First concentration camps established. Surge in Jewish immigration to Palestine.
1936	Arab general strike in Palestine, leading to a major military revolt against the British Mandate administration and the Zionist enterprise.
1937	British Peel Commission recommends partition of Palestine between Jews and Arabs.
1939	Outbreak of World War II. Escalation of Nazi persecution of Jews in Europe. British white paper limits Jewish immigration to Palestine. Jews start to organize "illegal" immigration.
1942	Wannsee Conference discusses "Final Solution" of the Jewish problem.
1945	End of World War II. Dimensions of Holocaust become generally known.
1947	United Nations votes to partition Palestine. Clashes between Jews and Arabs in Palestine escalate.
1948	British Mandate ends. State of Israel declared. Attempted invasion of Palestine by the armies of five Arab states.

1949	Israel and several Arab states sign armistice accords.

1949   Israel and several Arab states sign armistice accords.
         Transjordan takes over the West Bank and becomes King
             dom of Jordan.
         Egypt administers Gaza strip.
         Palestinian state, envisaged by the UN partition plan, is
             stillborn.

1956   A series of Palestinian terrorist infiltrations and Israeli
             counterstrikes escalates into the Sinai Campaign.
         Israel captures Sinai from Egypt but is forced to withdraw.

1959   The Fatah paramilitary force is established by Yasser Arafat
             in Kuwait.

1964   The Palestine Liberation Organization (PLO) is set up un-
             der Egyptian patronage, with the declared aim of liberat-
             ing Palestine from the Jews.

1967   Six-Day War; Israel takes West Bank, Gaza, Golan
             Heights, and Sinai. Sets up a military administration in
             these territories.
         Reestablishment of Kfar Etzion, south of Bethlehem, a
             village the Jews lost in 1948.

1968   The Fatah and other militant groups take over the PLO.
         PLO units launch attacks against Israeli targets but are
             forced to regroup in Jordan.
         Israel establishes "security settlements" in Sinai, Jordan Val-
             ley, and Golan Heights.
         An unauthorized Israeli group settles in Hebron.

1970   "Black September." PLO forced out of Jordan; sets up bases
             in South Lebanon.

1973   Yom Kippur War launched by Egypt and Syria.
         After initial defeats, the Israel Defense Forces (IDF) ad-
             vance into Egyptian and Syrian territory.
         United States helps negotiate cease-fires on both fronts.

1974   PLO officially recognized as representing the Palestinians
             by an Arab summit.
         Arafat addresses the UN General Assembly.
         Gush Emunim movement for Jewish settlement in the
             West Bank and Gaza established.

1975	After initial opposition, Israeli government approves first Jewish settlements in northern part of West Bank.
1977	Right-wing Likud Party elected in Israel. Egypt's president Anwar Sadat visits Jerusalem.
	Jewish settlement in the West Bank and Gaza stepped up.
1978	Decisive Israeli–Egyptian negotiations at Camp David.
1979	Israel–Egypt peace treaty signed.
1982	Israel completes withdrawal from Sinai but continues to occupy the Gaza strip, the West Bank, and the Golan Heights.
	IDF invades Lebanon, reaching Beirut.
1985	Israel withdraws from most of Lebanon, retaining a security zone in the south.
	Members of the "Jewish underground" (extremist settlers) are tried and imprisoned.
1987	Palestinians in the West Bank and Gaza launch the Intifada, an uprising against the Israeli occupation.
1991	First Gulf War: Iraq expelled from Kuwait. Large-scale deportation of Palestinians from Kuwait.
	United States convenes Madrid Conference on Middle East Peace.
	PLO officially excluded but de facto approves the Palestinian delegation.
1992	Israeli Labor Party wins election. Yitzhak Rabin becomes prime minister.
	Unofficial channel opened between Israel and the PLO.
1993	Israel and the PLO recognize each other and sign Oslo Accords.
1994	Israel–Jordan peace treaty signed.
	Israel withdraws from Gaza and Jericho.
	Yasser Arafat returns to Gaza. Palestinian Authority established.
1995	Israel withdraws from all major West Bank towns, which are taken over by the Palestinian Authority.
	Yitzhak Rabin assassinated. Further Israeli withdrawals halted.
1996	Benjamin Netanyahu of the Likud elected prime minister of Israel.

Israel withdraws from Hebron, but Jewish settlement in the territories stepped up.

1999   Labor's Ehud Barak wins election as prime minister of Israel, pledges to continue Rabin's path; embarks on ambitious schedule of talks with Syria and the Palestinians.

2000   Breakdown of crucial Israeli–Palestinian talks at Camp David.

A second Intifada meets with a harsh Israeli response.

Both sides fail to control the escalating violence.

2001   Ariel Sharon elected prime minister of Israel.

Forms National Unity Government with Labor Party.

Reacts with extreme force to Intifada. Declares that Yasser Arafat is "irrelevant."

Palestinians escalate violence, notably suicide bombings.

Unprecedented casualties on both sides.

2002   IDF reoccupies almost all the West Bank and much of Gaza.

Yasser Arafat restricted to his Ramalla government offices.

Palestinian Authority effectively abolished.

Extreme poverty in Palestinian territories. Economic difficulties in Israel.

2003   Sharon's Likud Party wins new Israeli election.

Labor and Left in Israel sharply reduced.

Extreme right-wing Israeli government formed.

United States and Britain gain swift victory in second Gulf War.

Palestinian Authority elects Mahmoud Abbas as prime minister.

United States, United Nations, European Union, and Russia present Israelis and Palestinians with "road map" for Middle East peace.

President George W. Bush convenes separate summit meetings with Arab leaders and with the Israeli and Palestinian prime ministers.

Prime Minister Abbas declares an end to "armed Intifada."

Prime Minister Sharon pledges to remove "unauthorized outposts."

Palestinian terror attacks and Israeli retaliations continue and even intensify.

INTRODUCTION

A Superfluous Confrontation

Every new development in the Middle East prompts a sickening feeling of déjà vu. No sooner had President George W. Bush banged Israeli and Palestinian heads together in June 2003, eliciting positive pledges from both sides, than the violence exploded with a new fury. It is unlikely that anyone was surprised. We have become familiar with the disappointment, accustomed to the "cycle of violence," used to the despair. The very phrases have become tired clichés, illustrating a situation of hopelessness. Israeli–Palestinian violence is like a volcano, sometimes relatively dormant, often erupting with sudden frenzy.

Is the Bush "road map" different? Does it represent a chance for a real breakthrough, or is it destined to go the way of so many other initiatives, processes, plans, and schemes of the past three years?

Following the past thirty-six months of almost continuous killings, it is almost impossible to remember that 2000 was the most encouraging year in the region since the heady days of the Israel–Egypt peace accord two decades earlier. Israelis and Palestinians were poised to terminate a century of conflict between them, effectively concluding the regional confrontation. Seven years after the historic Oslo agreement, the peace process was behind schedule but still appeared to be on track. Israel had withdrawn from Gaza and from much of the West Bank. A Palestinian Authority had been established. The Israeli economy was flourishing as never before; the Palestinian economy was starting to take off; the stage was set for an era of peace and prosperity such as the region had never known. Despite this, in September 2000, the whole endeavor collapsed in a horrendous explosion of violence. A time of hope was succeeded by a period of mutual recriminations, suspicion, and despair.

1

How on earth did it happen? Palestinians and Israelis are quick to blame each other for the collapse of the process. Each side accuses the other of bad faith and breaking agreements. The Israeli version is that, in the summer of 2000 at Camp David, Prime Minister Ehud Barak offered the Palestinians the best deal any Israeli leader had ever proposed, and he was answered not just with rejection but also with gratuitous violence. The Palestinian Authority had already been established in Gaza and the main population centers of the West Bank, proving Israel's sincerity. Despite this, an armed conflict was deliberately planned and launched by the Palestinian leaders, who had never really sought peace.

The Palestinians counter that Barak's proposal was a blatant attempt to bully them into accepting a truncated and unsustainable Palestinian state. Despite the establishment of the Palestinian Authority, most of the territory was still under Israeli control. In the years following Oslo, the Jewish settlements in the West Bank and Gaza expanded faster than ever before. An oppressive system of closures was introduced that made the Palestinians' lives unbearable, so that the frustration and fury of their people built up until it burst forth spontaneously.

The violence was horrifying and tragic. Above all, it was unnecessary. It was not, as many contend, inevitable. The differences that remained between the two sides were profound, but they do not explain the explosion. The issue of what the Palestinians call the "Right of Return," the demand that Israel admit hundreds of thousands of Palestinian refugees, has been put forward as one of the reasons for the breakdown of the peace process. An alternative theory blames the conflicting claims of the two sides regarding the Holy Sites in Jerusalem. Another intractable problem that remained to be settled was the disagreement over the border between Israel and the prospective Palestinian state. Although all these problems are indeed complicated, none of them is insurmountable, and further progress could have been made toward an arrangement.

The Israeli government and the Palestinian Authority were both aware of the danger of an explosion, but, strangely, neither side took serious steps to head it off. Instead, they blundered into an unnecessary conflict that neither had the wisdom or good sense to control. It brought no benefit to either side and caused enormous harm to both of them. Once it started, the confrontation gathered momentum, escalating in an almost classic progression of violence and counterviolence.

It is generally accepted that the trigger that set off the disorders was the visit of Ariel Sharon (at that time leader of the Israeli opposition) to Temple Mount at the end of September 2000. Insensitive as the visit was, though, it was a pretty feeble excuse for the severity of the Palestinian demonstrations that followed. Sharon did not enter any Muslim shrine, and the demonstrations were rowdy rather than violent. It was not until the following day that there were fatalities. The Palestinian riots were ferocious, but the response of Israel's security forces was clumsy, inept, and exaggerated.

Even after the initial clashes, it was possible to cool down the situation. The Palestinian Authority could have exerted discipline; the Israel Defense Forces (IDF) could have exercised restraint, but both sides manifestly lacked the will. Inside Israel, where there were also riots, thirteen Arabs were killed by police fire. In this instance, although the scars remain, the situation was swiftly calmed. On the Palestinian front, however, the violence was allowed to continue unchecked; no serious action was taken to calm things; the situation on the ground lurched totally out of control.

As the initiators of the violence, the Palestinians must be apportioned much of the blame, although the accusation that they never wanted a settlement with Israel and planned their Intifada uprising in advance does not stand up. Many experts on both sides are agreed that the Intifada was directed as much against the Palestinian Authority as it was against Israel. Furthermore, in the first week of the violence, sixty Palestinians were killed, compared to five Israelis, a proportion that was maintained for several months. Yasser Arafat, the Palestinian leader, may well be cynical enough to sacrifice the lives of his citizens to attract international sympathy to his national cause, but even he would hardly have started an uprising against himself.

Nevertheless, even if they did not plan the uprising, the Palestinians started it. Israeli proposals were on the table, and they failed tragically—as they had done so often in the past—to respond to them adequately. Some accounts now assert that there were Palestinian counterproposals, and even some former Israeli negotiators make this claim, but they were not reported at the time. The Palestinians did nothing to counter the impression that they were rejecting the Israeli suggestions without putting forward alternative proposals of their own.

Blaming Arafat and the Palestinians does not, however, absolve Israel, the stronger side, and the one holding most of the cards, from responsibility. Instead of taking steps to cool the situation on the ground, Israel played a significant part in escalating the clashes. Intelligence officers of the IDF had been maintaining for months that the Palestinians were planning violence, and the events of September 2000 would seem to prove them right. At the same time, it must be said that the behavior of the IDF in reacting to admittedly violent riots with extreme brutality helped to turn its predictions into a self-fulfilling prophecy. The initial months of the Intifada, with their steadily increasing level of violence, were bad enough, but the election of Ariel Sharon as prime minister, at the start of 2001, launched Israel on a policy of aggressive retaliation that escalated the death and destruction to previously unimagined levels. Sharon's accession to power can be seen as a ghastly historical accident, the responsibility for which must be shared by Ehud Barak and Yasser Arafat.

Barak, who had won the Israeli election handsomely in May 1999 as the Labor Party candidate, running on a platform of peace, virtually handed the nation over to Sharon less than two years later. A successful soldier and a man of brilliant intellect, Barak proved singularly inept as a political leader. He offended his colleagues, quarreled with his coalition partners, and rashly staked his future on a make-or-break effort at peace with the Palestinians. When this failed, he blundered into an election, which he lost humiliatingly. Yet, while Barak must take a large share of the blame, Yasser Arafat made his own unique contribution to the election of Ariel Sharon. A majority of Israelis believed that Barak had made a fair offer at Camp David—many thought he had been far too generous—and Arafat's failure to respond was deeply resented. In addition to this, Arafat cannot escape responsibility for the Palestinian rioting. He may not have given direct orders for the outbreak of violence, but he showed no manifest desire to calm the situation. The resulting turnaround in Israeli public opinion was swift and extreme.

Demonized in the Israeli media for decades, Arafat had become more acceptable to Israelis in the post-Oslo years, but it was a conditional acceptance. Following Camp David and the subsequent Palestinian uprising, most Israelis lost their belief in the good intentions of the Palestinian leader. A significant majority thought that Barak had blundered and concluded that the aggressive Ariel Sharon was just the man to deal with

Yasser Arafat. Consequently, Sharon won the direct election for prime minister by an unprecedented margin.

Sharon's longtime belief in the use of force was a matter of record. It had started, when, as a junior IDF officer in Israel's first years as a state in the 1950s, he led a series of savage reprisal raids against Jordan and Egypt. It culminated when, as minister of defense, he launched the Lebanon War in 1982. Sharon was eventually blamed for that disastrous adventure, which was to cost the lives of more than six hundred Israeli soldiers, and forced to resign in disgrace. However, with incredible stamina and guile, he had worked his passage back, until he became the leader of the right-wing Likud. In the eighth decade of his life, Sharon was all set to serve out a few years as leader of the opposition, before retiring to his farm in the Negev desert. In the event, he fulfilled his lifelong ambition to become prime minister of Israel.

It must be admitted that Sharon learned the lessons from his Lebanese experience very well indeed, although it can be argued that he learned the wrong lessons. He didn't learn that it is dangerous to go to war. He didn't learn it is counterproductive to use exaggerated force. He didn't learn it is inadvisable to be careless of casualties. What he learned was how to get away with all of these actions. He neutralized the opposition Labor Party, which had eventually opposed his Lebanon adventure, by forming a National Unity Government. He proceeded slowly, step-by-step, only gradually escalating the violence. He was notably helped by Barak, who, time and again, reiterated his version of what happened at Camp David and afterward. Thus, most Israelis, blaming the Palestinians for the situation, approved of Sharon's policy of force and more force.

Sharon also had his share of luck. The election of George W. Bush to be president of the United States, followed by the shocking terrorist attack on American targets on September 11, 2001, created a situation in which Sharon had a freer hand than any Israeli leader before him. At any other time, a U.S. administration would have protested his extreme actions, and exerted effective pressure on him to tone them down. Traumatized by 9/11, the Bush administration has found it difficult even to criticize—far less take measures against—Sharon's proclaimed antiterror campaign. What is more, Arafat's mixture of impotence and venality has helped Sharon every step of the way. It wasn't just that he missed his opportunities with Israel. The Palestinian leader also failed to win the confidence of any of the American officials who met with him. He totally lost the trust of President Bush. As a result, the violence and counterviolence proceeded almost unchecked.

Following a particularly violent Palestinian suicide bombing in the spring of 2002, the IDF moved into most of the area that Israel had ceded to the Palestinians. The forces were subsequently withdrawn, only to move back in permanently a few weeks later. Only the Gaza strip remained partly in Palestinian hands. With Yasser Arafat besieged in the Mukkata, his government offices in Ramalla, Israeli control was almost total: towns and villages were blocked off from Israel and from one another; IDF patrols moved freely throughout the territory. The Palestinian Authority managed to deliver some basic services but effectively ceased to exist. There was a daily loss of Palestinian lives, as Israeli troops continued with their search and destroy operations. The rate of attrition on the Israeli side was for a time somewhat reduced, but every now and then a suicide bombing restored the balance of blood, which remained approximately three Palestinians for every Israeli killed.

The lack of respect for life by both Palestinians and Israelis was horrifying. The Palestinian suicide bombings are by their very nature indiscriminate. The helpless and the disabled are particularly vulnerable. The bombs kill babies, the aged, and the infirm, along with vibrant teenagers. They rip into human flesh, splinter bones, and splatter brain tissue over a wide area. They disable people for life and cause horrible disfigurement. Apologists for the Palestinians term them "weapons of the weak," or "tools for resisting oppression," but they have been rightly described by organizations such as Amnesty International and Human Rights Watch as "war crimes."

Many Israelis argue that the "collateral damage" caused by the IDF is morally less repugnant than the deliberate indiscriminate slaughter of the bombers. Israeli soldiers, they maintain, do not set out deliberately to kill innocent civilians. For the most part this is true, but, in the face of the statistics, it has to be admitted that the fingers of the Israeli soldiers have been appallingly light on the trigger.

The escalation has been quite simply incredible. In the two and a half years following September 2000, more than seven hundred Israelis lost their lives to suicide bombs and other terrorist strikes. Such an intensity of terror attacks has never occurred in the five decades of Israel's existence.

On the Palestinian side, in the same period, over two thousand were killed in Israeli military actions. Among those killed by Israeli forces were hundreds of children. Palestinian sources put the number at over four hundred; Israeli estimates are considerably lower, but the IDF officially announced that 365 of the Palestinian civilians killed by its troops had "no connection with terrorist activity." To this must be added two international peace activists and two Israeli security guards, who could in no way be described as "terrorists." Some two hundred schools were damaged by Israeli bombing, shelling, and gunfire.

Thousands of Israelis and Palestinians were wounded, hundreds of them horribly disfigured or disabled for life. Some ten thousand Palestinians have been imprisoned; millions have lived for months under closure and curfew. In addition to the large-scale demolition of buildings, there has been deliberate despoiling of farmland.

As we have seen, most Israelis supported the military action and were indifferent to the civilian casualties, including women, children, and old people, because they blamed the Palestinians for initiating the violence. For their part, a majority of Palestinians applauded the suicide bombings, which kill the innocent indiscriminately, as it seemed to them the only way to hurt the Israelis. Despite the hardship on both sides, Sharon and Arafat continued to command wide support in their communities.

The question of cause and effect is debatable. Israeli security experts argue that a forceful military response to the Palestinian suicide bombings and other terror strikes has proved itself. Had the IDF not pursued such a policy, they assert, there would have been many more such attacks. It is, of course, impossible to prove this either way. What is indisputable is that each Palestinian attack has been followed by Israeli retaliation—and vice versa. The policy of hitting back hard has been pursued ruthlessly and has resulted in unprecedented levels of casualties on both sides. It is difficult to believe that a policy of restraint would have resulted in more Israeli casualties.

In the Palestinian areas, deprivation has been almost universal. According to a report issued by the World Bank in March 2003, while there was no actual starvation, malnutrition had become a real problem. More than 60 percent were living below the line of poverty of US $2 per day. Before the violence erupted, there were some six hundred thousand poor

Palestinians; two and a half years later the number had increased to two million. The report paid tribute to the resilience of Palestinian society and the level of mutual help among the Palestinians. Despite its virtual destruction, the Palestinian Authority continued to deliver many basic services. Outside donations helped to prevent total collapse.

Although the Palestinians have suffered far more than the Israelis, both sides have been harmed. There has been enormous damage to the Israeli economy; the Palestinian economy has been all but destroyed; the continuous disruption of both societies has resulted in irreparable harm to both national psyches.

The collapse of Sharon's coalition toward the end of 2002 initially changed the situation for the worse. Traumatized by the cycle of violence, the Israeli public lurched even further to the right. The system of direct elections for prime minister—which had elected in turn Benjamin Netanyahu, Ehud Barak, and Ariel Sharon—was repealed, and the former system of proportional representation was reestablished. Sharon's Likud Party emerged as by far the largest in the new Knesset (Israel's parliament). Other right-wing parties also gained in strength, as did the center. The Labor Party, under a new moderate leader, was thrashed, and the dovish Meretz Party lost half its strength. The current Israeli government is the most right-wing the nation has ever had.

Nevertheless, there were some positive developments: Under enormous pressure from the United States and Europe, the Palestinian Authority started to reform itself. Arafat, under siege for many months, managed to hang on, but his power was eroded with the appointment of a new finance minister and the election of a prime minister, Mahmoud Abbas, popularly known as Abu-Mazen.

Even more significant, the president of the United States once again became directly involved. Following the swift American victory in Iraq, Bush moved decisively to bring the Israeli and Palestinian prime ministers together and also convened important Arab leaders to guarantee their support.

For a few hours he managed to calm the volcano, but only for a few hours. The next eruption was not long in coming and, if the immediate violence was upsetting, the long-term outlook was even more discouraging. The conflict of the past three years has not moderated opinions—quite the reverse. In 2003, the positions of the two sides were much farther apart than they were at Camp David three years before. It was clear that an awful lot of work remained to be done.

It is not the purpose of this book to chronicle the horrors of the recent period in Israel and the Palestinian territories. These have been dramatically projected on our television screens and graphically described in our newspapers and on our websites. My aim is to explain the background to the conflict by putting these recent events in perspective. This brief introduction sets the scene for the following chapters, in which a historical review of the main events of the past century is succeeded by profiles of sixteen Israelis and Palestinians. These portraits are intended to flesh out the narrative and give it a human dimension. The personalities chosen do not include top leaders of either people, but neither are they simply man-in-the-street figures. They compromise a mixture of people, involved to a greater or lesser extent in their national sagas. Each of them illustrates a different aspect of the story.

In the final chapters, possible ways ahead for both peoples are examined. It must be stressed that the views expressed in these chapters are solely those of the author, and they in no way obligate anyone else—least of all the sixteen people whose stories appear in the following pages.

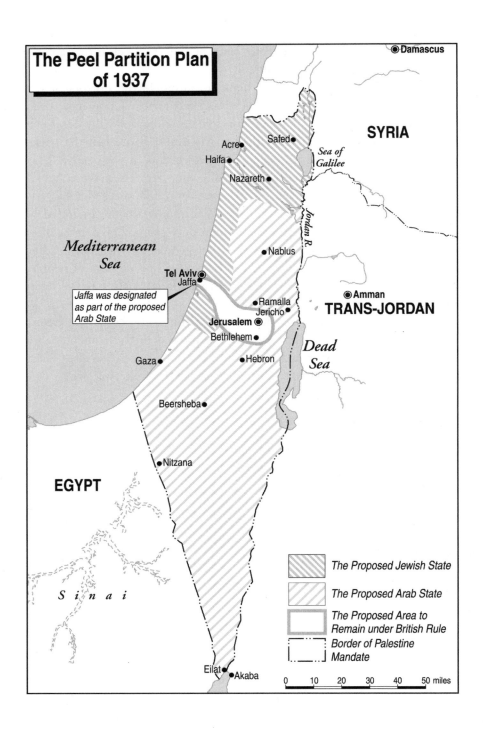

The Peel Partition Plan of 1937

Damascus

SYRIA

Acre
Safed
Haifa
Sea of Galilee
Nazareth

Mediterranean Sea

Nablus

Jordan R.

Tel Aviv
Jaffa

Jaffa was designated as part of the proposed Arab State

Ramalla
Jericho

Amman
TRANS-JORDAN

Jerusalem
Bethlehem

Dead Sea

Gaza
Hebron

Beersheba

EGYPT

Nitzana

Sinai

Eilat
Akaba

The Proposed Jewish State

The Proposed Arab State

The Proposed Area to Remain under British Rule

Border of Palestine Mandate

0   10   20   30   40   50 miles

Territorial Compromise with Israel Annexing "Settlement Blocs"*

LEBANON

SYRIA

Golan Heights

Sea of Galilee

◉ Damascus

Acre

Safed

Haifa

Nazareth

Mediterranean Sea

Tel Aviv ◉

Nablus

WEST

BANK

Ramalla

Jerusalem ◉

Jericho

◉ Amman

JORDAN

Jordan R.

Bethlehem

Hebron

Dead Sea

Gaza

GAZA

Beersheba

Arad

ISRAEL

Nitzana

EGYPT

Negev

Sinai

*Drawn by Yossi Alpher in 1994, and published by the Jaffee Institute for Strategic Studies, Tel Aviv University. Prime Minister Barak's proposals at Camp David in the summer of 2000 followed the concept represented by this map.

Eilat

Akaba

Annexed to Israel

Area of Israeli Army Deployment

International Border

"Green Line"

0   10   20   30   40   50 miles

The State of Israel
1948–1967

Damascus ◉

SYRIA

Demilitarized Zone

Acre ●   Safed ●

Haifa ●

Sea of
Galilee

Nazareth ●

Mediterranean
Sea

Jordan R.

● Nablus

WEST

Tel Aviv ◉

BANK

● Ramalla

◉ Amman

Jericho ●

Jerusalem ◉

JORDAN

Bethlehem ●

● Hebron

Dead
Sea

Gaza ●

GAZA STRIP

Beersheba ●   Arad ●

ISRAEL

● Nitzana

EGYPT

Negev

Sinai

Eilat ●
● Akaba

Area Administered
by Egypt

Demilitarized Zone

International Border

Armistice Line

0   10   20   30   40   50 miles

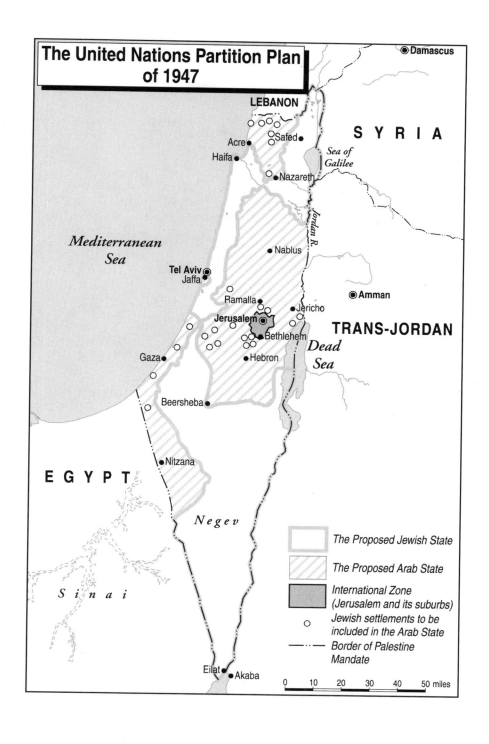

The United Nations Partition Plan
of 1947

Damascus

LEBANON

S Y R I A

Acre
Safed
Haifa
Sea of
Galilee
Nazareth

Mediterranean
Sea

Nablus

Jordan R.

Tel Aviv
Jaffa

Ramalla
Jerusalem
Jericho
Bethlehem
Hebron

Amman

TRANS-JORDAN

Dead
Sea

Gaza

Beersheba

Nitzana

E G Y P T

N e g e v

S i n a i

Eilat
Akaba

The Proposed Jewish State

The Proposed Arab State

International Zone
(Jerusalem and its suburbs)

Jewish settlements to be
included in the Arab State

Border of Palestine
Mandate

0   10   20   30   40   50 miles

Part I
YESTERDAY

CHAPTER 1
THE UNSOLVED PROBLEM
One Country, Two Peoples

The Israeli–Palestinian issue has been correctly described as complicated, but the basic problem is simple: Two peoples lay claim to the same piece of real estate. Somehow it has to be shared, and the complications emerge in working out how. Because of the differences in the historical backgrounds, religions, cultures, and aspirations of the two contenders, the generally preferred model for sharing has been partition of the land into two separate states. That is where the complexity begins, because Israelis and Palestinians live among each other, entwined in a deadly, unbreakable embrace.

There are Arab towns, villages, and neighborhoods in Israel; Jewish settlements are located all over the West Bank and Gaza, which are the areas designated for a Palestinian state. Jerusalem is a mixed city that has to be shared but is difficult to divide. Virtually all the problems in working out a solution have involved the technical details of separating the two peoples from each other. Attempts to include West Bank Jewish settlements in Israel and Israeli Arab villages in Palestine produce maps with borders as grotesque as they are indefensible. And then, of course, there is the matter of the refugees. So, despite the remarkable ingenuity that has been exercised in proposing solutions, every time that an agreement seemed imminent, it has disappeared at the last minute, like a Middle Eastern desert mirage.

An examination of the history of the conflict points to the inevitable conclusion that there is no right or wrong here—simply different angles of vision. Where you stand depends on where you sit. If you are sitting in Jewish Tel Aviv, the situation looks very different from the way it looks viewed from Arab Nablus. Unfortunately, distance has not always led to detachment. Observers sitting in New York, London, and Paris often vociferously adopt a Tel Aviv or a Nablus point of view.

The Palestinian Arabs maintain that they were living contentedly in Palestine, a region of the Ottoman Turkish Empire, when they were faced with the intrusion of Jewish immigrants from Europe. Starting toward the end of the nineteenth century, the Jews arrived in ever-increasing numbers, until they became strong enough to establish their state. Creating Israel by force of arms, they expelled hundreds of thousands of Arabs and destroyed the indigenous Palestinian society.

The Jews contend that Palestine is the biblical Land of Israel, where the Jewish people and religion were born. There never was an Arab nation of Palestine, they say, simply Arab residents of a Turkish province, who neglected the land and allowed it to deteriorate. Most of the present-day Palestinians arrived comparatively recently from the surrounding lands, attracted by the growing economy of Palestine, which was largely driven by Jewish development. The Jews made every effort to reach an agreement with the local Arab inhabitants, but their attempts at conciliation were always rejected.

The Palestinians trace the start of their national movement to the middle of the nineteenth century, when local leaders in Acre and Nablus mobilized militias in an attempt to achieve a greater measure of autonomy in the Ottoman Empire. Further stirrings of nationalism emerged in Syria, Lebanon, and Palestine in the 1880s, but it was an *Arab* national awareness, centering on all three territories. Even after the establishment of Israel in 1948 and the departure of some six hundred thousand residents from Israeli-controlled territory, United Nations resolutions referred to the *Arab* refugees, rather than the Palestinian refugees. It must also be pointed out that, following the creation of Israel, a Palestinian state was not established. The West Bank was incorporated into Transjordan, which then became Jordan; Gaza was placed under an Egyptian military administration. Although a Palestinian consciousness existed for many years, it developed into an effective national movement only after the Six-Day War of 1967.

The Jewish national movement was better organized and more sharply focused. Although most Arabs see Zionism as a classical imperialist enterprise, the Zionist movement drew its inspiration from a powerful sense of Jewish communal identity, from millennia of abuse and oppression, and from the nineteenth-century European movements for national self-determination. Despite differing streams within the movement, there was a clear consensus favoring Jewish immigration to Palestine, with the eventual establishment of a Jewish national entity there. At the same time, it is fair to point out that most Jews were not Zionists, even after the establishment of Israel. A Jewish consensus supporting Israel emerged only after 1967.

As early as the turn of the century, Arab leaders expressed concern at the prospect of a Jewish influx. Yussuf Khalidi, a member of one of Palestine's leading families, conceded in a letter to a leading French rabbi that the Zionist idea was "natural, fine and just." He continued, "Who can contest the right of the Jews to Palestine? God knows, historically it is indeed your country, but there must be somewhere in this wide world where the Jews can settle. There is no room for them here. It will lead to bloodshed."[1]

There were indeed violent clashes between the early Jewish settlers and the local population, but most of the settlers viewed their attackers as gangs of bandits. This impression was reinforced by the fact that Ottoman Palestine was not a conspicuously law-abiding land. Bedouin tribesmen frequently raided local Arab villages, so it was natural to view the attacks on the Jewish communities as normal behavior in Palestine at that time. For some years, the Jewish settlements employed Arab laborers and Arab guards, but the later Jewish immigrants believed in self-reliance. They insisted on doing their own work and formed their own groups of guards, which were eventually combined in the Hagana, the Jewish self-defense organization.

For its part, the Ottoman administration, understandably suspicious of both Christian and Jewish designs on the Holy Land, generally refused to grant entry visas to the Jewish newcomers. Nevertheless, although the early immigrants were certainly not welcome, the first serious local opposition to Jewish plans did not come until after the British army's conquest of Palestine in World War I.

While the guns were still firing, Britain had made promises to both Arabs and Jews. As a reward for rising in support of the Allies against the Turks, the Arabs were promised independence. In 1915, Hussein, the sharif of Mecca, demanded support for a kingdom composed of the Arab parts of the empire in return for leading a revolt against the Ottomans. The British high commissioner in Egypt, Sir Henry McMahon, promised to recognize "the independence of the Arabs," but he also mentioned certain areas of

Syria, in which France had an interest, that would be excluded from Arab rule.

Britain's foreign secretary, Arthur James Balfour, issued a declaration in favor of the Jews that was rather more specific, although also hedged around with conditions:

> His Majesty's Government view with favor the establishment in Palestine of a National Home for the Jewish people, and will use their best endeavors to facilitate the achievement of this object, it being clearly understood that nothing shall be done which may prejudice the civil and religious rights of the non-Jewish communities in Palestine.[2]

After the war the Arabs achieved independence in Arabia, Iraq, and (later) Transjordan. The French ruled in Syria and Lebanon. The British were given a "mandate" for Palestine by the League of Nations, on the understanding that the Balfour Declaration would be carried out. As it tried to balance the two contradictory sentiments of the declaration—facilitating a Jewish national home without harming the local population—British policy veered this way and that, sometimes promoting the Zionist enterprise, sometimes seeking to control and limit it. Nevertheless, despite Arab resistance that was often violent, the Jews made giant strides toward their goal under the mandatory administration.

The first serious Arab riot occurred even before the British formally received the mandate. Arab mobs rampaged in Jerusalem in 1920, causing the deaths of six Jews, the wounding of two hundred, and widespread destruction of property. A similar number of Arabs were killed and wounded by British troops and police. The British military administration responded by stopping Jewish immigration, detaining the senior Zionist official in Palestine, and arresting several members of the (still unofficial) Hagana Jewish defense force, including its commander. A few months later, the British Mandate was endorsed, and a British Jew, Herbert Samuel, was appointed the first civilian high commissioner.

From the outset, the British played the imperial game of "divide and rule," both between Jews and Arabs and among the Arabs themselves. The two most important families in Palestine were the Husseinis and the Nashashibis. They owned real estate, groves, and farms all over Palestine, exercising considerable economic and political power. Following the 1920 riots, the military governor of Jerusalem had dismissed the nationalist mayor of Jerusalem, Kazem Husseini, and appointed Ragheb Nashashibi in his place. To balance this, the mandatory administration engineered the election of Haj Amin Husseini as mufti of Jerusalem.

Although there was concern about his reputed extremist stance, Husseini's appointment initially seemed to be justified. When the next wave of violence broke out in 1921, nearly fifty Jews and Arabs lost their lives in clashes in Jaffa and the coastal plain area, but Jerusalem remained quiet. Reacting to the new violence, the administration again suspended Jewish immigration, and, in 1922, a white paper was issued that clarified the Balfour Declaration, stating that it "did not contemplate that Palestine as a whole should be converted into a Jewish National Home, but that such a Home should be founded in Palestine." Furthermore, the territory of Transjordan was detached from Palestine and made into an Arab emirate.

British attempts to set up a legislative council in 1923 to involve both the Arabs and the Jews in the administration of Palestine were unsuccessful. The Jewish side was prepared to go along with the scheme. On the Palestinian side, the Nashashibis, who controlled many of the municipalities, were inclined to cooperate with the British—if not directly with the Jews—but the Husseinis, who controlled the Palestine Arab Executive and the Supreme Muslim Council, ensured that the proposal was turned down. As a result, the two communities developed separately.

With Palestine relatively quiet between 1921 and 1929, both Jewish and Arab communities grew, but the Jewish increase was larger. In 1918, there had been about 700,000 Arabs in Palestine and 60,000 Jews. A census in 1931 showed that there were 880,000 Arabs and 175,000 Jews. In fact, the Jews had hoped for an even faster rate of growth, but the Arabs were seriously alarmed, and in 1929, a simmering dispute about the Western Wall in Jerusalem came to a head. The Muslims had been in control of the Temple Mount compound, the site of the ancient Jewish Temple, since their final defeat of the Crusaders in the thirteenth century. They built the Aksa Mosque and the Dome of the Rock there, called the compound Haram al-Sharif (the Holy Sanctuary), and regarded it as the third most holy site of Islam, after Mecca and Medina.

For their part, the Jews revered the Western Wall as the last remnant of the Temple. It was, in fact, a containing wall of the Temple Mount compound, dating back to the time of Herod the Great. The Jews would pray and lament the destruction of the Temple by this wall, which is why it was for a long time called the "Wailing Wall."

From time to time, there were minor clashes. The Jews accused the Muslims of deliberately dislodging rocks on the worshippers from above, unloading garbage, and driving donkeys and goats along the narrow passage by the wall to jostle those at prayer. The Arabs objected to the construction of a partition, separating male and female worshippers. In 1929, angered by what they saw as "Muslim provocation," a group of nationalist Jews organized demonstrations and mass prayer meetings at the Wall. A few days later, Haj Amin Husseini (by now termed the "grand" mufti of Jerusalem) preached an inflammatory sermon to the thousands of worshippers, assembled on the mount for Friday prayers, accusing the Jews of planning to destroy the Muslim shrines. The construction of a prayer partition, he intimated, was only a first step in the rebuilding of the ancient Jewish Temple.

Angry Muslims poured out of the compound. Murderous attacks were made on Jews in Jerusalem, followed by massacres in Hebron in the south and Safed in the north. Some 130 Jews were killed. When Jewish settlements were attacked, Hagana units fought back, inflicting casualties on the Arabs. About eighty Arabs were killed by British troops and the Hagana.

Despite the religious dispute that sparked the riots—and which made them all the more severe—the fundamental reason behind the violence was Arab alarm at the growth of the Jewish community in Palestine and resentment of land purchases by the Jews, which led to Arab farmers being evicted from their fields. Two British Inquiry Commissions came to Palestine and subsequently recommended limiting both Jewish immigration and land sales to Jews. These proposals angered the Zionists, and strenuous diplomatic efforts on the part of Zionist leader Chaim Weizmann managed to persuade the British government effectively to annul them.

After the coming to power of Adolf Hitler in Germany in 1933, the rate of Jewish immigration was even faster. By 1936, the size of the Jewish community in Palestine had more than doubled. The Jews also acquired more land, establishing more communal and cooperative settlements, the kibbutzim and moshavim. Most of the land was purchased from absentee landlords, but even ostensibly nationalist Arab owners frequently found themselves unable to resist the high prices offered.

The rivalry between the Husseinis and the Nashashibis continued, with the former demanding violent resistance and the latter espousing co-operation with the British mandatory authorities. During the 1930s, the Husseinis became increasingly dominant, and in 1936, a series of violent clashes between Arabs and Jews led to the formation of local committees and eventually the establishment of an Arab Higher Committee, which declared a general strike. All over Palestine, attacks were launched on Jewish and British targets. The British brought in twenty thousand extra troops, but initially official policy was restrained. The Arab Higher Committee, chaired by Haj Amin Husseini, denied involvement in the rebellion. It was, of course, deeply engaged, but it did not exercise full control over the local committees.

The strike had a positive effect on the Jewish economy, which had been developing separately but now further freed itself from dependence on the Arabs. An important example was the strike at the port of Jaffa, which resulted in the creation of a new (Jewish) port in Tel Aviv. The British sent another inquiry team, the Peel Commission, and the strike was called off. Under the influence of the Husseinis, the Arabs initially boycotted the Peel Commission, but in the end Haj Amin Husseini personally gave testimony.

The commission came up with the first of what would be several plans for the partition of Palestine between the two peoples. The Jews were awarded Galilee, the plain of Jezreel, and much of the northern coastal plain; the Arabs were to have the southern coastal plain, the Negev desert, and the West Bank, which would be united with Transjordan in an independent Arab state; the British would retain control over a strip of land between Jaffa and the Jerusalem–Bethlehem area. Peel also recommended a "voluntary transfer of populations," to ensure that the Jewish area had a clear Jewish majority.

The Arab Higher Committee rejected the Peel recommendations and launched the next stage of the uprising. This became a full-scale rebellion in the towns and the countryside, which lasted until 1939 and cost the lives of some 6,000 Arabs, more than 450 Jews, and about 100 British soldiers and officials. Many of the Arab casualties were the result of fighting among the Arabs themselves. The Nashashibis had withdrawn from the Arab Higher Committee, which was subsequently disbanded by the British. The Husseinis, aiming for complete control of the Palestinian

Arabs, launched a wave of violence against the Nashashibis and other opponents of their policy of insurrection.

Since its establishment in 1920, the Hagana Jewish defense force had espoused a policy of relative restraint, fighting back when Jewish districts or settlements were attacked but for the most part not initiating action. Dissident Jewish members of the breakaway Revisionist Zionists attempted some retaliation operations, and, as the Arab Revolt continued, the Hagana partly revised its previous policy. With the help of Orde Wingate, a British intelligence officer, the Jews formed mobile attack forces. Operating from kibbutzim, they were known as the Special Night Squads. These units, which would become the Palmah, the Hagana's strike force, operated effectively against Arab rebels, but in general terms it can be said that the British army smashed the rebellion. It was helped by the vicious infighting among the Arabs. Several thousand Arabs who did not support the rebellion left Palestine in fear of assassination. Most of them subsequently returned.

Despite its shortcomings, the Arab Revolt was successful in that it forced a radical change of British policy. Another commission was sent to Palestine and recommended a different partition plan, but at the same time a white paper (an official British government report) was published rejecting the idea of partition altogether. Representatives of Palestinian Jews and Arabs, along with others from a number of Arab nations, were invited to London for talks. As the Arabs refused to sit with the Jews, the British were forced to hold separate talks with the two sides.

The Arab attitude seemed to pay off, when, following the London talks, a new British proposal limited Jewish immigration to a total of seventy-five thousand over the next five years, set severe limits on Jewish land purchases, and favored the establishment of an independent Palestinian state. The stunned Zionists bitterly protested what they called the British "betrayal," all the more so as the situation of the Jews under Hitler had become desperate and they needed Palestine as a refuge. Jews fleeing Europe were denied haven not only in Palestine but in numerous other countries around the world as well. Despite this, the Palestinian Arabs persisted in their rejection of all British proposals.

When World War II broke out in 1939, both sides acted predictably: the Jews supported the British against Nazi Germany, the deadliest enemy the Jews had ever known. Large numbers of young men and women volunteered for the British army; the Arabs were lukewarm, when they were not hostile. The Nazis made use of the conflict of interests between Britain and the Arabs. Haj Amin Husseini was invited to Berlin. From there he called on the Arabs of Palestine to rise against the British and the Jews. British policy, which had veered toward the Arabs in 1939, remained unchanged. During the war Palestine remained quiet, and the Jewish economy prospered as it mobilized to serve the large Allied forces stationed in the Middle East. The Hagana set up a secret organization to smuggle Jews out of Europe and bring them to Palestine in defiance of the British.

After the war, when the full dimension of the Holocaust was confirmed, a Jewish state became a raging need. Six million European Jews had been murdered, and the Jews of Palestine were determined to gather in the traumatized survivors. To this end, unofficial immigration, termed "illegal" by the British authorities, was stepped up. For their part, the Arabs did not see why they should pay for the crimes of others. In Britain, the Labour Party, which had a record of support for Zionism, won the postwar elections, but the new government proved hostile to Zionist claims. Now it was the turn of the Jews, many of whom had gained military experience in the British forces, to launch a revolt. A number of British targets were hit, most famously the southern wing of the King David Hotel in Jerusalem, where British civil and military administrative offices were housed. Unofficial British forces retaliated, blowing up the Jewish Agency offices and several other buildings in central Jerusalem. The final days of the British Mandate saw a three-way battle among the Jews, the Arabs, and the British.

The war-weary British, after trying to hold some sort of a balance in Palestine, and doing their utmost to stem the illegal Jewish immigration, surrendered their mandate to the United Nations, which produced yet another partition plan, this time dividing the area of mandatory Palestine roughly 50:50 between the Jews and the Arabs.

When the British forces withdrew from Palestine in 1948, David Ben-Gurion, the pugnacious but pragmatic leader of the Jewish community, declared the establishment of the state of Israel in the areas allotted to the Jews under the partition plan. He became the new state's first prime minister. The Palestinians stepped up their attacks and five Arab states joined the war against the Jews. In the subsequent fighting, which was periodically interrupted by UN-sponsored truces, the newly formed Israel Defense Forces expanded Jewish territory beyond the scope of the UN plan. Some six hundred thousand Arabs fled from the Israeli-controlled areas, most of them expelled by the IDF. The Israelis called the war *Milhemet Hashihrur*, the "War of Liberation" (usually termed the War of Independence in English). The Arabs refer to 1948 as the *Nakba*, the "Disaster."

Israel signed armistice agreements with the neighboring Arab states in 1949. By then, it controlled just over twenty-one thousand square kilometers of the twenty-seven thousand in Palestine. Left with some six thousand square kilometers, the state of Palestine was stillborn: Egypt administered the so-called Gaza strip; the West Bank of the River Jordan was incorporated into Transjordan, which changed its name to Kingdom of Jordan. The refugees remained in camps in Jordan, Syria, Lebanon, and the Gaza strip.

Despite continuing enmity between Israel and the Arab nations, the new Jewish state developed and flourished during the next two decades. It tripled the size of its population by bringing in Holocaust survivors from Europe and also by receiving hundreds of thousands of Jews from Arab and other Middle East countries. One of the first pieces of legislation to be enacted by the new state was the "Law of Return," which stipulated that any Jew, from anywhere in the world, could come to Israel and automatically receive citizenship. This law, which some have termed "racist," was regarded by the legislators as a vital gesture of affirmative action. The memory of ships bearing Jews fleeing Europe, being shuttled from port to port around the world until they were forced to return to Nazi-ruled Europe, had not been forgotten.

For their part, the Palestinian Arabs who had gone (or been forced) into exile adopted the concept of the "Right of Return." This notion, conditionally accepted in a number of UN resolutions, was that Arabs who had formerly lived in Palestine should be permitted to return to their homes. The Israelis resisted the return of potentially hostile citizens, many of whom had fought against the establishment of the state. They argued that the refugees had lost their homes as the result of a war started by the Arabs themselves and therefore had no moral right to return. The Law of Return and the Right of Return would in the course of time come to symbolize the intractable nature of the Israeli–Palestinian problem.

Relations between Israel and the Arab states remained tense, and there was continuous infiltration into Israel from across the border. In some cases, Palestinians were merely visiting their former homes or even harvesting their olives, but the incursions became deadly, with an increasing number of Israeli civilian casualties. In addition to this, the Arab countries remained officially at war with the Jewish state, despite the fact that they had signed armistice agreements with it.

As a result of this situation, all Israelis were required to serve in the IDF. Following their years of conscript service, IDF soldiers performed at least one month of reserve service every year. Two groups received exemption from military service. The country's Arab citizens, approximately 180,000, who had remained in Israel and had become citizens of the new state, were excused, along with a few hundred ultra-Orthodox Jewish students, who studied in Yeshiva religious colleges.

The Arabs were exempted on the ground that they would feel ambivalent—at the very least—about serving in the army, which was engaged in an ongoing conflict with their fellow Arabs (although members of the minority Druze and Circassian communities did serve in the army, and a number of Bedouin volunteers performed valuable work as scouts and trackers). The ultra-Orthodox were excluded, as a sad remnant of the Yeshiva colleges that had been wiped out in Europe. It was felt that something should be preserved of the former scholastic institutions. In the event, they were so successful at rebuilding the Yeshiva seminaries that the few hundred exemptions grew over the years to hundreds of thousands, and today a bitter controversy persists in Israel on the matter.

In its first two decades, Israel successfully absorbed the huge increase in its Jewish population. Two groups, the Middle Eastern, or Sephardi, Jews and the Arabs who remained in the new state, were less successfully integrated. The Sephardi Jews were for some years economically deprived and felt a strong sense of discrimination. In the course of time, though, they would become fully integrated citizens of Israel.

For the Israeli Arabs, life was more problematic. On the positive side, they elected their representatives to the Knesset, they administered their own towns and villages, and they were members of the Histadrut Trade Union Federation, with all the protection that it afforded. Furthermore, they were free of the obligation of military service. On the other hand, they lived under a military administration that restricted their movements, the government provided less funds for their development than it did for Jewish towns and villages, and—particularly in the case of the Bedouin—much of their land was expropriated. Many of their small villages were not officially recognized. Although the military government was abolished in 1965, and they were on the whole more prosperous than their neighbors in Lebanon, Syria, Jordan, and Egypt, the Israeli Arabs were manifestly second-class citizens in Israel.

The Palestinians who had left during the 1948 war were of course in a worse situation, continuing to live in poverty and deprivation in the refugee camps in the neighboring Arab countries. Israel has been critical of the failure of the Arab nations to absorb the Arab refugees from Palestine, contrasting it with their own successful absorption of Jewish immigrants, many of them refugees from the Arab countries. The Palestinian refugees, it is suggested, were deliberately kept in deprivation to be used as a political weapon against the Jewish state. While this contention contains a measure of truth, it should be pointed out that the Arabs in general never became reconciled with the Jewish influx and the establishment of Israel. They saw it as a historic injustice and did not see why they should be required to assist in its perpetuation by accepting the refugees as citizens. It should also be pointed out that, after Israel took over the West Bank and Gaza in 1967, no serious efforts were made to abolish or rehabilitate the refugee camps in those areas.

In its first years, Israel maintained a policy of restraint against the infiltration from across the border, but in the early 1950s, a new doctrine was formulated, with the support of Prime Minister Ben-Gurion. It was a young IDF officer, Ariel Sharon, who implemented the new policy on the ground. The process of infiltration and reprisal eventually escalated into the Sinai Campaign of 1956.

In the Sinai Campaign, the Israelis took advantage of Egypt's seizure of the Suez Canal and the combined French–British raid on Egypt to capture the Egyptian-controlled territories of the Gaza strip and Sinai. The following, however, combined pressure by the United States and the Soviet Union forced Israel to withdraw its forces. Ten years of relative quiet followed, disrupted by a military confrontation that erupted in 1967 with dramatic suddenness. The Israelis, certain that an Arab alliance of Egypt, Syria, and Jordan, led by Egypt's president Gamel Abdel Nasser, intended to wipe them off the map, saw the Six-Day War as a "war of survival." The

Arab side quickly came to regard Israel's sweeping victory, in which the Jewish state took Gaza and Sinai from Egypt, the West Bank from Jordan, and the Golan Heights from Syria, as a "war of aggression." Recently released documents indicate that Egyptian blustering and Soviet duplicity led both sides to miscalculate, and blunder into a war that neither wanted or needed. The Soviet Union deliberately deceived the Egyptians and Syrians into thinking that Israel planned to attack them.

The 1967 conflict reversed the de facto partition of Palestine that had resulted from the UN plan and the 1948 war. After it, Israel ruled all of Palestine, as well as the Syrian Golan Heights and the Egyptian Sinai Peninsula. The Palestinians of the West Bank and Gaza, including the inhabitants of the festering refugee camps, now came under Israeli administration. For the most part, Israelis were convinced that, as in 1957, they would be forced to withdraw from the conquered territories, and they rushed to see parts of Sinai and the West Bank, "before giving it back." The general assumption was that Israel would withdraw from these territories and that peace accords, or at least nonbelligerency agreements, would be signed with Egypt, Syria, and Jordan. The Arab states were not, however, in a peaceful mood. At an Arab summit conference in Khartoum, they resolved that there would be no negotiations, no peace, and no recognition of the Jewish state.

The Israelis, who had established a temporary military government framework to administer the new territories immediately after the war, started to dig in for a long stay. At the same time, a growing number of religious Jews saw the conquest of the territories as the fulfillment of the divine promise to the Jewish people, and a significant number of secular-minded Israelis welcomed borders that seemed more defensible.

Initially, the government set up a number of military camps and paramilitary settlements in the Syrian Golan Heights and the Jordan Valley, which were seen as strategically important in the event of further hostilities. In September 1967, however, a different type of settlement was approved. The first Jewish settlement in the West Bank was in the so-called Etzion Bloc, south of Jerusalem, where four Jewish villages had been overrun in 1948. The children of former villagers led this "return to Eztion." Not long afterward, in the spring of 1968, other settlers "returned" to Hebron, which had a far longer association with Jewish history. Fifty-nine Jews had been massacred in Hebron in the 1929 riots. Moreover, the town contained the Machpela cave, where tradition says the biblical patriarchs are buried. As if this were not enough, King David's capital was in Hebron before he moved to Jerusalem. It was indeed the historical Jewish heartland. This private initiative was the real start of the Jewish settlement project that would eventually result in the existence of some 200,000 Jewish settlers in more than 150 settlements all over the West Bank and in Gaza.

Apart from the Golan Heights, the Jordan Valley, and Sinai, the settlement movement was the result of such private initiatives—not governmental policy. Often acting secretly and at night, the mainly religious settlers saw themselves as obeying the divine commandment to settle the Land of Israel. Several members of the Labor governments that ruled Israel in the first decade after 1967 saw them as the successors of the pioneers of the 1920s and 1930s, who had founded kibbutzim in defiance of the British authorities. Thus, the settlements were created by a combination of religious zealotry and subterfuge, tendentious Zionist nostalgia, and governmental indifference and impotence.

The Jews were not, however, the only ones looking for answers to the situation created by the Six-Day War. The Palestinians stepped up the armed raids that had been a feature of the situation ever since 1948. The Fatah organization, established by Yasser Arafat in Kuwait in 1959, had carried out raids against Israel even before the 1967 war. In the fall of 1967, the Fatah launched some fifty attacks, but the Israeli security forces quickly destroyed its network, and its fighters withdrew across the river into the Kingdom of Jordan.

Several smaller Palestinian military groups had been established over the years, and, in 1968, they and the Fatah took over the Palestine Liberation Organization (PLO). Originally set up by Egypt, Syria, and Iraq, the PLO supported the destruction of Israel and the establishment of a Palestinian state in its place. Now under the command of Yasser Arafat, the PLO launched raids across the Jordan, and its various factions hijacked aircraft and launched attacks on Israeli and Jewish targets around the world.

This international terror campaign is certainly a stain on the Palestinian national movement. It included such targets as Israeli athletes competing in the Olympic Games and Jewish synagogues and community centers that had no connection with Israel. From Lisbon to Buenos Aires,

Adelaide to Oslo, synagogues hired security guards and surrounded themselves with razor wire. Very often, their locations were deliberately disguised. Israelis traveling abroad were made to feel like lepers, shunted to special sections of the airports, inspected, searched, and questioned. Even white South Africans of the apartheid era, purportedly reviled by the civilized world, never had to put up with this kind of treatment.

By 1970, the PLO had become a state-within-a-state in Jordan, threatening that country's integrity. King Hussein launched a strong attack on the Palestinian forces in his kingdom. This confrontation is still called "Black September" by the Palestinians. Most of them fled to Syria, Lebanon, Iraq, and Egypt, with some even finding refuge in Israel and the West Bank. The PLO set up its new headquarters in South Lebanon.

In 1973, Egypt and Syria launched the October War, with the aim of recovering their lost territories in Sinai and the Golan Heights. As in 1948, the different names given by the sides indicate the different ways they viewed events. The Arabs called 1973 the "War of Ramadan," after the holy Muslim month in which it was launched. The Israelis called it the "Yom Kippur War," as it started with a surprise attack on Yom Kippur, the Day of Atonement, when many Israelis were praying in synagogue. Following early Arab successes on both fronts, the IDF managed to fight back and reestablish its control over Sinai and the Golan Heights, even crossing the Suez Canal. However, despite its recovery, the war was traumatic for Israel, and a State Commission of Inquiry was established to look into the intelligence failures and initial setbacks. Although the commission laid the blame on Israel's military leadership, a public outcry in Israel forced the political leaders, Prime Minister Golda Meir and Defense Minister Moshe Dayan, to resign.

The subsequent period of soul-searching in Israel did not lead to fresh thinking about the situation; it only served to reinforce previously held opinions. About half the population continued to believe that Israel should withdraw from territories conquered in the Six-Day War in order to reach agreements with the Arabs; the other half persisted in its belief that Israel must hold on to the territories taken in 1967 for strategic reasons. The religious nationalists stepped up their settlements in the conquered territories.

In the Arab world, too, the 1973 conflict polarized attitudes. Some remained more determined than ever to wipe Israel off the map; others began to accept that they would have to live with a Jewish state in their midst, and thought in terms of limiting its size and strength rather than destroying it.

Egypt's president Anwar Sadat, who planned and waged the 1973 war, proved as adventurous and unpredictable in peace as he had been in war, coming to Jerusalem in 1977 and addressing Israel's parliament. His initiative led to a peace agreement between Egypt and Israel, involving the IDF's withdrawal from Sinai and the dismantling of the Jewish settlements there. It was a notable step in the direction of peace in the Middle East, but it failed to solve the Palestinian problem that was at the heart of the Israeli–Arab confrontation.

The right-wing Likud-led government, which made peace with Egypt, was much less flexible when it came to the Palestinians. It stepped up the construction of Jewish settlements, particularly in the West Bank. The PLO continued to attack Israel from Lebanese soil, and, in 1982, shortly after the final stage of the Sinai pullback, Israel launched a war against the Palestinians in South Lebanon. Ariel Sharon, now the minister of defense, played the leading role in planning and executing the campaign. He presented the government with a plan for a limited foray into Lebanon to "push the PLO out of range of Israel's northern border." In the event, the IDF went all the way to Beirut, and Israel was stuck in Lebanon for eighteen years.

In the first stage, the Israeli invasion was effective in that the PLO was expelled from Lebanon and forced to set up its headquarters in faraway Tunisia, but the success was short-lived. Prime Minister Menachim Begin, who had expressed the hope that the campaign in Lebanon would give Israel "forty years of peace," was deeply depressed by the continuation of the fighting and the large number of Israeli casualties. He resigned and went into seclusion. It was a sad end for the man who signed the peace treaty with Egypt.

Despite the distancing of the PLO to North Africa, the Palestinian problem did not go away. At the end of 1987, the Intifada, a civil uprising, broke out. Mobs of Palestinians, many of them youngsters, confronted Israeli security forces in Jerusalem and all over the West Bank and Gaza. There was a partially successful boycott of Israeli goods, and shops were closed down for half-days, in an attempt to show that the Palestinians were in charge in the territories. The spontaneous confrontation initially took the IDF by surprise, and the slow reaction of the Israeli military enabled the uprising to gain momentum.

Interestingly, the Intifada also took the exiled Palestinian leadership in Tunisia by surprise, but the young rioters quickly recognized the leadership of the PLO, which became increasingly involved. Although the uprising would eventually run out of steam, the scale of the violence convinced a number of key Israeli leaders that the occupation of the Palestinian territories could not continue.

In 1990, Iraq conquered Kuwait and the United States established a coalition, which included Saudi Arabia, Egypt, and Syria, to expel the invading army. The PLO lined up with Iraq, thereby losing support, not only in the United States and other Western nations but also in the Gulf states, particularly Kuwait. To the Americans the defeat of Iraq and its expulsion from Kuwait seemed an appropriate time to launch a new Israeli–Palestinian peace initiative. The 1991 Madrid Conference, convened by Washington, was attended by Israel, Egypt, Syria, Lebanon, and a joint Jordanian–Palestinian delegation. The Palestinians were officially "non-PLO," but the members had been approved by that organization, and they constantly consulted with PLO headquarters in Tunis.

Little progress was achieved at Madrid, but the following year the Labor Party won the elections in Israel, and the new prime minister, Yitzhak Rabin, adopted a much more pragmatic policy toward the Palestinians. A series of unofficial, semiofficial, and (finally) official talks and discussions produced an accord in Oslo in 1993. The agreement was officially signed on the White House lawn in Washington. For the first time, Israelis and Palestinians recognized one another's claims, and set about trying to reconcile them. To put it simply: At Oslo, the two peoples stopped trying to win the argument and began trying to solve the problem. The proposed solution, as in the past, was partition of the land claimed by both peoples. They were not seeking a just solution but rather a *realistic* one: an arrangement with which both sides could live. For the first time, both Israelis and Palestinians agreed to the principle of partition, even if they didn't see eye to eye on the details. The Palestinians wanted the pre–June 1967 borders, as the official border between the two states; the Israelis demanded adjustments to improve their security and permit at least some of the Jewish settlements to remain under Israeli sovereignty. Israel demanded that Jerusalem remain its united capital; the Palestinians wanted East Jerusalem as their capital.

There were ups and downs during the 1990s, but the sides continued to move toward a solution. A land-for-peace deal was discussed with the Syrians, and Israel signed a peace treaty with Jordan. The IDF withdrew from most of the Gaza strip and from the large towns of the West Bank. A "Palestinian Authority" was created to administer those areas. Most of the Palestinians were liberated from the direct rule of the Israeli military. Elections were held, and Yasser Arafat became chairman of the Palestinian Authority, in effect the Palestinian president.

The Jewish settlers in the West Bank and Gaza and their supporters, however, realized that an accord with the Palestinians would include the dismantling of at least some of their settlements. Accordingly, they waged a virulent campaign against what they termed the "sellout" to the Palestinians. In a series of vicious demonstrations, right-wing politicians and settler leaders termed Rabin a "traitor." Several rabbis from the settlements issued a *din rodef,* a virtual death sentence, against him for "betraying the Land of Israel." He was pictured wearing a *keffiye,* an Arab headscarf, and even wearing the uniform of an officer of the Nazi SS.

Rabin's supporters belatedly rallied to his defense by organizing a demonstration in favor of peace. Held in Tel Aviv on November 4, 1995, the rally was a huge success, but it ended in tragedy. Leaving the speakers' platform, the prime minister was gunned down by a right-wing student who had manifestly been influenced by the extremist rabbis and other right-wing leaders. Rabin's successor, Shimon Peres, lost a subsequent election to the right-wing Benjamin Netanyahu, and for some three years, the peace process was more or less brought to a halt.

In 1999, Israel held another election, in which Ehud Barak led the Labor Party to victory, pledging to continue Rabin's path toward peace and compromise with the Palestinians. Again progress was made on both the Syrian and the Palestinian fronts. In particular, peace with the Palestinians seemed to be within grasp, but an American-sponsored conference at Camp David in the summer of 2000 failed to bring an agreement. For this failure, both sides must take responsibility.

There is no doubt that, at Camp David in the summer of 2000, Ehud Barak made an offer that was extremely generous by Israeli standards. He proposed that Israel withdraw from over 90 percent of the West Bank and offered a compromise on Jerusalem. The scale of the pullback offered by Barak, even if unacceptable to the Palestinians, was more than had ever been put on the table before, but it was the proposals about Jerusalem that were remarkably daring. Even Israelis to the left of Barak's Labor Party had feared to talk about sharing Jerusalem with the Palestinians. It was extremely courageous of Barak even to contemplate such an idea. He defied an Israeli axiom and shattered a strong taboo.

At the same time, it should be acknowledged that Yasser Arafat is the first Palestinian leader ever to accept even the idea of a Jewish state. At Oslo, Arafat not only recognized Israel—in itself a revolutionary decision—but also recognized the 1967 borders. That meant that he accepted a Palestinian state in the West Bank and Gaza, which constitute some 22 percent of the area of Palestine. Most Israelis, who emphasize the magnitude of Barak's concessions at Camp David, do not appreciate the extent of this compromise by the Palestinian side. Nevertheless, in failing to come up with a serious counterproposal at Camp David—even when U.S. president Bill Clinton intervened with further compromise suggestions—Arafat made a disastrous mistake.

Ehud Barak's mistake had occurred several months earlier, when he threw the basic idea of Oslo out of the window. The Oslo agreement was based on a step-by-step approach, in which trust would be gradually restored between Israelis and Palestinians. Each step would build more confidence in the goodwill and sincerity of the other. It is true that trust had not been built, because both sides were deficient in keeping their promises. In addition to this failure of confidence building, Barak saw Israel continuously giving up pieces of territory, which were its bargaining chips. By the time the final deal was imminent, he feared, the Israeli negotiating team would be sitting at the table with an empty hand. He resolved to save his chips for the final deal. In junking step-by-step and going all-out for a final agreement, Barak was acting logically—even bravely—but he disregarded the vitally important psychological factor. He failed to discern just how thin the patience of the Palestinians was wearing.

It was unfortunate that the start of the Oslo process coincided with two painful blows to the Palestinian economy. The Gulf War of 1991—and Yasser Arafat's ill-advised support for Iraq—led to the expulsion of hundreds of thousands of Palestinians from Kuwait. This resulted in an enormous loss of income from Palestinians who had been working in Kuwait and sending money home. At the same time, the Israeli policy of "closures" (shutting off Israel to the Palestinians of the territories), which had started during the Gulf War, meant that much of the income formerly earned by Palestinians working in Israel was lost to the Palestinian economy. This double deprivation was partly replaced by the foreign aid that started flowing in after Oslo. Moreover, the Palestinian economy was starting to develop in a healthier manner, but this was not yet clear to the residents of the West Bank and Gaza.

In some ways, it is true, the lives of the Palestinians had improved, but memories are short. For three decades, the IDF had been stationed in the West Bank and the Gaza strip. For thirty years, Israeli soldiers had been omnipresent in the lives of the Palestinian inhabitants: patrolling their streets, entering their homes, stopping their cars for inspection, demanding their papers, interrupting their games of dominoes and backgammon, spoiling their evenings at the local coffeehouse, interrupting their sleep. Their presence was a continuous irritant to the citizens, an intrusion on their privacy, and a violation of their self-respect. Understandably, the Palestinians were euphoric when the Israeli soldiers pulled out of Gaza and the main West Bank towns. They were thrilled that Palestinian mayors were running their towns, and delighted to be received by Palestinian officials in the municipal offices. The IDF officers who ran their lives seemed to be gone forever. Yet, only a month or two later, the Palestinians were complaining that the situation was "worse than before."

To be fair, it was not only their short memories that caused this feeling. The closures, first introduced during the Gulf War, that prevented Palestinians from working in Israel were bad enough. Before long, however, the closures were extended into the Palestinian areas, and a series of checkposts and roadblocks was set up that prevented free movement between the Palestinian towns and villages. Despite the existence of the Palestinian Authority, the Israelis were manifestly still in charge on the ground. It became impossible to go from Nablus to Ramalla, from Hebron to Bethlehem, and (above all) from any of them to Jerusalem without passing through Israeli checkpoints. Very often the soldiers manning the checkpoints behaved unpleasantly and arrogantly. Old men were humiliated; women were treated with a lack of appropriate respect. This situation became an increasing source of frustration and anger for the Palestinian residents, particularly as officials of the Palestinian Authority had special VIP passes that permitted them to pass swiftly through the barriers.

At the same time, it has to be pointed out that the closures were set in motion because of terrorist actions carried out by Palestinians. During the year after Oslo, it was opponents of the agreement—the extreme Muslim groups, Hamas and the Islamic Jihad—that carried out these attacks. Did the Palestinian Authority make sufficient effort to prevent terror? There were periods when the Palestinian Authority tried to stop terrorism, often with a measure of success. There were also times when the Authority and its chairman seemed to ease up on the terrorists. Israel justifiably complained about the "revolving door" policy of arresting terrorists and releasing them after a few weeks or even days.

It is certainly true that Arafat and his colleagues did not directly challenge Hamas and the Jihad. No attempt was made to smash these organizations. Was this because Arafat wanted "a bit of terror" to nudge the Israelis in the ongoing negotiations, or because of the nature of Palestinian Arab society, which prefers consensus and compromise to a clear-cut decision? Or was it because the chairman was quite simply afraid of the Islamic groups? It may well be that the truth is a combination of all the above.

It is worth recalling that, faced with a similar situation just after the establishment of Israel in 1948, Israel's first prime minister, David Ben-Gurion, smashed the main dissident organization, the Irgun Zvai Leumi. In a famous incident, he ordered his forces to fire on and sink the *Altalena*, an arms ship, brought in by the Irgun. Several Irgun members were killed. Ben-Gurion also disbanded the Stern Gang and the left-wing Palmah, insisting that there could be only one authority and one military force in the state of Israel. Interestingly, right-wing Israelis, who have been complaining for years—often in extreme terms—about Ben-Gurion's "crime" in attacking the *Altalena* were the ones who in the 1990s urged Yasser Arafat to prove himself worthy of leading a state by "behaving like Ben-Gurion."

The Palestinian Authority certainly could and should have done more to control terrorism in the post-Oslo years, but the Israeli governments could have done much more to create trust. They could have been more forthcoming about releasing Palestinian prisoners, but here again the Palestinian failure to control terror must be noted. The matter of the settlements was not mentioned in the Oslo agreement, but their continuous expansion was surely against its spirit. Israel could have done more to limit the settlements and to control the aggressive behavior of the settlers toward the Palestinian population. The government could also have given clearer orders to the IDF about the conduct of its soldiers at the checkposts and eased the closures between the territories and Israel, permitting more Palestinians to come to work.

It is difficult to sustain the Israeli contention that the Intifada was planned and deliberate. The Palestinians certainly always felt that they had the option of renewing the Intifada if the Israeli side didn't deliver on Oslo. They knew that their uprising of 1987–1991 had brought them substantial gains. They were also aware of the anger and frustration building up during 2000, and did nothing to defuse it. That does not mean the violence was deliberately initiated. No direct orders by Yasser Arafat launching the Intifada were ever discovered. The meticulous search of Palestinian documents, seized by Israel in the summer of 2002, conspicuously failed to come up with a "smoking gun" of this type. This is clear from *Authority Given*, a book by Israeli journalist Ronen Bergman, which, along with other accounts and interviews, presents the IDF case against Arafat, based on the seized documents. Moreover, in the first two months, less than a third of the incidents involved Palestinian shooting. Stone throwing was countered with tear gas, rubber-coated bullets, and often with live fire by the IDF.

Israeli spokesmen have repeatedly charged that Arafat spoke with two voices: one directed at Israel and international opinion, another directed at his own people and their Arab and Muslim allies. A case in point is Arafat's famous Johannesburg sermon, in which he compared the Oslo Accords to the Prophet Muhammad's *hudna* (truce) with the quraish of Mecca at Hudaybiya in 628 C.E. The truce, the Israelis gleefully point out, was deliberately broken by Muhammad two years later, when he had become stronger. This proves, they maintain, that Arafat had no intention of keeping to Oslo. The problem with this seemingly convincing argument is that it wasn't Muhammad who broke the truce. A look at the history books (an elementary precaution apparently quite beyond the competence of our present crop of politicians, journalists, and commentators) discloses that it was the quraish. Some historians allege that Muhammad provoked the quraish into breaking the truce, but this is far from certain. It can of course be argued that Arafat was cynically counting on the Israelis to break the agreement, and this might be true, but it is hardly the same thing. Nevertheless, Arafat was guilty of double-talk. He frequently condemned terror, but just as frequently he glorified the *shaheed*, "martyr bombers."

Despite his courage, Ehud Barak cannot be absolved from responsibility for the breakdown of the peace process and the subsequent confrontation. After the failure of the Camp David conference in the summer, the Israeli prime minister ostensibly continued to search for a solution, holding talks with the Palestinians notably at Taba, on the Israel–Egypt border, but his subsequent accounts of these events have been inconsistent.

In an interview with historian Benny Morris in the *New York Review of Books* on June 13, 2002, Barak insisted that the "Clinton Parameters" (new suggestions put forward by the American president) offered to the Palestinians at Taba in January 2001 were significantly better than the proposals they had been offered six months earlier at Camp David.

Had they, even at that late date, agreed, there would have been a peace settlement, he told Morris. Three months later, September 6, he was telling journalist Ari Shavit in the Israeli *Ha'aretz*, "It was plain to me that there was no chance of reaching a settlement at Taba. Therefore I said there would be no negotiations and there would be no delegation and there would be no official discussions and no documentation. The only thing that took place at Taba were non-binding contacts between senior Israelis and senior Palestinians."

It doesn't matter very much which of Barak's two versions is the true one. By the time of the Taba talks, Barak had lost his parliamentary majority and was immersed in the election campaign that he lost to Ariel Sharon. Subsequent events are described in the introduction.

Although the renewed diplomatic activity that followed the second Iraq war is extremely welcome, the gulf between the positions of the Israeli government and the Palestinian Authority remains vast. Once the two sides get down to detailed negotiations, even with the most energetic American arm twisting, it will be difficult to reconcile the Israeli prime minister's intention to retain most of the Jewish settlements in the West Bank and Gaza with the Palestinians' assumption that their state will be based on the 1967 borders. I return to this matter in the final section of the book.

Although it has been argued that the latest confrontation could, and should, have been prevented, it is correct to describe the events of the past century in Palestine as an unavoidable collision between two entirely different entities. A relatively undeveloped indigenous population, the Arabs, was confronted by a restless, dynamic immigrant community, the Jews.

For a close-up on this confrontation, let us now examine more closely the lives of two individual protagonists. Both achieved some degree of leadership and influence; both sought, in different ways, to promote conciliation and compromise. Unfortunately, neither was able to exert a lasting influence on events.

Born in 1920, Nasser Eddin Nashashibi is the scion of one of the dominant families in Palestine. His uncle and role model, Ragheb Nashashibi, was a deputy in the imperial Ottoman parliament and for fourteen years mayor of Jerusalem. Nasser Eddin, diplomat, politician, and journalist, has spent much of his life in exile but now lives in Jerusalem. Only a few months younger, Arie Lova Eliav is a Jewish immigrant from Russia, an army commander, an illegal immigrant runner, an expert in regional development, and a significant political figure. He still inhabits the house his immigrant father built in Tel Aviv in 1925.

Nashashibi and Eliav have never met, but the Israeli–Palestinian confrontation is in many ways embodied in the clash between the very different worlds of these two men.

Notes

1. From the Central Zionist Archives, Jerusalem, 1.3.1899, cited by Neville Mandel, *Middle Eastern Affairs* (Oxford, U.K.: Oxford University Press, 1965).

2. The Balfour Declaration, British Foreign Office Papers, November 3, 1917, cited in Daniel Gavron, *The Kibbutz: Awakening from Utopia* (Lanham, Md.: Rowman & Littlefield, 2000).

CHAPTER 2
NASSER EDDIN NASHASHIBI, PALESTINIAN PATRICIAN

Good morning, Mr. Gavron," boomed Nasser Eddin Nashashibi, getting up to shake hands. "What a bloody mess! I don't know what the hell is going to happen, do you?"

It was December 1987, just a few days after the outbreak of the first Intifada. All over the West Bank and Gaza, and in Jerusalem itself, young Palestinians were confronting Israeli soldiers and police with stones and gasoline bombs. Nashashibi had played a considerable part in the century-long confrontation between Jews and Arabs in Palestine, but he had not been politically active for some years, and the recent violent turn of events seemed rather beyond him.

We had arranged to meet in the lobby of the American Colony Hotel, on the seam between the Jewish and Arab parts of Jerusalem and still the most popular location for encounters between Israelis and Palestinians. The hotel was founded by an American family, which continues to involve itself in the administration, although it is now run by a Swiss chain. Most of its employees are Palestinians, and its ambiance is distinctly Arab. Nashashibi was manifestly at home in the lounge, with its pink marble floor, Persian rugs, and low brass-topped tables. The waiters bustled around him, removing his slippers, putting on his shoes, bringing him strong, sweet Turkish coffee.

He had returned to Jerusalem to supervise the rebuilding of his home in the neighborhood named after his family. A taxi was waiting for him outside, and it took us to the building site. The traditional Jerusalem stone house was being rebuilt tastefully and expensively. He related to the foreman and the other workers with the same mixture of peremptoriness and geniality that he had shown toward the waiters in

41

the hotel. He was courteous, even friendly, but there was no doubt who was the boss.

I was to have other meetings with Nasser Eddin over the years, most recently at the Carlton Towers Hotel, near his apartment in London's elegant Lowndes Street. There he demanded an extra chair from a passing waitress, and placed his hat and cane on it, before ordering coffee. The American Colony and the Carlton Towers were appropriate settings for the silver-haired Arab gentleman, with his dark blue blazer and club tie, equally at home in London and Jerusalem—and in Beirut, Cairo, Geneva, and Paris, for that matter—but not entirely at ease in the new millennium, where a second—and much more deadly—Intifada is now raging.

Nasser Eddin Nashashibi is a Palestinian Arab of the old school. When he was born, there was already a Zionist presence in Palestine, which grew rapidly during his lifetime and became the state of Israel, but he still manages to personify the atmosphere of the sleepy backwater of

Nasser Eddin Nashashibi

the Ottoman Empire that was Palestine before the Zionists came. His lifelong hero is his uncle, Ragheb Nashashibi—or to give him his proper Ottoman title, Ragheb Bey Nashashibi—mayor of Jerusalem in the early years of the British Mandate. He likes to quote Ronald Storrs, the British military governor of Jerusalem, to the effect that Ragheb Bey was "unquestionably the ablest Arab in Palestine. He was gifted with an imagination, a swiftness of perception and of action, and an absence of fatalism and *laissez-aller* infrequent among his coreligionists." This patrician remains a role model for his nephew today.

Sitting in London, Nasser Eddin recalls a recent visit to Jerusalem, when he drove past the junction between Jaffa Road and King George Street.

"You know the café that was blown up? I told my driver to stop and got out. On one side of the crossroads was the café, still boarded up; opposite was a plaque commemorating the opening of King George Street by Samuel, Ronald Storrs, and my uncle. I thought, On the one side peace, tolerance, life, and understanding; on the other strife, intolerance, death, and ignorance. What a pity! If only they had listened to the right people, we would not have reached this stage at all."

(The café to which he was referring is the Sbarro Pizza Bar, where fifteen Israelis were killed and some forty wounded by a suicide bomber on August 9, 2001. The plaque across the road from the Sbarro reads in English, Hebrew, and Arabic, "King George V Avenue, opened by His Excellency Sir Herbert Samuel, High Commissioner for Palestine in the presence of Ronald Storrs, Governor of Jerusalem and Ragheb Bey Nashashibi, Mayor of Jerusalem, 9th December, 1924.")

By listening to "the right people," Nasser Eddin meant that the Palestinians should have espoused the diplomatic approach of his family, rather than the violent policy of their rivals, the Husseinis.

The two most important families in Palestine were the Nashashibis and the Husseinis. They owned urban real estate, olive and citrus groves, farms, and businesses. Both families exercised considerable economic and political power, and they were fierce rivals. In 1920, when the mayor of Jerusalem, Mussa Kazem Husseini, marched at the head of an unruly demonstration against the Zionist offices, it was natural for the British mandatory authorities to appoint a Nashashibi in his place. Since then, a widespread perception has cast the Husseinis as staunch Arab nationalists, and the Nashashibis as corrupt politicians, who collaborated with the British and the Jews. Nasser Eddin strongly rejects this version, and, in view of the fact that the eventual result of Husseini-led confrontation was the establishment of Israel, there is more than a little force in the Nashashibi claim that the cause of Arab Palestine would have been better served by their basic approach.

Nasser Eddin recalls sitting in his uncle's home in the Egyptian city of Alexandria in the autumn of 1948, some four months after the establishment of Israel. Ragheb was talking to the son of Hassan Shukri, former mayor of Haifa, who had married an American diplomat.

"'If you see [Israeli prime minister] Ben-Gurion,' he says, 'tell him that, if he decides to erect statues of the heroes who built the state of Israel, he should not forget to put up a memorial to the Arab leader, who kept saying, no, no, no!'

"I am not qualified to identify the person he had in mind," remarks Nasser Eddin with a smile. "You can draw your own conclusion, but this was the pain and grief of a man in his eighties, who failed in his mission."

In his book, *Jerusalem's Other Voice*, he quotes Ernest Bevin, the pro-Arab British foreign minister, as telling Mussa Alami, a political ally of the Nashashibis, that Britain was giving up the mandate for Palestine: "Whenever we suggest a solution you always reject it. You would never come up with a better solution, never with a counterproposal. But we have tried and tried, and you know how much I have personally tried, and we fail the whole time. What else can we do but surrender the Mandate?"

When I showed this passage to Nasser Eddin, he remarked sadly, "It could be today, couldn't it?"

The Nashashibis trace their connection with Jerusalem back some six centuries, when the Mamluk sultan of Egypt ordered one Nasser Eddin Nashashibi to bring relief to the people of Palestine, who were suffering from famine and drought. From that time on, the family played an important role in Palestine, and particularly in Jerusalem. They included political leaders, scholars, teachers, lawyers, and doctors. They also contributed to the charitable *waqf* institutions, which ran schools, mosques, and kitchens for the poor and needy. One of the most worthy was the Syrian Orphanage Foundation, where the children wove carpets and used brass, mother of pearl, olive wood, and black stone from the Dead Sea shore to make attractive artifacts.

"We grew up with a tradition of service," explains Nasser Eddin. "We knew we had to help people. I remember visiting prisons. We even helped Jews. I was proud to be a Nashashibi, but I knew it involved obligations."

Osman Nashashibi, Nasser Eddin's grandfather, was a member of the Ottoman parliament. Haj Rashid Nashashibi, his great uncle, was a big landowner and a member of the Jerusalem city council. An uncle, Is'af, was a writer and teacher, with an enormous library. Is'af's cousin, Azmi, who was a graduate of the London School of Economics, became the director of the Public Information Office in Jaffa and later the head of Arabic Broadcasting during World War II. Aref, one of Ragheb Bey Nashashibi's cousins, was the top man in the department of the Muslim charitable foundations, in Jerusalem.

"In every branch of the administration and in every institute of learning, you could always find a Nashashibi," says Nasser Eddin proudly. (There is even a Nashashibi, a distant cousin, in the present Palestinian Authority.) Ragheb Bey, apart from serving in the Ottoman parliament, was an engineer and town planner, a graduate of the University of Constantinople. He was district planner in Jerusalem before becoming mayor and was responsible for building the southern town of Beersheba. He served as Jerusalem's mayor for fourteen years.

Nasser Eddin remembers his uncle as abstemious in his habits, apart from smoking eighty Turkish cigarettes a day in an amber holder. His suits were made by the best tailors in London and Paris. He had an enormous collection of walking sticks, some with ivory handles, which he matched to his suits, and he always wore his crimson tarboosh. He was the first person in Jerusalem to own a large American limousine, a dark green Packard, which was changed every year.

He was married to a Roman Catholic, whom he met while studying in Constantinople. Always known as Madame Nashashibi, she spoke English, French, Italian, Turkish, and Arabic. She was beautiful and intelligent, and she was a superb hostess. Some nationalist circles criticized Ragheb for marrying a Christian, but he never tried to persuade her to change her faith.

In his memoirs, Storrs pens an amusing description of Nashashibi's administration:

> His attitude toward his municipal councilors was that of a solo instrument toward an entirely muted orchestra . . . he was an oriental incarnation of a Tammany Boss. To watch his expression as he submitted to me some budgetary proposal based on cogent but quite unacceptable arguments was a satisfaction of which, though often repeated, I never wearied.[1]

Nasser Eddin does not entirely contradict this account. In his book, he approvingly quotes his uncle as saying:

> I have lived and filled the post of mayor of Jerusalem in my own way. I was the boss. I did not have to consult with anybody about anything, and I made my own decisions myself. . . . I alone decided on the budget of the municipality and its various plans. I alone acted, planned, ordered and executed. I refused interference from anybody.[2]

He goes on to argue that his style of government was unacceptable to the Jews, who turned against him in his last mayoral election, ensuring his defeat by the Husseinis and their allies. In conversation, though, Nasser Eddin stresses Ragheb Bey's overall tolerance and belief in coexistence with all the different elements that made up the Jerusalem of the time. He accepted the right of the Jews to have Saturday as their Sabbath, streets named after their prominent historical personalities, and their own slaughtering arrangements in line with their religious requirements. There was no conflict between Arabs and Jews when he was growing up, he maintains; Jerusalem was a city of many communities.

Contradicting the generally accepted picture of Turkey's Ottoman Empire as corrupt and degenerate, Nasser Eddin defends it as a regime of peace, tolerance, and protection, where each community could look after its own interests. The Arabs could rise to the highest positions, even though they were not Turks. Old Arab families of notables, with a tradition of learning and leadership, such as the Dajanis, the Alamis, the Khalidis, the Husseinis, and the Nashashibis, held official positions in Palestine. Other families were dominant in Syria and Iraq.

As an example of this tolerance and coexistence, he cites the tradition of foster brothers, whereby neighbors giving birth at more or less the same

NASSER EDDIN NASHASHIBI, PALESTINIAN PATRICIAN   47

time would suckle each other's children. For example, when Mussa Alami (later a political ally of the Nashashibis) was born in 1897, he was suckled by the wife of a neighboring Jewish grocer, and her son was suckled by Alami's mother. The two boys were regarded as foster brothers, and they continued to be friends and visit each other on Muslim and Jewish festivals. Their friendship ended in the 1920s, when hostility between Jews and Arabs in Palestine escalated.

Nashashibi describes the Jerusalem in which he grew up as "an Arab city," albeit sacred to three faiths: Islam, Judaism, and Christianity. The Old City of Jerusalem, that part surrounded by the wall built by Sultan Suleiman in the sixteenth century, was divided into four quarters: Muslim, Christian, Jewish, and Armenian. There was, he says, more than mutual tolerance among the communities; there was active cooperation.

In fact, statistically, the Jews had been a majority of the population since the last decades of the nineteenth century, and around the time of Nasser Eddin Nashashibi's birth, well over half of the population of Jerusalem was Jewish. Nevertheless, the administration, even after the British ruled Palestine, was largely in the hands of the Arabs. Of Ragheb Bey's six councilors, two were Muslim Arabs, two Christian Arabs, and two were Jews.

Looking back on the years between his birth and the establishment of Israel, Nasser Eddin forcefully rejects the depiction of his family as collaborators. He insists that the Nashashibi policy of cooperation with the British—and even with some Jewish personalities such as Judah Magnes, who favored a binational state for Jews and Arabs in Palestine—would have produced better results for his people.

"Believe me, Ragheb Bey and his cousin, Fahri Nashashibi, understood both the power of the Arabs and that of the Jews," he argues. "In particular, they understood the *limitations* of both our power and that of the Jews. They were men of the world. All the leading personalities involved, Englishmen, Arabs, and Jews, visited their homes."

Nasser Eddin was educated at St. George's School and Bishop Gobat School in Jerusalem, both modeled on English public schools. There he wore a cap and blazer, learned to play cricket and football, joined the Boy Scouts, and attended Christian prayers. Everyone knew he was a Muslim, but there was mutual respect. Many years later, when he was director of the

Jordanian Broadcasting Service in Ramallah (today in the territory of the Palestinian Authority), he was famous for his Christmas broadcasts about Jesus.

Outside the school, he remembers tanks rumbling through the streets, curfews, being stopped and searched by British troops. His parents told him of the promises to the Arabs and the Balfour Declaration. He and his friends could not understand how the British could give away his country to somebody else. He says that early on he learned the difference between what he was taught at school and the reality outside.

After matriculation, Nasser Eddin went to the American University of Beirut, where he studied political science, but he is adamant that his real political education was in "the wonderful school of Ragheb Bey Nashashibi." After graduating in Beirut, he lived with his uncle, and they discussed politics every night. He is indignant that many historians—even some Israeli scholars—minimize the role of his uncle and praise Haj Amin Husseini, the mufti of Jerusalem, for his control of "the street."

He notes that in 1935, when Ragheb Nashashibi formed his National Defense Party (NDP), he had the support of the ten leading mayors of Palestine, including those of Jaffa, Haifa, Nablus, Tulkarm, Ramle, and Jericho. There are no reliable statistics, he concedes, but the NDP did have support in Palestine. It lost to the Husseinis for a number of reasons, at least partly because it received no help from the Arabs of neighboring countries, no help from the British, and no help from the Jews.

In view of the fact that its constitution included a pledge "to fight for the full independence of Palestine, with guaranteed sovereignty over all of Palestine, and without acknowledgement of any international guarantees that might lessen, influence, or damage that Arab sovereignty," it is perhaps not surprising that the NDP did not receive help from the Jews. Nevertheless, Nasser Eddin has a point. If there was an Arab element in Palestine that was ready to talk, it was the Nashashibis, and it can be argued that the Jewish side did not take sufficient advantage of this. On at least one occasion, the Jerusalem municipal elections of 1934, the Jewish side ganged up with the Husseinis against them.

"Today the whole world talks about fighting terrorism," declares Nasser Eddin with bitterness, "but in those days Ragheb and Fahri Nashashibi stood alone in opposing the terrorism of the Husseinis. In 1936, Ragheb sent Fahri to the Jaffa port workers, telling them to call off their strike. He warned them that the Jews would build their own port in Tel Aviv—and that, of course, is exactly what happened."

Threatened by the Husseini party during the Arab Revolt, Fahri asked for protection from the police, who sent him to the army. He was shuttled back and forth between the two forces, with neither offering any assistance. He was shot and wounded in Jaffa in 1937, shot at in Jerusalem in 1940, and finally assassinated in Baghdad in 1941. Nasser Eddin himself claims to have been a target of assassination on three separate occasions.

In 1939, when the British issued their white paper, which virtually abrogated the Balfour Declaration, Ragheb Nashashibi had been certain that the Arabs were about to accept the recommendations of the British government that would have given them an independent state, and limited both Jewish immigration and land purchases. He told the Egyptian press that the conference in London had been a success. However, once again, the Palestinian Arabs rejected the British proposals.

Many years later, when the state of Israel was an established fact, Ragheb Bey ruminated on the past: "I do not know who did more harm to the Palestinian people . . . the man who was reasonable and accepted the rule of the Arab majority, with the Jews as a minority, or the Palestinian leaders who kept on saying no, until the Jews became a majority."[3]

It is true that the moderates lacked a certain will to claim power, admits Nasser Eddin. His uncle did not boast all the time how suitable he was to be a leader. He was a thoroughly honest man who said publicly the same things he said in private. He did not cheat or lie. He lost out to opponents who were more ruthless than he was.

"Since the days of Socrates, modesty has been the characteristic of the real intellectual," says Nasser Eddin with feeling. "Ragheb Bey was humble. It is a matter of character."

Another moderate who always rejected a leadership role was his friend Mussa Alami. Nasser Eddin credits Alami with the Arab success at the 1939 London conference and the publication of the white paper limiting Jewish immigration and land purchases. Alami continued his involvement right through to the end of the British Mandate in 1948, frequently meeting with British foreign secretary Ernest Bevin. In the 1930s, he had held several meetings with David Ben-Gurion, who became Israel's prime minister in 1948. He even met Ben-Gurion after the 1967 war, but through it all, Alami insisted that he was not a leader and had not been authorized by anyone to represent the Palestinians. He also was the target of many assassination attempts.

As a graduate of the American University of Beirut, Nasser Eddin thinks he understands the Americans, and Jewish influence on American policy. He recalls talking to members of the Anglo-American Committee of Inquiry, which came to Palestine in 1946, having first visited the survivors of the Holocaust in Europe and a number of Arab capitals. The committee rejected partition and recommended the British Mandate should continue as a UN trusteeship. It also recommended that entry visas be immediately granted to 100,000 Jews currently living in displaced persons camps in Europe. Nasser Eddin said he spoke to Bartley Crum, an American member of the committee. In 1947, Crum wrote an impassioned account of his mission, explaining how he became converted to the Zionist point of view after seeing the Holocaust survivors' camps in Europe and the achievements of the Jews in Palestine. Nashashibi remembers it differently.

"Bartley Crum told me that the decisions of the committee had nothing to do with anything they had seen or heard," he relates. "He said he was representing President Truman and would pursue American national interests. Unlike the Europeans, the Americans are not hypocritical. They say straight out what they mean."

Nasser Eddin does not, as do some Arab spokesmen, play down the Holocaust. He notes that "Western sympathy for the plight of the Jews was a formidable force that the Arabs could not possibly match. It is right not to forget what Mr. Hitler did, but we have to move on, to continue with our lives."

I suggested to Nasser Eddin that the Palestinians and other Arabs never really understood Zionism.

"Our struggle against Zionism came before our understanding of it," he agreed. "But the Zionists did not help us. They didn't try to explain themselves. Since the 1930s, Ben-Gurion and the other leaders came with demands. You can't expect us to be pragmatic, when the other side isn't."

Although he looks back on the Anglo-American Committee with some skepticism, Nasser Eddin had a completely different attitude toward the United Nations Special Committee on Palestine (UNSCOP), which came to Palestine in 1947. He was in Cairo when the committee was appointed, and Haj Amin Husseini asked him to go to Palestine and inform the local Arab leaders that they must boycott the new committee. In vain did Nashashibi plead the cause of the UN body. It was "the new international child of an international father," he suggested. It had been appointed by the UN General Assembly and its members belonged to small states, which were neutral. UNSCOP also had some important Muslim members, such as the representatives of India and Iran.

The mufti was adamant; he was determined that Nasser Eddin should make it plain that any Arabs cooperating with the committee would be regarded as traitors and would be punished accordingly. In the end, Nasser Eddin agreed to telephone his Uncle Ragheb, who remarked sarcastically that he had "full confidence" in the mufti and would "abide by his wise decisions concerning this problem." Haj Amin was delighted with this response from his old rival. The Palestinian Arab leaders obeyed the mufti's orders, with the single exception of Mussa Alami. After UNSCOP left Palestine, without hearing the Arab side, Alami wrote to Geneva, offering to present them with the Arab point of view, but he received no reply.

The result was the UN partition plan of 1947, which was approved by the General Assembly and led directly to the establishment of the state of Israel the following year. As the fighting raged in Jerusalem, Ragheb Nashashibi's house was severely damaged, and he and his wife decided to leave for Alexandria. After 1948, notes Nasser Eddin, some members of his family went to live in Cairo and Alexandria, and others were forced to leave Jerusalem for Amman and Damascus. Many left for the United States; others went to Kuwait and Saudi Arabia. Is'af Nashashibi's magnificent library was destroyed in the 1948 war, and some of its volumes can be found today at the Hebrew University. He is buried in Cairo. Azmi Nashashibi is also buried in Cairo. Nasser Eddin's mother died in London; his aunt, Madame Nashashibi, in Alexandria. Many other relatives were buried far from Jerusalem. Like the other Palestinian refugees, says Nashashibi, the members of his family have three alternatives: living in refugee camps, living under Israeli administration, "as second- or third-class citizens," or trying to earn a living in countries (including Arab countries) where they feel far from welcome.

In September 1948, the mufti proclaimed the "Arab Government of all Palestine" in Gaza, which was recognized by all the Arab states except Transjordan. After a few days, the Egyptian government ordered the mufti to leave Gaza and come to Cairo. The Arabs were chronically divided, recalls Nashashibi, with Egypt, Syria, and Transjordan each blaming the others for the loss of Palestine.

In December 1948, King Abdulla of Transjordan incorporated the West Bank into a united kingdom that he called Jordan. The all-Palestine government never got off the ground, and Haj Amin Husseini moved to Beirut. Abdulla invited Ragheb Nashashibi to become governor-general of the West Bank. The Jordanian prime minister, a known supporter of the mufti, continuously interfered with his administration. Ragheb, who by then was an ill man, complained to Abdulla, who responded by appointing him guardian of Haram al-Sharif and custodian of the Holy Sites.

Nasser Eddin, who had become a political adviser to the Royal Hashemite Court, brought the appointment to Ragheb at the American Colony Hotel in Jerusalem and personally wrote his uncle's formal acceptance speech. The two went to the Rawda College near Haram al-Sharif for the ceremony. Despite the grandeur of the occasion, Nasser Eddin says that he and his uncle felt that the appointment was marginal and only served to emphasize how much of Jerusalem the Arabs had lost. The division of Jerusalem between Israel and Jordan was for them "a blasphemy and a blight on civilization."

He recalls that it was not only the Israelis who refused to recognize his uncle's new appointment; representatives of the Christian churches protested vehemently. A few months later, Ragheb was admitted to Augusta Victoria Hospital, suffering from cancer of the liver. Abdulla came to visit. Recalling his meetings there with Winston Churchill, Herbert Samuel, and Lawrence of Arabia in 1921, the king told Nasser Eddin that the place was cursed, a symbol of bad luck. So many Arab misfortunes had occurred there, when it was the seat of the British high commissioner. Two days after the visit, Ragheb Bey died. He was buried in Jerusalem. His old house was demolished and is now the site of the Ambassador Hotel.

Three months after Ragheb Bey's death, Abdulla was assassinated at the entrance to the Aksa Mosque. After a short interregnum, his grandson Hussein became king of Jordan, but Nasser Eddin Nashashibi did not remain at the Hashemite Court for long. Like his uncle before him, he could not handle the intrigues: The king wanted one thing, the prime minister something else; the Iraqis were competing for influence with the

Saudis. He found himself walking a tightrope, fearful of falling to the left or the right. He left Jordan and went to work for the Egyptian paper, *Akbar al-Yawm*. Subsequently he served as roving ambassador for the Arab League, interspersed with assignments for leading Egyptian papers.

The Israeli media has treated Nasser Eddin Nashashibi as a sort of éminence grise, a prestigious behind-the-scenes operator, with the ears of Arab kings and presidents and Israeli leaders. Certainly he has moved around the Middle East with remarkable freedom, but it has to be said that the cautious Nashashibi gives contradictory signals about his later role.

Both in his book and in conversation, he describes a meeting with Israel's prime minister Levi Eshkol, shortly after the 1967 Six-Day War. Eshkol, who was by then a sick man, told him he could give him thirty minutes but then talked to him for three hours. Eshkol emphasized that Jerusalem's holy places were open to all, offering to helicopter King Faisal of Saudi Arabia to the Aksa Mosque so that he could pray there.

Nasser Eddin countered that Eshkol should declare that Israel had no interest in the territories conquered in 1967 and was prepared to withdraw to its previous borders. He suggested the prime minister declare that every Arab who left Jerusalem during or after the war would be permitted to return. Bringing an Arab monarch by helicopter to pray in Jerusalem was not the answer, he told the prime minister. He should not annex Jerusalem to a small state, when its sovereignty belonged to heaven.

He left the meeting feeling that neither side liked what the other had said, but he sensed that Eshkol realized that the occupation of Jerusalem was a problem for the Jews themselves.

"I liked Eshkol," he says emphatically. "He was a gentleman!"

The Israeli prime minister died shortly afterward and was succeeded by Golda Meir, who was much less accommodating toward Palestinian aspirations.

Nasser Eddin says that he sent a report of his meeting with Eshkol to Egypt's President Nasser, but he insists that he had absolutely no authority from Nasser or anyone else to represent anybody. He is simply an ordinary citizen of Jerusalem. He was given a VIP travel permit by the Israeli military authorities, but they refused to renew it after he criticized Israel on various Arab television stations. His criticism concerned the Jerusalem municipality, which took some of his land to build Road Number One, which cuts through the eastern part of the city, and refused to compensate him.

"I understand that I was not compensated for property I lost in 1948," he says reasonably. "There was a cutoff date for that compensation, but Road Number One was built in the mid-1990s. Taking my land for that without payment is sheer robbery, and I have said so."

He characterizes the refusal to renew his VIP permit as "childish." He can do without it. The permit merely made crossing the Allenby Bridge, or entering via the airport, a bit smoother. He has homes in London, Geneva, Paris, and Beirut. He doesn't have to come to Jerusalem at all, although he still regards it as his home. He feels that the Israelis should want him to come to Jerusalem, and this is where he becomes inconsistent.

This "ordinary citizen of Jerusalem" says mysteriously that the Israeli leaders know all that he has done for peace between Israelis and Arabs. He was a good friend of Yitzhak Rabin, and, before her death, his widow, Leah Rabin, had testified to that. Israeli cabinet ministers Shimon Peres and Ephraim Sneh also know all about this, he claims. Bearing in mind his history, Nasser Eddin must surely be referring to contacts between King Hussein of Jordan and various Israeli prime ministers, including Rabin, whom the king manifestly liked and with whom he signed a peace treaty. But Nasser Eddin is of a generation that does not always spell out everything explicitly.

"If there is anyone who has done more than me for peace, I'd like to meet him," he declares. "As for the present Israeli mayor, Ehud Olmert, he can go to hell!"

(Since our conversations, Olmert has left his position as mayor of Jerusalem and now serves as minister of Industry and Commerce. Peres and Sneh are no longer cabinet members.)

After our last meeting in London, Nasser Eddin looks forward to meeting again in Jerusalem and sitting in his garden. Is he intending to go back soon?

"Of course," he says, pointing at the leaden sky, "look at the weather here."

He is nostalgic about the Jerusalem of his youth, the Jerusalem of Ragheb Bey Nashashibi.

"The Jerusalem he knew and built and served and loved does not exist anymore. His Jerusalem was peaceful, calm, romantic, poetic, friendly, and beautiful. The Jerusalem of today is just the opposite. His old Jewish friends were noble people: advocate Eli Eliachar, Professor Magnes, Dr. Mandel, and many others in the fields of literature, the arts, and politics.

"A walled city, set on its seven hills, with the Dome of the Rock and the Mosque of al-Aksa in the Haram al-Sharif, dominating the foreground . . . a bit more building outside the walls, certainly, but not those hideous, high-rise concrete blocks which today overwhelm the city from all sides. Now Jerusalem is being rapidly transformed by developers to look much like a bustling American city. It has been robbed of its unique character, robbed of the beauty which used to strike visitors as forcibly as that of Venice."

The overidealization does not lessen the sincerity. As observed previously, Nasser Eddin Nashashibi is yesterday's man. He does not know today's leaders of the Palestinian national movement, he says, but he points out that they too will not live forever. A solution must be satisfactory to the Palestinian people as a whole.

"My dear sir," he proclaims, "it is nonsense to talk of insoluble problems. Every problem has a solution. Reason can solve everything. But bombs, rockets, and bullets have no place anymore. Believe me, every aspect of the Arab–Jewish problem can be solved in one month.

"However, if the solution is not realistic, wise, and practical, it won't last. You can't just build villages all over the West Bank, wherever you want them, but, if you make peace, it will open doors to Israel all over the world. I would like to see this happening; it is part of the solution."

Notes

1. Ronald Storr, *Orientations* (London: Nicholson & Watson, 1939).
2. Nasser Eddin Nashashibi, *Jerusalem's Other Voice* (Exeter: Ithaca, 1990).
3. Nashashibi, *Jerusalem's Other Voice*.

CHAPTER 3
LOVA ELIAV, ISRAELI PIONEER

As I drove west along the black ribbon of road that cut through the dusty, rust-colored plain of the western Negev, I realized that I was actually leaving behind the problem I was seeking to address. The West Bank, the Gaza strip, and the populated part of Israel were to the north. That was where the violence was raging. I was on my way to Nitzana, a peaceful academic community, almost completely divorced from our current problems. Furthermore, I was going to see a man who was no longer directly involved in the Israeli–Palestinian confrontation.

Arie Lova Eliav would be turning eighty in three months. He was engaged in building a new center for education and research, a miraculous green jewel in the arid desert wastes. Palestinian, Jordanian, and Egyptian students had once been invited to this desert campus. Their visits, in which they studied desert farming and ecology together with Israeli students, had been a huge success, but since the outbreak of the new Intifada, such joint projects were in a deep freeze. Today, Eliav is busy raising money for buildings and equipment, educating Israeli youngsters and assisting new immigrants from the former Soviet Union and Ethiopia to become Israelis. He is fostering desert agriculture, solar energy, archaeology, and Jewish roots.

Despite his lack of direct involvement in Israeli–Palestinian affairs, he represents both the problem and the solution to the conundrum. A passionate Zionist, who has done as much to build the state of Israel as any other man, he was also the first mainstream Israeli to recognize the Palestinian situation and to try to do something about it.

Eliav played a major role in settling the mass immigration that flooded into the new state of Israel in its first years. He directed the development of the Lachish region, southwest of Jerusalem, setting up a barrier of Jewish settlements between Gaza and the West Bank. He established the town of Arad and its regional industries, creating a Jewish presence in the empty eastern Negev and the Judaean desert. Today, he is involved in developing the western Negev and opposes a proposal to transfer a portion of this area to the Palestinians in a land swap for some of the West Bank Jewish settlements.

At the same time, Eliav was the first figure from Israel's political establishment to advocate a Palestinian state in the West Bank and Gaza, alongside Israel. As early as 1968, Eliav promoted this policy, and he paid for it with his political career. As secretary-general of the ruling Labor Party, Eliav was effectively the number two man in the state of Israel, but he abandoned his position, becoming the first mainstream Israeli to meet with representatives of the PLO.

Today, the concept of two states for two peoples is the basic international consensus, but it was not always so: When Eliav proposed the idea in 1968, he was regarded as a traitor to the Zionist vision and pushed to the fringes of Israeli political life.

As with Nasser Eddin Nashashibi, I held several conversations with Lova Eliav, mostly in his bungalow in Nitzana and in the Tel Aviv apart-

Lova Eliav

ment building, where he has lived since 1925. The two locations—the desert outpost and the austerely furnished flat—are appropriate to the balding veteran, with his open-necked shirt and sandals. Unlike Nashashibi, who sat quietly during our meetings, content to summon his memory, Eliav was constantly jumping up to bring me a book, or a pamphlet, or a newspaper cutting, or a photograph to illustrate his point.

I first met Eliav in Arad in the early 1960s, when I and my family were among the very first residents of that new town overlooking the Dead Sea in the eastern Negev desert. He had resigned as director the previous year, but the team of architects, engineers, technicians, and builders who had founded the town still looked to him for inspiration and guidance. Many of the team were my friends, and, when Eliav paid a visit, the introduction was swiftly made. It was the start of a warm friendship. For me, Lova—he is still generally addressed by his Russian name—has always been the quintessential Israeli: at once idealistic and pragmatic, with a restless energy that he channeled into concrete achievement. The more I got to know him, the more astounded I became at the sheer volume of his achievement, the extraordinary number of tasks and missions he had carried out.

Born in Moscow, Lova Eliav arrived at the port of Jaffa in 1925, with his mother, half-brother, and twin sister. He was three and a half years old. His first memory is being torn from his mother's skirts by an Arab boatman, "a frightening looking man with gold teeth and a big mustache," who gently lowered him from the deck of the *Lenin*, in which they had sailed from Odessa, onto the small skiff that took them ashore. Not long afterward, he was introduced to his father, "a nice-looking man with a white beard." His father, a once-prosperous merchant, who lost most of his money during World War I, had preceded them to Palestine. He had enough left to buy a plot of land in Tel Aviv, where he built a single-storied house. Three stories were subsequently added, and today the small apartment bloc houses the extended Eliav family, with Lova and his wife occupying the top floor.

The Tel Aviv of those days was a young city of white buildings on golden sands. He remembers swimming in the sea, playing on the beach, catching lizards in Wadi Musrara (today the location of the Ayalon Freeway, Tel Aviv's main ring road), and having picnics by the River Yarkon.

For some years, it was an idyllic childhood, and then, in 1929, when he was seven years old, he heard shots being fired from neighboring Jaffa. Running with his friends to Hadassah Hospital on nearby Balfour Street, he saw trucks arriving with dead bodies. He remembers sensing something negative about Jaffa, where the Arabs lived, but the bad vibrations soon passed. His life continued with membership in the scouts, camping, and field trips.

Three major personalities stand out in the Tel Aviv of his youth: Meir Dizengoff, the mayor; Rabbi Uzziel, the chief Sephardi rabbi, who was preceded everywhere by an elegant *kavass* (major-domo), with a staff that he banged on the ground; and Chaim Nahman Bialik, the poet of the Hebrew renaissance. When Eliav was ten, he won a school essay competition, which led to a friendship with the childless poet. Written on a photograph of the two of them is the message, "To Arie, may you be as light as a deer, as heroic as a lion, to accomplish the labor of your people." *Arie* means lion in Hebrew, *Lova* means lion cub in Russian, but Eliav has been obsessed all his life with the concept of the deer. He married a woman with the family name of Zvi, meaning deer. He called his children Zvi, Ofra, and Ayal, names for different types of deer; his grandchildren are named Yael and Ayala (ibex and gazelle). When he wrote his book about sharing the land with the Palestinians, he called it *Eretz Hazvi*, "Land of Splendor," a traditional name for the Land of Israel, but it also means "Land of the Hart."

When he was fifteen, his personal age of innocence was over. It was 1936, the year of the Arab Revolt and general strike. In Herzliya High School, a light shining in his eyes, his hand on a Bible, he was sworn into the Hagana defense force.

"I knew it would happen," explains Eliav. "My elder brother was already a member. It was the done thing in our crowd. All of us joined."

In the school cellars they underwent weapons training. Outside they took messages from one Hagana unit to another, either running across the dunes or riding their bicycles down the streets and paths. At sixteen, he and his friends were recruited into the Ghaffirs, the official British-sponsored supernumerary police, the members of which served unofficially in the Hagana. Of that experience, Eliav recalls, "We had rifles bigger than we were. We used to be sent at night to defend isolated settlements. Our unit was stationed in a moshav of Yemenite Jews, south of Tel Aviv, which was coming under fire from two large Arab villages, Yazur and Beit Dejen. We lay in the dunes, not thirty meters from the Arabs.

"One night I heard somebody crawling through the scrub opposite me. I saw the flare of his match as he lit a grenade. I fired at the light and the grenade exploded. In the morning I saw his dead body. The grenade had blown him to bits.

"I wasn't thinking about Zionism that night—just about survival. I didn't want him to throw the grenade and kill me. That was the situation: them or us."

From his teachers, his youth movement and Hagana commanders, through field trips and hikes in the desert, to the Jordan River and sites such as Masada, Eliav developed a knowledge and love of the land. His father inculcated him with the knowledge of Jewish sources and a love of tradition. It was difficult for his father, who became a parent late in his life, to live with the knowledge that his young son was out every night and probably in danger, but he accepted the situation. There was no question of his not going. Everybody went. As a bourgeois, his father had fled from Soviet Russia. As a "Zionist to the very depths of his soul," he had come to Palestine. Now he was forced to face the consequences. He didn't like it, but he didn't flinch.

In 1939, with the outbreak of World War II, Eliav and his Hagana comrades had to make a choice: either to join the Palmah, the kibbutz-based mobile strike force of the Hagana, or to enlist in the British army. Eliav decided on the army, serving first in the Royal Artillery and later in the Royal Engineers. After service in the Western Desert, he embarked with thousands of British, Indian, African, and Palestinian troops at Port Said in Egypt, sailing from there to the Allied bridgehead in southern Italy in 1943. His service in Europe brought him into contact with the Jewish survivors of the Holocaust and led to his volunteering after the war in organizing Aliya Bet, the "illegal" immigration of Jews to Palestine.

"Until then, I was like a surfer," says Eliav today. "I just did what all my friends were doing: scouts, Hagana, Ghaffirs, army. In the supernumerary police, I was a simple constable; in the army, I was a sergeant; but now, in Aliya Bet, I took a leadership role." He performed this vital work for two years and has chronicled one of his most important missions, commanding the refugee ship, *Ulua,* in a book, which relates how he returned to Europe in 1946, with a forged Dutch passport in the name of William van Groot. He and some colleagues had made their way from Palestine in a series of rickety Greek, Turkish, and Italian vessels to Italy and from there to Marseilles in France to take command of a ship that would bring Jews to Palestine.

The *Ulua* was an American Coast Guard vessel that had been adapted for escort purposes during the war, was subsequently used as a cargo boat, and was now due to be refitted yet again for running Jewish refugees. The flag was Honduran, the crew mostly American Jewish volunteers, three of them formerly of the U.S. Navy.

The cabins and mess rooms of the *Ulua* were eliminated, partitions were ripped out, and the ship was converted into one huge dormitory, with showers and lavatories, which would take some two thousand passengers in crowded conditions. The first pickup point was Trelleborg in Sweden, where thousands of Jewish women, rescued from Nazi concentration camps by the Swedish Red Cross, were living. The British were making strenuous efforts to block the movement of Jewish immigrants to Palestine, so everything was accomplished by subterfuge. Officially, the Jewish refugees were being taken to the French port of Le Havre for eventual transport to Cuba for "rehabilitation and resettlement."

The ship's "doctor," a former medical corpsman from the U.S. Marine Corps, dispensed aspirin to all the passengers, whatever their ailments, but he won them over with an impeccable bedside manner. Tanya, a Hebrew-speaking children's nurse from Kovno in Lithuania, whose entire family perished in the Holocaust, volunteered to assist the doctor. In due course she was to become Mrs. Eliav.

Despite all sorts of problems, the *Ulua* took on more passengers, until it was crammed with some two thousand men, women, and children, all survivors of the concentration camps, and sailed east. Reaching the coast of Palestine south of Tel Aviv, it was intercepted by a British destroyer and ordered to stop. The crew hoisted the Israeli flag, and all of the passengers burst into the Jewish national anthem, *Hatikva* (The Hope). British troops boarded the vessel to be met with violent resistance. After the soldiers had overcome the refugees and crew, the *Ulua*'s passengers were loaded onto British warships and taken to Cyprus, where they were interned in a transit camp.

Eliav and his comrades quickly escaped from Cyprus and returned to Palestine. It took the *Ulua* refugees a little longer, but they eventually arrived in the state of Israel. Lova, who had become an officer in the new state's navy, married Tanya and took her to the family home in Tel Aviv. In an advanced state of pregnancy, she came under sniper fire from Jaffa, while standing near her new home.

Describing this incident laconically, Eliav stresses that the Israeli–Palestinian conflict is one involving two sets of refugees: the Jewish refugees, who created Israel, and the Palestinian refugees, who were expelled. He readily concedes that most of the Palestinians who fled in 1947–1948 were expelled by the IDF. He points out, however, that where the Arab side won, in East Jerusalem, the Etzion Bloc of settlements south of Jerusalem, and in the Jordan Valley, the Jews were the ones to be expelled.

"Luckily for us, we won more battles than they did in 1948," he observes, "so there were many more Arabs expelled."

After the war, Eliav played a leading part in the settlement of Jews from Europe and the Middle East, who flooded into the country, tripling its population in the first few years. The early years were chaotic, with the newcomers dumped in former Arab neighborhoods, tented camps, and hastily built shantytowns. Eliav urged his superiors to improve the methods of settling the immigrants, and in 1954, he became the director of the Lachish Development Region, roughly the area between the southern West Bank and Gaza. There he planned and executed the development of an area, with kibbutzim, moshav farming villages, and regional service centers, around a newly built town, Kiryat Gat.

Subsequently, he planned the development of Arad, east of Beersheba. Lachish became the prototype for properly organized regional development; Arad was Israel's first properly planned new town. After his time in Arad, Eliav was sent to coordinate the rehabilitation of the Chavzin Region in Iran, following an earthquake in 1962. Subsequently he headed similar missions in Nicaragua and Morocco, after earthquakes in those countries.

Between Lachish and Arad, he had served in the diplomatic post of first secretary in Israel's Moscow embassy, where he also performed intelligence duties. Later he would serve in an intelligence capacity on missions to Morocco and Kurdistan. In 1965, he became a member of the Knesset, Israel's parliament, and was appointed a deputy cabinet minister, first in the Ministry of Industry and Commerce, and then in the Ministry of Immigrant Absorption.

After the Six-Day War of 1967, he arranged with Prime Minister Levi Eshkol and Defense Minister Moshe Dayan to visit the newly conquered territories of the West Bank and Gaza. He envisioned development projects for the Palestinians, similar to those he had carried out in Lachish and Arad. It was a turning point in his life.

"I suddenly realized that there was a people out there," he says, "a people with its own national movement, its own culture, literature, poetry, its own institutions—above all its own refugees."

He admits that, prior to this, he had not thought a great deal about the problem of the Palestinians. Like most Israelis of his generation, he was occupied with building a new nation. The Palestinians were simply a nuisance, an enemy who infiltrated the borders, carrying out murder and sabotage. Now, he perceived the reality of the Palestinians of the West Bank and Gaza. In particular, the inhabitants of the refugee camps struck a chord with the man who had spent two years of his life bringing Jewish refugees to Israel.

He reported to Eshkol on what he had learned about the Palestinians. In fact, he must have spoken to the Israeli prime minister just around the time of the latter's conversation with Nasser Eddin Nashashibi. Unfortunately, Eshkol did not have long to live, and he was succeeded by Golda Meir, "the strongest prime minister Israel ever had, even including Ben-Gurion," according to Eliav. He sent her a pamphlet that he had written, *New Challenges for Israel*, in which he argued that Israel could fulfill its Zionist mission within its previous borders; the West Bank and Gaza should be kept as a "peace deposit" and an eventual independent Palestinian state. Meir never read the pamphlet.

Shortly afterward, Eliav was elected secretary-general of the ruling Mapai Party, with a mandate to unite it with Ahdut Avoda and Rafi, two factions that had broken off in the past. In the new situation after the Six-Day War, it was felt that past doctrinal differences had become irrelevant. Elected to this key position, Eliav was interviewed by *Time* magazine, and this time the American-educated Meir did read it. The prime minister was shocked to learn about his views on a Palestinian state. She proposed a debate in the party, but Eliav declined, suggesting that they should postpone their confrontation while he proceeded with the party merger. He convened a congress at which the reunited Israel Labor Party was successfully launched, but he had been sidelined from Golda Meir's "kitchen cabinet," where the important political decisions were made. Realizing he no longer had Meir's trust, he resigned from the position of party secretary-general to write *Land of the Hart*, in which he elaborated his ideas regarding a two-state solution to the Israeli–Palestinian problem.

Meir continued to be dumbfounded by Eliav's behavior and asked everyone she met, "What on Earth has happened to Lova?"

She simply did not grasp what he was talking about. As far as she was concerned, the Arabs had quite enough states. There was no such thing as a Palestinian people, she argued. If anyone was Palestinian, *she* was, and she had her old (mandatory) Palestinian passport to prove it. Lova Eliav of all people should not hold such unthinkable views. He had served in the Hagana, the IDF, and the diplomatic corps. He had engaged more than anyone else in the "sacred" task of absorbing immigrants. He had created Lachish and Arad. He had joined the right party and become its secretary-general. He was one of the young leaders in line to succeed Golda Meir herself.

"What indeed happened?" I challenge him. "You yourself said that when you shot an Arab villager in 1937, it was 'us or them.' Surely Golda was saying just the same."

"What happened was that we had achieved our state, which by 1967 was strong enough to defeat Egypt, Syria, and Jordan," he replies. "The Palestinians had nothing. We had our part of Palestine; it was time to let them have their part."

It is important to stress that the Israeli settlement enterprise in the West Bank, Gaza, Sinai, and the Golan Heights, the territories captured in the 1967 war, was started by the Labor Party. Moshe Dayan, the powerful defense minister, was a sort of "governor of the Territories" and endeavored to create a pattern of coexistence. The Palestinians in the territories would go on living their daily lives and be free to earn their living in Israel and also be able to stay in touch with the Arab world via Jordan. The matter of their political rights was never considered. His political rival, Yigal Allon, the deputy prime minister, worked out a new partition scheme for keeping the maximum amount of the territories, with the minimum amount of Arabs. Meir's senior adviser, Cabinet Minister Yisrael Galili, drafted a document to facilitate settlement in the territories.

A number of Jewish settlements were established in the territories, more or less according to the partition plan that Allon had proposed.

Golda Meir herself sat tight, not doing very much but strongly resisting any idea of relinquishing anything. Everyone else shut up, leaving Eliav to wage a lone battle in the Labor Party. Others shared his views, but none of them dared stand up to the formidable prime minister.

In 1973, Eliav published a newspaper article called "The Seagull": A seagull flies in front of the ship, seeing that it is headed inexorably for the rocks. He tries to tell the captain and the crew about the danger facing their vessel, but they don't hear—or, if they hear, they don't understand. Eliav's "rocks" appeared soon enough, in the shape of the Yom Kippur War, which shook Israel to its foundations. Meir and Dayan were eventually forced out, but the new leadership team of Yitzhak Rabin and Shimon Peres continued the old policy. Twenty years later, Rabin and Peres were to find their way to the Oslo agreement with the Palestinians, but the first time around Prime Minister Rabin was as unimaginative as Golda Meir had been, and Defense Minister Peres was pushing Jewish settlement in the territories for all he was worth.

Eliav spent the year after the Yom Kippur War working as a volunteer hospital orderly, while functioning as a rebellious Labor Knesset member. He subsequently resigned from the Knesset and the Labor Party, formed the Council for Israeli–Palestinian Peace, and launched into a series of talks with Palestinian leaders in Europe. As the meetings were being arranged, someone suggested that the members of the Israeli side present themselves to the Palestinian side as part of the "Israeli peace movement," but the creator of Lachish and Arad was not about to deny his identity.

"I insisted that I was a Zionist and that they recognize Zionism as the National Liberation Movement of the Jewish people," he recounts. "In return, I was prepared to recognize the PLO, as the National Liberation Movement of the Palestinians."

"And did they?" I query.

"They understood," says Eliav, after a brief pause. "They did not refuse to talk to me, as a self-declared Zionist."

His Palestinian interlocutor was Issam Sartawi, a Boston-educated doctor from Acre in Galilee, who was a political official of the PLO. The Israeli and Palestinian teams held secret discussions for two days in a villa outside Paris. At the start, the atmosphere was exceptionally tense and emotional, but over the two days of talk, food, and drink, the atmosphere thawed.

Today, it is difficult to remember the atmosphere of the 1970s. In talking to the "enemy" at that time, Eliav and his colleagues were doing the unthinkable. Many in Israel regarded them as traitors. And of course this was even more true of the Palestinian side. PLO chairman Yasser Arafat gave Sartawi and his colleagues permission to talk to Eliav and company, but he was ambivalent about it, and Sartawi insisted on absolute secrecy. When news of the meetings leaked out, Farouk Kaddoumi, Arafat's "foreign minister," denied all knowledge of the contacts and termed Sartawi "an insignificant, marginal figure."

The talks had started at the instigation of a group of former Egyptian Jews, but both sides sought more authoritative mediators. Former French premier Pierre Mendes-France, Austrian chancellor Bruno Kreisky, President Leopold Senghor of Senegal, and Houphet-Bouigny of the Ivory Coast were among those hosting, sponsoring, encouraging, and assisting. At one stage Eliav and Sartawi were due to meet in Tunis publicly in the presence of Tunisian President Bourghiba, but Arafat torpedoed the plan at the last minute.

When Egypt's president Anwar Sadat made his dramatic visit to Israel in 1977, he met individually with each party in the Knesset. His encounter with Eliav, by then the leader of the small pro-peace Sheli Party, was notable for its extreme warmth.

"I'm watching you," the Egyptian president told him. "I know what you are doing."

Two years later Eliav and Sartawi were jointly awarded the Kreisky Prize by the Austrian Trade Union Movement. An impressive ceremony had been scheduled in Vienna, when Sartawi received a call from Arafat at the last minute, ordering him not to show up. White-faced but resolute, Sartawi informed Eliav and the others that he was disobeying orders.

Following the ceremony, Sartawi returned to Paris, where he lived with his wife and children. Eliav went to take up a fellowship at Harvard, where he lectured before the Kennedy School of Government on his vision for the future: a confederation of Israel, Palestine, and Jordan, to be called Isfalur (a combination of the three names.) Drawing on his experience in regional development, Eliav laid out a practical program for joint exploitation of resources. In Isfalur, Israel, Palestine, and Jordan would each preserve its sovereignty but would cooperate on a range of projects.

Assuming that, following its withdrawal from the West Bank and Gaza, Israel would also reach agreements with Syria and Lebanon, Isfalur could work out a rational distribution of the northern water resources, with Lake Kinneret as a water reservoir for irrigating land on both sides of the River Jordan. The Jordan Rift (the southern part of the Jordan Valley, which is Palestinian territory) would become a major area for settling Palestinian refugees. A canal from the Mediterranean to the Dead Sea, parallel to the Jordan, would be a source of hydroelectric power for all three entities, and there could be several lakes, with desalination plants. The lakes would also be utilized for recreation and tourism.

The Dead Sea would be jointly exploited by the three nations of the confederation, and the Arava, south of the Dead Sea, would become a shared region of modern farming, supplying winter fruit and vegetables to Europe. Palestinian, Jordanian, and Israeli towns would be built in the area, which would also be available for the absorption of Palestinian refugees. Saudi Arabia and Egypt would be invited to cooperate in the creation of harbors and multicity complexes on the Red Sea and the Mediterranean. These urban conglomerates would be "the Rotterdam and Antwerp of the Middle East," flourishing ports and centers of modern industrial and tourism projects, on the crossroads of three continents, and three great religions. He forecast the practicalities of "a new Middle East," more than a decade before Shimon Peres coined the phrase.

Although both he and Sartawi had been neutralized, their joint activities were not quite over. After Israel invaded Lebanon in 1982, Prime Minister Begin asked for Eliav's help in securing the release of Israeli prisoners held by the Palestinians. It was a complex business, as the Palestinians had no official national framework, but Kreisky and Sartawi both agreed to lend a hand. As a result, there were two prisoner exchanges between Israel and the Palestinians, and an exchange of bodies with the Syrians.

However, Sartawi's days had been numbered ever since he defied Arafat and accepted the Kreisky Prize. He was gunned down at a meeting of the Socialist International in Lisbon. Eliav looks back with sadness on his meetings with Sartawi.

"I never met another Palestinian of his quality. He was special. I don't want to give the impression that it was easy. The talks were exceptionally tough, but conducted with tremendous mutual respect. We reached agreement on many issues. With regard to the Right of Return, he once told me, 'I know I won't come back to live in Acre, but my son will play football for Nablus against Acre.'

"He used to joke, 'The first bullet will be for me, Lova, the second one for you.' It was always assumed that Issam Sartawi was killed by a Palestinian extremist, probably from the Abu Nidal group, but I have never believed that. I have always thought that Arafat personally ordered his murder. I don't trust Arafat. I never have. He gave Sartawi just enough rope to hang himself. He is cunning and untrustworthy, and very bad for his own people. He doesn't want a Palestinian state. He wants to be an eternal rebel, an Arab Che Guevara."

Eliav was well out of the loop by the time Peres and Rabin achieved the Oslo breakthrough. From his research center in the desert, he applauded Oslo, but he stresses it was not his sort of agreement: All those finicky details, with Areas A, B, and C, under different degrees of Israeli and Palestinian control—that wasn't his style, nor was it the style of Issam Sartawi.

Since the Oslo agreement and the subsequent progress toward a solution, I point out, the Israeli–Palestinian confrontation has again escalated in hatred and violence. How can the two peoples find their way out of the present deadlock? Eliav is not directly involved, but that does not mean he has lost interest in the problem. Recently he laid out his ideas in a joint newspaper article with Meir Amit, a former head of both Military Intelligence and the Mossad Intelligence Service.

There should be two states, Israel and Palestine, side by side, based on the pre-1967 borders, with minor adjustments, they wrote. This means no Right of Return into Israel for the Palestinians, but it also means dismantling most of the Jewish settlements in the West Bank and Gaza. The settlements should be left intact, as part of Israel's contribution to solving the refugee problem. The Palestinian capital will be the eastern part of Jerusalem.

Eliav adds a postscript: "I didn't write it in the article, but we should return the Temple Mount to the Palestinians *with our thanks!* After the destruction of our Temple two thousand years ago, the Romans made the site into a garbage dump, deliberately to insult us. It remained defiled for four centuries. Then the Muslims came along and cleaned it up. They built two of their holiest, most beautiful shrines there. We should thank them for their wonderful gesture and hand it over. We will, of course, keep the Western Wall, as our shrine."

Eliav refuses to despair. He never said it would be easy, he stresses, quoting from his *Land of the Hart:* "We have to talk, even though the argument will be, in the biblical phrase, 'as bitter as wormwood.' At first we will sow our seed on the dry rocks. For every ten wells we dig, nine will be dry or saline."

Today, Israel has arrived at the eighth well, or the ninth, he suggests, and it must persist in its search for a negotiating partner among the Palestinians. Certainly it will be tough, but he never had any illusions regarding that. There is no other way.

Lova Eliav and Nasser Eddin Nashashibi represent the past. Both men, in their different ways, endeavored to point the way to alternative paths far more rational and sensible than those their peoples actually took. If the Palestinians had followed the Nashashibi route map, they would have saved themselves much suffering. If the Israelis had listened to Lova Eliav, the entire Middle East would be different today.

In looking at the lives and views of the two men, I have sought to explain the background to the confrontation. Now the time has come to describe the present situation from the points of view of today's Israelis and Palestinians. Subsequently, I consider alternative scenarios for the future and offer a personal assessment of the best solution to our problem.

Part II
TODAY

CHAPTER 4
THE RELUCTANT WARRIORS

Abdulla Abu-Hadid: For a Two-State Solution

f I have to, I will go on fighting to defend myself, to defend the Palestinian people, but I would prefer to see an agreement. I don't want to be a killer. I don't want my children to remember me as a fighter. I want them to see me as an honest, patriotic man. I would like to point out that I was elected to my present position—not nominated. When the fighting stops, I intend to continue in public life. It is generally accepted that the mayor of Bethlehem must be a Christian, so I can't do that, but I will find a way to serve our people and our society."

This surprising declaration comes at the end of a long interview with Abdulla Abu-Hadid, a senior commander of the Fatah in Bethlehem. The surprise is not in his professed support for an agreement, which could easily be a public relations ploy, an example of the interviewee telling the interviewer what he wants to hear. The surprising feature of his statement is the clear indication that the speaker is thinking about the future, anticipating the day that the shooting stops.

On the wanted list of Israel's security services, Abu-Hadid is far from being a "lover of Zion." For the past two years he has been leading an armed campaign against the Jewish state. Nevertheless, a conversation with him evinces a man without deep hatreds, a reluctant warrior, who feels he has been pushed into taking up arms and is genuinely waiting for the day that he will be able to lay them down.

"It isn't true that we want to throw the Jews into the sea," he remarks at one point. "I want to establish a Palestinian state inside the 1967 borders. And, believe me, that is what will happen in the end. I have been fighting for this since I was sixteen years old. After all the death and destruction, the time has come for the two sides to live in peace."

Challenged on the matter of suicide bombers, who have come from his Fatah organization as well as from the extremist Islamic groups, Abu-Hadid is evasive. He denies ever sending a suicide bomber on a mission but will condemn the phenomenon only in very general terms. He is "opposed to killing innocents." That is his "own personal opinion."

His evasion reflects the complex relations within the loose, improvised coalition of Palestinian groups that was formed soon after the outbreak of violence and that is supposed to be directing and coordinating the uprising. In fact, the process has been chaotic and unorganized.

"Every organization started establishing its own military force," relates Abu-Hadid. "Every faction has its own armed group."

If there has indeed been coordination, it hasn't been very effective. Even inside the various Palestinian groups, forces, and factions, decisions appear to be ad hoc, taken personally by specific leaders. At the same time, these leaders are reluctant to criticize one another. The suicide bombings, which were initiated by the Hamas and the Islamic Jihad, extreme Muslim elements, were taken up by some Fatah groups. The Fatah has remained officially opposed to suicide attacks but is not ready to condemn them specifically. (The Fatah units fighting in the current confrontation are often called the Tanzim, which simply means the "organization." The fighters themselves prefer to continue with the old name, Fatah, an acronym for Movement of Liberation.)

To reach Abdulla Abu-Hadid, I have to pass through Checkpoint 300 on the Jerusalem–Bethlehem road. It is a grotesque new feature in the landscape: a vast, ugly concrete wall, nine feet high and reinforced by razor wire. Some trucks and other vehicles cross over from time to time. As an ordinary visitor I must leave my car on the Israeli side. After walking between high walls up a specially constructed narrow alley at the side of the barrier, I wait for the Israeli border police officer to pass me through. Once on the Palestinian side, I am met by N, my Palestinian contact, a handsome, lanky figure, dressed in a tricot shirt and jeans, fashionable sunglasses perched on the top of his head. On the Israeli side, he would blend in perfectly, not drawing a second glance, even in these tense times.

The taxi, colored yellow in the style of the New York cabs, speeds past Rachel's tomb, which is starting to be walled off, the coarse gray concrete contrasting with the honey-colored stone of the Bethlehem buildings.

We pass by the Palace Hotel, its glass frontage boarded up. My guide informs me that it was badly damaged by IDF tanks during the recent incursion. A fifteen-minute drive through narrow, winding streets, up steep dirt roads, and across unpaved areas brings us to an unexceptional two-story apartment block.

"He has to move around a lot," explains N. "The Israelis are looking for him all the time."

Abu-Hadid is small and stocky, with a short beard and mustache. He has a distinct facial resemblance to Marwan Barghouti, the head of the Fatah in the West Bank, captured in Ramalla by the Israeli security forces and put on trial. He has a severe limp, the result of a wound he says he received in the Ketziot prison camp in the Negev desert. He has a ready smile and often jokes, even when the subject matter is distressing. There are four young men in the room, one of them wearing a traditional *abaya* tunic, the others in jeans and T-shirts. From time to time young children wander in and out. Abu-Hadid is married, with three girls and two boys.

I asked questions in Hebrew; Abu-Hadid replied in Arabic; N translated. Later I checked the recording with another translator, finding only insignificant discrepancies between the two versions of Abu-Hadid's answers.

Abdulla Abu-Hadid was born in 1968, just over a year after the Six-Day War. His mother comes from the Jerusalem suburb of Beit Safafa, divided between Israel and Jordan before 1967. His father lived in Bethlehem, but he also had some land in Al-Auja, a few miles north of Jericho. Abdulla went to school in Bethlehem but spent the summer months down in Al-Auja, where the family kept goats and grew oranges.

His first meeting with Israeli soldiers occurred down there when he was six years old. It was a hot day, he recalls; the soldiers offered him and his friends fruit juice and invited them to sit in the shade. The situation was not threatening in those days; the soldiers related to the Palestinians as human beings. A very small group of people were involved in political activities, but the population as a whole did not feel oppressed by the occupation.

Not long after his first encounter with the soldiers, Abdulla had his first experience of the *fidayun*, Palestinian resistance fighters. He and some friends were bathing in a stream near his home, when he saw three young men in colored T-shirts. Like the soldiers, they had weapons, but he knew they were different from the soldiers. He heard that they had crossed the border from Jordan, and that Israeli soldiers were looking for them.

"I was an inquisitive child," he relates, "and I asked my father who they were, why they came across the valley, where they were going, who was in charge in Jordan—that sort of thing."

His father refused to answer and warned him to steer clear of politics, but his grandfather, who owned an old "Bren" submachine gun, used to tell him stories with a nationalist slant. When the soldiers came to search the house, the old man threw his gun into the well and denied he possessed a weapon.

Most of the time, however, Abdulla lived in Bethlehem, where his father drove a cab to supplement the family income. They were poor, he recalls, but not hungry. They wore plastic sandals, which broke, and shared the school uniforms that their Christian school insisted on. Their trousers had holes and patches. He remarks with a laugh that they would be "the height of fashion" today.

His first demonstration against the Israeli administration was a Balfour Day protest at the age of twelve:

"We burned tires and started blocking the roads with rocks. The soldiers arrested some fifty of us from our school. I remember the officer was known as Abu-Fayid. He took us to the local military headquarters and made us clean the offices and the latrines. In the evening we were released. That was when I started thinking. I wanted to know who this Balfour was and what he had promised. I had participated in a demonstration without having the faintest idea of what it was all about."

He laughs uproariously at the memory. In 1985, his uncle from Beit Safafa was arrested, put on trial, and sentenced to three years in prison for membership in the Popular Front for the Liberation of Palestine (PFLP), led by Ahmad Jibril. He remembers going with his mother to visit him in jail and learning that some of the prisoners were serving terms of fifteen years and more. He joined the Fatah, which was led by students from Bethlehem University, and painted graffiti against the Israeli occupation.

"What set us off was the confiscation of our land," he explains. "For example, we were told that they built the Jewish settlement of Tekoa on land belonging to the Ta'amra tribe. Efrata was also built on our land. We were furious about the land!"

According to Abdulla, he and his friends did not actually do very much at this time. They held fierce discussions on all sorts of subjects. Apart from the land confiscation, he recalls, they talked about the expulsion of the PLO from Lebanon and the humiliating treatment of "Abu-Amar" (Yasser Arafat) in Jordan. The group of youngsters felt personally insulted, and resolved to restore Palestinian honor by active resistance in the territories. As he remembers it, it was mostly talk at that stage, but he and his friends found themselves taken in for questioning by the Shin Bet security service. He recalls a "Captain Mussa," who issued dire threats about what would happen to them if they did not behave themselves. Despite this, they became more active, spurred on by the shooting of a Bethlehem University student, who had climbed up on the roof to hang a Palestinian flag.

"There are Israeli flags all over the place," he remembers telling a friend, "and we can't even put up one of our own flags."

After the shooting, their Fatah group expanded from five or six to over twenty members. It was centered in the university, but many of the members came from the nearby Dehaishe Refugee Camp. They made a practice of throwing stones at the settlers' cars as they passed by Dehaishe, on their way to the Jewish settlements farther south. Rabbi Moshe Levinger, a settler leader who lived at the Jewish settlement in Hebron, started to walk through the camp, shooting in the air. He also had a one-man sit-down strike opposite Dehaishe, demanding an end to the stone throwing.

"He was a menace," says Abu-Hadid. "Our old men used to say that he carried evil with him."

In 1987, Abu-Hadid was due to take his matriculation exams, when he and several of his friends were arrested at night and taken to the Farrah detention center. They were accused of throwing stones and beaten by the jailers. From there, they were taken to a building near Dahariya, which appeared to be a stable for horses. There were feeding troughs and piles of hay. He and his friends were put to building work, breaking openings for doors and windows.

"There were all sorts of humiliations," he recalls. "At line-up, we had to stand with our hands on our heads. The officers cursed us and ordered us to treat them with respect. We could hear the screams of prisoners being beaten."

When he was released after a month, too late to take his exams, he felt that he was prepared to die for the cause. The bus that took him and his fellow prisoners from Dahariya stopped on the way, and the soldiers who were guarding them got off for a break. While they were absent, the bus driver took a stick and started beating them.

"I said to him, 'You are the driver—it's not your job to beat us,'" recounts Abdulla. "That made him beat us much harder. He was really violent!"

His experiences in Dahariya convinced him to step up his activities in the struggle against the Israeli occupation. There was no alternative, he felt, the occupation had to go. Those were the days leading up to the first Intifada, and the general atmosphere became much more tense. The soldiers started shooting at stone throwers. Some of the Israeli soldiers behaved decently, he allows, but many behaved with increasing brutality. It was not the economic situation that led to the Intifada, in his view, but a growing frustration with the political situation and a general feeling of hopelessness.

With the outbreak of the Intifada, Abdulla Abu-Hadid was in the thick of it. He was on the run from the security forces, sleeping at a different location every night. Early one morning in the spring of 1988, he returned to his own home to sleep, and he was arrested by soldiers and Shin Bet security personnel. Shortly after his arrest, he and his fellow prisoners were informed of the assassination in Tunis of Hallil al-Wazir, better known as Abu-Jihad, by an Israeli hit team. Abu-Jihad, Arafat's second in command, was the PLO contact man with the Intifada activists.

"Of course, we didn't believe them," recounts Abu-Hadid. "We thought they were just trying to demoralize us, but they brought in a radio, and we realized it was true."

After his trial, Abu-Hadid was told he was being taken to a "special" new prison. He remembers traveling for several hours through the desert in old buses and the engines becoming overheated. He was to spend just over six months at Ketziot in the Negev. Abu-Hadid says he doesn't want to dwell on the conditions in Ketziot but then spends the next quarter of an hour doing just that. There were snakes and scorpions, he recalls, and a diet consisting mainly of beans. Tea made an appearance only after two months. The latrines stank, and "little creatures were swarming around them." Showers were permitted only once in two weeks.

"Despite the heat, you had to keep your shirt buttoned up," he relates. "If you opened it, you could be put in a *tzinok* [tiny cell] as a punishment, or you had to sit on the ground in the sun for five hours." He demonstrates, sitting with shoulders hunched, hands behind his back.

Four months after his arrival, the prisoners were informed that a "very important visitor" was coming, and they were made to clean out the whole camp. They were sure it was a delegation from the Red Cross or some other humanitarian organization, but the visitor, who arrived by helicopter escorted by hundreds of soldiers, was none other than Yitzhak Rabin, Israel's minister of defense.

Rabin addressed the prisoners in harsh tones. Outside, the Intifada had moved into high gear, and Rabin had made his much-publicized statement (subsequently denied) about "breaking their bones." He now told the prisoners that, if their comrades outside continued to make trouble—"He called it trouble, not an Intifada," interjects Abu-Hadid, with a smile—he would react with severity.

"We'll put you all in Ketziot," he declared, "and we can built seven Ketziots!"

By the end of the Intifada, Rabin had almost fulfilled that promise, observes Abu-Hadid. Not long before he was due to be released, the other prisoners heard that it was his birthday and announced they would give him a party. Many youngsters were imprisoned during the Intifada, he notes, but he was the youngest in that section of Ketziot. The cigarettes committee gave him an extra ration, other prisoners hung up decorations made out of green and white toilet paper, and a third group made fruit juice from their jam ration.

The party somehow degenerated into a riot. Abu-Hadid is vague about how this happened, but at some point all the prisoners stood up and started shouting "*Allah hu akbar*" (God is great). Stones started to fly, and the guards replied by firing tear gas canisters. Abu-Hadid remembers two prisoners who were shot dead, Ali Samudi from the village of Yamun, near Jenin, and Assad Shawa from Gaza. Samudi had shown him a picture of his seven children the day before.

In the midst of the rioting, Abu-Hadid lost consciousness, and when he woke up, he was handcuffed to a bed in Soroka Hospital in Beersheba. He had been shot in the leg. He pulls up his trouser to show me the scar.

"I decided I would never celebrate my birthday again," he remarks with a laugh. "I have bad memories of my birthday. The only good thing was that, soon after it, I was released."

He spent 1993 in "administrative detention for a whole year." (Under laws introduced during the British Mandate, the British authorities could imprison without trial people they suspected of underground activity. The law was used against Jews and Arabs alike. Ironically, the Israelis applied it against their own Arab citizens and, after 1967, against Palestinians in the occupied territories.)

He claims it was for speaking out openly against the Oslo agreement. He remained doubtful about Oslo, but when he was released, he decided to give it a chance, and he even tried to persuade his friends to accept it. In retrospect, however, he thinks his suspicions about Oslo were justified.

He feels very bitter toward the PLO people who came back from Tunis after the Oslo agreement was signed. They behaved as if the achievement was all theirs, he maintains, and had no respect for the people who had actually fought in the Intifada. The outsiders were the ones who received all the benefits: jobs, money, tax-free cars, permits to move around. The permits were a particular source of anger, as the Israelis established more and more roadblocks and checkpoints. The VIPs, officials of the new Palestinian Authority, could pass through without delay, whereas the others had to wait, sometimes for several hours.

"Every little shit with a tab on his shoulder was suddenly a big shot," he complains. "In some ways it was worse than the Israeli military government. The Israelis imprisoned us during the Intifada and charged us with various offenses. Now you could be imprisoned without any reason being given. There were no interrogations, no proper procedures."

Abu-Hadid describes vividly the growing frustration of the post-Oslo years. He had the feeling that the economy was deteriorating, that the rich were getting richer and the poor were becoming poorer. Palestinians who had sold land to Israelis were not put on trial, as they should have been. If anything, they were given preferential treatment over those who had fought and been in prison. Instead of building schools, hospitals, youth centers, and universities, the Palestinian Authority was more concerned to build interrogation centers and jails. All sorts of different security services were established. In effect, there were private armies. It was as if everyone from Tunis wanted his or her own state.

"Look at me," he says. "I was a person who made a contribution. I sat in jail for our cause. What did I get? Nothing!"

On the political front, all that seemed to be happening from his point of view was the expansion of the Jewish settlements. Before Oslo, there had been 80,000 settlers in the West Bank, and in the years after the agreement, they increased to 150,000. All this happened, notes Abu-Hadid, under the umbrella of the peace process. When he and his friends tried to speak out, the leaders told them that everything was under control, that negotiations were under way and everything was going to work out fine. True, the Palestinian Authority condemned the settlement expansion, but that is all it did. It was only words.

For their part, the Israelis did not seem enthusiastic about the new agreements either, he suggests. They assassinated their own prime minister, Yitzhak Rabin, who really did seem serious about peace. Abu-Hadid doesn't have a good word to say about any of Rabin's successors. Peres, in his view, vacillated. Netanyahu and Barak were no better than Sharon, and Sharon has deliberately provoked the Palestinians.

The current Intifada, says Abu-Hadid, was a reaction to all of this. The Palestinian Authority, in his opinion, lost all control. Nobody took any notice of its officials anymore. He was the local Fatah commander, and quite a few of the Authority's police joined the mass demonstrations that erupted. He is adamant that the Palestinians only took up arms in response to Israeli shootings. If the Israelis had used only tear gas, the Palestinians would have continued throwing stones, as in the first Intifada.

This time, weapons were available, he points out, so when the Israelis fired at them, they fired back.

"The Israelis thought it would be like the tunnel riots, and be over in a matter of weeks," he continues. "They thought that if they hit us hard, we would stop our campaign, but we were determined that this time we would solve everything: the roadblocks, the settlements, law and order for the Palestinians, get rid of the corruption in the Palestinian Authority. It was against the Authority as well as being against the Israelis.

"I don't say that it is right when people are killed on both sides, but we are fighting to get rid of the bad things. In the first weeks of the Intifada, we lost 140 people, whereas only 2 or 3 Israelis were killed. We had no choice. Stones were no good against live fire. The Israelis started coming in to our areas, so we defended ourselves. We have no choice except to fight the Israelis in every way we can."

Abu-Hadid is exaggerating, as five Israelis were killed in the very first week of the Intifada, but his point about the negative ratio of the casualties is valid. On November 9, Hussein Abayat was killed in the first Israeli "targeted assassination." The Israelis announced that they had killed the Bethlehem commander of the Tanzim, but in fact, claims Abu-Hadid, he was the commander, even then. Abayat was his friend, a simple man who had sat in jail for five years.

Abu-Hadid won't go into detail about his actions. He denies ever having operated inside Israeli territory, terming it "a lie put out by your security services." His activities have been confined to the West Bank. He also denies ever dispatching a suicide bomber. He says he is against harming civilians. He doesn't actually say it is justifiable to kill settlers but emphasizes that "the children of the settlers are not to blame for being there and should not be harmed. It was their parents who brought them there." The hint is clear. The settlers must realize, he intimates, that they are taking their lives in their hands every time they set out on a trip.

In his view, both the Israelis and the Palestinians are suffering from the existence of the settlements. He is in favor of an agreement, based on the 1967 borders. He is sure that an Israeli initiative on these lines would find a ready response among the Palestinians. The two states can live side by side as neighbors. He dismisses the fears of some Israelis that the Palestinians regard this as only the first step. He repeats that the Israelis are neighbors, "and you don't kick out your neighbors."

But what about the Hamas and the Islamic Jihad?

He considers his answer thoughtfully. Yes, he concedes, there are extremists on the Palestinian side also. He thinks they are influenced by the outside. The Hamas in particular draws its inspiration from the Hizbolla, the fundamentalist Lebanese Islamic movement.

"Look what happened with the Hizbolla," he says. "They said they would fight until they conquered Jerusalem, and today all they are talking about is Shaba!"

He is referring to the fact that Hizbolla, which fought against the Israelis when they were occupying the so-called security zone in South

Lebanon, is now calling for a further Israeli withdrawal from a small area called Shaba.

"Give both Israelis and Palestinians peace and independence," he concludes. "There has been too much death and destruction."

To what extent does Abdulla Abu-Hadid represent the Palestinians still pursuing their armed struggle against Israel in the West Bank and Gaza? On the face of it, he is a reluctant warrior, but is his reluctance genuine, and do his comrades feel the same way? And what about other movements and factions, particularly the Hamas and the Islamic Jihad? It is difficult to accept his rather simplistic reassurance, citing the Hizbolla. Quite apart from the fact that the Hizbolla still poses a threat to Israel's northern border, the Palestinian Islamic groups show no sign that they will give up their view that Israel is an illegitimate entity in the region.

To take the Fatah first: When journalist Gideon Levy interviewed five armed fighters in the early months of the Intifada for *Ha'aretz*, the young men said more or less the same things that Abu-Hadid said in our conversation. Like him, they refused to be specific about their actual operations; like him, they justified targeting settlers; like him, they said that there will be negotiations and an agreement in the end. More recently, Amira Hass and Akiva Eldar reported a split in the Fatah over declaring a cease-fire, but here again the Fatah statement of policy insisted that they were seeking peace: "The only choice we have is to live side by side in two neighboring states in security and peace."

In an interview in *Yediot Aharonot* with journalist Nahum Barnea to mark the first year of the Intifada, Fatah leader Marwan Barghouti spoke in a similar vien.

"The Intifada united the Palestinians around one aim: to end the occupation and to establish an independent Palestinian state in the 1967 borders," he said. "We will remain neighbors. We don't want to break you; we want to break your occupation mentality."

At the opening of his trial, Barghouti shouted to reporters in Hebrew, "Two states for two peoples—that is the only solution!" These are just three examples of many. The second Intifada might lack coordination, but the expressed aims of the Fatah leaders and fighters are almost identical.

The same cannot be said of the suicide bombers. It is, of course, impossible to interview "successful" suicide bombers, but several young men and women who, for one reason or other, failed to detonate their bombs have been interviewed in the Israeli and foreign media. A couple spoke to Israeli defense minister Benjamin Ben-Eliezer in the presence of journalists, so there are a few clues about their feelings and motives.

It is popular in Israel to paint the bombers as naive people of low intelligence who might have suffered personal misfortune and are ruthlessly exploited by their leaders, both in the Islamic movements and in the Fatah. Specifically, the men are offered "seventy virgins in Paradise" if they die in a suicide operation. There is indeed a documented case of a failed suicide bomber waking up in Hadassah Hospital in Jerusalem's Ein Kerem neighborhood and demanding his seventy virgins, but, of course, there are also nonbelievers among the bombers. It is generally accepted that there is no standard profile of a suicide bomber. Psychologists agree that the bombers are not "abnormal." No one has claimed that he or she could have identified a bomber in advance.

The official Islamic version depicts dedicated fighters, videotaped making militant declarations before going out to strike blows for freedom, even at the cost of their own lives. Some Fatah sources have spoken of the despair of their youngsters over their inability to prevent the Israelis from killing and imprisoning their people. The suicide bombers, they suggest, are the only real weapons they possess, the Palestinian equivalent of the Israeli fighter aircraft, helicopters, and tanks.

Of course, all these explanations hold a measure of truth, but what must strike anyone reading the interviews, confessions, and declarations is, above all, a sense of confusion. There is no coherence in the interviews. The young people are hopelessly muddled in their approach to life.

Palestinian intellectuals tend to rationalize the phenomenon, saying it is a direct consequence of despair. Israeli experts who have researched the matter, both by talking to families of suicide bombers via Palestinian colleagues and by interviewing unsuccessful survivors, say that it is primarily a matter of organization and social pressure. First, there must be the plan and the resources to carry it out. Second, the candidate is recruited and indoctrinated, either in a long process or sometimes in a few days. The candidates are told about "the crimes of the Zionist enemy."

They are told about acts of heroism on behalf of Islam in the past. A major factor is the enormous social approval, particularly after Israeli actions such as incursions and targeted assassinations. The young suicide bomber, say Israeli experts, has a status similar to that accorded to the young Israeli soldier of an elite IDF unit. It must also be noted that the families of the bombers have received considerable financial assistance, both from the Palestinian Authority and from Iraqi and Saudi Arabian sources.

It is difficult to argue that the attacks are totally random and irrational. If violence breaks out, there are many suicide attacks. During a period of relative calm, there are many fewer. Lowering the intensity of the confrontation creates a positive cycle of calm, just as acts of violence create a negative cycle of destruction.

Talking to Abdulla Abu-Hadid, and examining the various statements both of his Fatah colleagues and of the more extremist elements among the Palestinians, does not convey a vital patriotic movement of fighters, thirsty for action. Undoubtedly, some Palestinians are determined to continue the war against Israel by all means. There are leaders, particularly but not exclusively from the Islamic factions, who are clearly resolved to continue to sacrifice young lives in what they see as a "sacred cause."

Following the new American push for an Israeli–Palestinian agreement, based on the so-called road map, several Arab nations that had shown symapthy and even support for Palestinian attacks against Israel came out clearly against such violence. On the other hand, the Hamas, the Islamic Jihad, and the more militant Fatah fighters tried to step up their strikes—sometimes with a measure of success. Despite this new pro-peace atmosphere, generated largely by the United States, these groups can do much to sabotage the peace effort. Nevertheless, although public opinion polls continue to show a large majority of Palestinians supporting the violence against Israeli targets—even suicide bombs—this doesn't mean that the Palestinians are irrevocably dedicated to fighting, no matter what happens. Given what they see as a fair deal, the overwhelming majority—even among those actually doing the fighting—would definitely greet it with a huge sigh of relief.

This majority, the reluctant warriors, have their counterparts on the Israeli side of the barricades.

Nir Shoshani: "Each Time It's More Difficult"

When IDF lieutenant Nir Shoshani reported to his paratroop company for reserve service in the Palestinian territories in the summer of 2002, his fellow soldiers were surprised to see him. Although he was scheduled to become deputy commander of the company, his dovish views were well known, and his friends were sure he had signed the public letter of refusal to serve, which had received a lot of publicity. He hadn't. He admits that each tour of duty is more difficult, but he doesn't think he will refuse. He realizes that, whether he is there or not, the company will continue to carry out its assigned tasks, and he feels a sense of obligation to his men.

Prior to one of his earlier stints of service, Shoshani wrote a letter to the newspaper *Ha'aretz*. He explained that his divisional commander had expressed concern that fewer soldiers might report for duty in the future because of the difficulty of continuous periods of army service. Shoshani wrote that the commander should have another cause for concern: the "nature of the service that the soldiers are required to carry out." He continued:

> Every citizen of Israel is entitled to have his life protected, and the IDF's task is to provide that protection. When I am called up, this is clear to me, but I assume that the state will not send me to war when there is an alternative. The state is obligated to prove to its citizens that their mobilization is absolutely necessary.
>
> Everyone agrees to the principle that the army must protect the citizens of the state, but does this apply everywhere, no matter what the price? Is the continued existence of Netzarim, Kfar Darom and their like, in the center of a Palestinian population, ethical and legitimate? Is the mission of the IDF to defend them a necessary war? Might the continued existence of those settlements [in the Gaza strip] cost too much in human lives, as in South Lebanon, or Joseph's Tomb, where the high number of casualties eventually led to withdrawal?
>
> Public opinion is often the major factor that causes a government to act. In Israel most of the army is made up of reservists, citizens who are part of the consensus or nonconsensus. When I am called up into the reserve, there is no iron curtain between my views as a citizen and my views as a soldier. The above questions that concern me as a citizen remain with me when I become a serving soldier. The missions do not become clear just because I put on a uniform. Israeli settlements in the

Nir Shoshani

Gaza strip and others in the West Bank are not legal under international law, and they are not ethical.

The increasing number of days of reserve service, coupled with the nature of the IDF's operations in the territories, are causing an ongoing erosion of the national consensus. If the situation doesn't change, this erosion will lead to increased refusal to serve and to the loss of confidence of the soldiers in those who send them on their missions.

Shoshani, a high school teacher, says that he was trying to point out that he remains a citizen, with a citizen's doubts, even after he has donned his uniform. Nevertheless, despite what he wrote, and despite his growing uncertainty, he doesn't think he has reached the stage of refusing to serve. He understands those who refuse, but he thinks they are wrong. He still reports for duty. He continues to obey orders. He is confident that he can continue to ensure that the soldiers under his command conduct themselves toward the Palestinians with a degree of respect and decency.

He has come to my home for the interview, first dropping off his equipment at the government office in Jerusalem, where he was temporarily employed as a security guard. He is ready to talk, keen to express his point of view. He is a slim, even slight, figure, his close-cropped hair topping a narrow, sensitive face. He is serious for the most part but sometimes lights up with a smile. He can pause for a full thirty seconds as he considers a question, but, once he starts answering, he is fluent and confident even when admitting to being confused over the moral issues of service in the territories.

Nir Shoshani was born in Jerusalem twenty-seven years ago. His father and grandfather were born in Jerusalem; his great-grandfather immigrated from Iran. His mother was born in Morocco. He attended Jerusalem's prestigious Rehavia High School, learned to play the piano, competed in long-distance running, and was a youth leader in the scouts. When he was at high school, he was selected to participate in a month-long visit to schools in the United States, spending most of his time in Seattle. He enjoyed it enormously and learned a lot.

When the time came for his army service, the athletic Nir volunteered for one of the elite IDF commando units, eventually ending up in the paratroops. Volunteering for an elite unit was "the done thing" in his circle. It wasn't an eagerness for fighting, he explains, so much as wanting "to make a contribution." After the tough six-month basic training course, he was pitched right into the maelstrom of the occupied territories, serving in Hebron, where the IDF functions as a wedge between the Jewish settlers and the Palestinian residents. Four months before Shoshani and his fellow soldiers arrived in the town, Baruch Goldstein, the doctor of Kiryat Arba, the Jewish suburb of Hebron, had shot and killed twenty-nine Palestinians while they were praying in the Ibrahimi Mosque. In the six days following the massacre, a further twenty-one Palestinians had been killed in protest riots all over the occupied territories. In Hebron the tension was still very high.

Three weeks after their arrival, a Jewish girl, Sarit Prigal, was murdered, and most of the population of Jewish Kiryat Arba descended on Arab Hebron. The task of Shoshani and his fellow soldiers was to block them from entering the Arab neighborhoods to launch reprisals. There were, he recalls, physical clashes between the young soldiers and the settlers.

"We were cursed, spat on, punched, beaten, and even wrestled to the ground. After that I had a very real understanding of the complexity of the situation in Hebron. Of course, I knew that there had been a Jewish community there for hundreds of years. I knew about the massacre of fifty-nine Jews there in 1929. I realized that the Jews had a historic right to live in Hebron, but when you are there, in the midst of it, you realize that terms such as 'historic rights' are utterly meaningless and irrelevant."

It became clear to Shoshani that, in exercising their *historic* rights by living in Hebron, the settlers were violating the *human* rights of the Arab inhabitants of the city. This was very much a personal perception. As opposed to a reserve soldier, whose civilian identity is dominant, a young conscript is more soldier than civilian. Chatting with his fellow soldiers, he learned that some of them had doubts, as he did, but there was no mass questioning of what they were doing. When a young man starts out in the army, he wants to do his utmost to be a good soldier, explains Shoshani. He was no different in this motivation, but nevertheless he found "civilian" questions worrying him.

He and his fellows patrolled the streets, stopping Palestinians and examining their papers. For his part, he always tried to perform his duties with respect for the residents of Hebron, but he was not always helped by the orders he received. There were big differences among their officers: Some behaved with humanity; others were harsh and unpleasant toward the local residents. This made it difficult for the soldiers, who were commanded on different days by different officers, with different attitudes. Part of the problem was that all the approaches seemed to be accepted as legitimate. There was no acceptable norm.

"Take the simplest thing," he says. "You stop a car and search it. That is your job, but how do you talk to the driver? What tone of voice do you use, polite or hectoring? I was determined to behave with respect toward the residents. But what is 'respect'? You are violating their freedom."

Particularly unpleasant was establishing lookout posts on the roofs of private houses. He never found himself actually wanting to disobey an order, but he felt extremely uncomfortable, walking into people's homes without permission. It was a clear violation of their privacy and their dignity.

Shoshani had his first leave after four weeks. He remembers going home and telling his father about Hebron. He stresses that he grew up in a family that was right of center politically. In elections, his parents always voted for the right-wing Likud Party. Membership in the scouts moved him slightly toward the center, he says, but that first month in Hebron moved his sharply leftward, a position he has held ever since. He notes, with some satisfaction, that his father has voted for the Labor Party in the last two elections. He thinks that his accounts of service in the territories have made his father more pragmatic and more aware of the complexity of the Israeli–Palestinian situation.

Shoshani served in Hebron for six months, before his unit was withdrawn and sent to maneuvers. He then signed up for the noncommissioned officers' course, followed by an officers' course. As a new lieutenant, he found himself commanding a platoon in South Lebanon. The nature of the service there kept his parents in a constant state of worry. He and his men manned fortified positions, conducted patrols, and lay all night in ambushes. It was much harder and more dangerous than Hebron, but he was much happier. The mission was clear: to prevent incursions or attacks across the border.

His next tour of duty in Hebron was even more difficult, although the implementation of the first stages of the Olso Accords had calmed the general situation. The first time he served in the town, he was mainly on the dividing line between Arab Hebron and the Jewish suburb of Kiryat Arba. This time, his unit was right inside Hebron, defending the isolated Jewish neighborhoods. It was particularly unpleasant in Tel Rumeida, at that time a few Jewish prefabricated homes, one kilometer from the Cave of the Machpela, and overlooking it. The Bible describes how the patriarch Abraham bought the cave for four hundred silver shekels, and the synagogue there is named Avraham Avinu (The Patriarch Abraham). The Muslims tacitly recognize the connection, calling their house of prayer at the site the Ibrahimi Mosque. As for Tel Rumeida, the archaeologists consider that Iron Age site to be the remains of King David's capital, before he moved to Jerusalem.

The group of Jews settled there are among the most extreme in all the territories, and Shoshani recounts how they sent their young children to block the tankers coming to bring water to the nearby Palestinian neighborhood. To his disgust, his battalion commander held talks with the settlers to resolve the problem.

"I couldn't see why on Earth we were talking to these people," he asserts. "I asked the battalion commander why, if the army is supposed to be in charge, we didn't simply do our job and remove the children."

Later he learned that the IDF general in command of the Central Front had personally ordered the local commander to enter into negotiations. Furthermore, today he justifies the decision.

"In the current situation, the best policy is to keep things quiet," he suggests. "As long as there is no progress on the political front, the army's job is to keep the flame as low as possible."

Shoshani would see service in Nablus and again South Lebanon, before completing his conscript service. Nablus consolidated his dovish views. They were not actually in Nablus but manning roadblocks outside the largest city in the West Bank. Back in 1996, there was no question of preventing pregnant women or sick people from getting to the hospital, he asserts, but he still felt uncomfortable controlling the lives of the Palestinians. Being on the spot gave him a different perspective, he notes.

"In Israel, everyone was saying that we had given back 90 percent of the territories, but that was nonsense. We were on the roads between the towns. The reason for our being there was to seize weapons and explosives and arrest people suspected of terrorist activities. That may have been necessary, but it meant that the Palestinians only really controlled about 40 percent of the territory in the West Bank."

Shoshani says that, here again, a lot depended on the commanding officer. He ensured that his soldiers behaved properly. The men under his command were older and more humane in their behavior than his earlier unit, but his discomfort remained. Another stint in South Lebanon completed his conscript service, and, three weeks after his demobilization, he was touring South America with three army friends.

It was a wonderful emotional release after three years of military service. His friends and he soon parted company, but he met up with a variety of backpackers from the United States, Italy, Germany, and Holland. A Dutch friend subsequently visited him in Israel. After seven months on the road, he returned to studies at the Hebrew University of Jerusalem. He was thinking of becoming a journalist, so he chose political science and Middle East studies. After a short while he dropped the latter, finding the course too academic for his taste, and concentrated on political science. His studies sharpened his perception that Israeli democracy was seriously flawed.

"Somebody once told me that an American child's first words are 'Mummy, Daddy, Constitution,'" he remarks with a smile. "In Israel we lack that value. We talk about democracy without really knowing what it is. What is happening in the territories is not consistent with democracy."

During his first year at the university, he constantly confronted the question of how liberal democracy applied to the situation in Israel. He was particularly horrified when suggestions were aired that there should be a referendum on withdrawal from the Palestinian territories but that only the Jewish citizens should have the right to vote. That, he felt, showed a complete lack of understanding about the nature of democracy. He started going to demonstrations of Peace Now, the movement that has been campaigning for an Israeli withdrawal from the territories for the past twenty-five years.

Shoshani's first reserve service was in the Gaza strip, and it was relatively quiet. He was now commanding a platoon of reserve soldiers, most of them considerably older than himself. There were soldiers from all walks of life and all shades of the political spectrum. There were settlers from the territories, with conventionally right-wing views, several left-wingers like himself, and others in the center. They discussed politics all the time. Their behavior, he maintains, was good. There was no difference according to political views. The older soldiers were distinctly more humane than the young conscripts he commanded earlier in his military career.

His next service was on the Green Line, the old border between Israel and the West Bank, at the edge of Tulkarm, about twelve miles east of the Israeli coastal town of Netanya. It was a period of relative calm in between the spring and summer incursions of the IDF in 2002. It was at this call-up that he surprised his fellow soldiers by reporting for duty. About to be appointed deputy company commander, Shoshani felt comfortable with the basic mission of preventing incursions from the West Bank into Israel proper, but concerned about the means. Until the spring incursion, the IDF did not enter the Palestinian towns on the whole, but afterward the towns were regularly patrolled. Units entered the towns in tanks and armored personnel carriers to enforce curfews and make arrests.

They didn't have much contact with the Palestinian population because they were in personnel carriers, explains Shoshani. He found himself questioning the tactics. What were they trying to achieve? They wanted to prevent terror—fine, but they were not doing anything to solve the major problem. They were merely reacting to the previous terror strike and trying to anticipate the next one. There were exchanges of fire, and one of the soldiers in the company was killed.

"We went in and occupied whole rows of houses, searching for armed men," he recounts. "Why weren't we on the Green Line, defending it? Our soldier was killed when we went in. Was it strictly necessary?"

With all his doubts, why does he continue to serve?

"I think the letter ["Courage to Refuse," published by a group of combat officers and soldiers] simply allowed the signatories to clear their own consciences," he says carefully. "It didn't make any real contribution toward rectifying the situation. I know some of the boys who signed, and they were not politically active before, or politically conscious. I don't have a political argument with them. We are on the same side. At the same time, I still think I can make a positive contribution when I serve, ensuring that my soldiers behave correctly."

He gives an example: The Shin Bet security services directed his platoon to a house where there was a suspected female suicide bomber. They arrested the eighteen-year-old girl and had to guard her for three days. They gave her a room of her own and treated her with scrupulous correctness.

"She looked like an ordinary university student, the type I see every day on the campus. Nobody reacted with hostility, despite the fact that she might have blown herself up in an Israeli market, discotheque, or shopping mall. Our Arabic speakers talked to her. She told them that she had parted from her boyfriend recently and had family problems. When the security men came to take her away, she cried bitterly. We all felt sorry for her."

Nir Shoshani has no doubts about what policy the government should pursue. First, it should cool things down—lessen military activity, stop the demonstrative shows of force. Second, there must be a withdrawal from the territories and the dismantling of Jewish settlements there. As long as the settlements are there, they have to be defended, and for that reason they should not be there. He does not want to go into detail. He knows discussions have been held about keeping some blocs of settlements, and he won't get into that.

"The vital thing is to relinquish control of the land and to stop violating the rights of the Palestinians," he asserts. "And that should happen yesterday! If there can be compromises, swaps of territory, that is fine, but in principle we must get out."

As to what will actually happen, Shoshani is trying to maintain a sense of optimism, but he doesn't think a change in the Palestinian leadership will solve anything. The Israeli leadership is no less of a problem, in his view. As long as Ariel Sharon is prime minister there will be no movement toward peace. He feels sympathy for the Palestinian struggle and compares it to the fight for a Jewish state in 1947. Nevertheless, he thinks that there is no justification for attacks on civilians.

Shoshani has just started teaching civics in a high school south of Tel Aviv, where he lives with his girlfriend. He doesn't contemplate leaving Israel. He is not prepared to give up on his family and his friends, but he wants to see a change. He rejects the dual system of values that exists in Israel today.

"We call ourselves democrats," he reiterates, "but we behave undemocratically in the name of security. We claim we are defending democracy, but you can't sell everything in the name of security."

He has not yet come up against the problem in his teaching, although the slogan "No Arabs: No Terror" was chalked on a blackboard in a classroom next door to his. He no longer sees his future in journalism but hopes to make his contribution as a teacher, fostering a sense of freedom and debate, instilling those democratic values that he finds lacking. It is possible to get through to high school students, he says. He is particularly hopeful about his special class of "difficult" students, stimulating them with questions on the rights of prisoners and other social matters.

On another level, he has bought a piano and started taking lessons again. He plays Rachmaninov, Beethoven, Chopin. He has a subscription to the Israeli Philharmonic Orchestra.

"It helps to keep me sane," he says with a smile.

Adi Eilat: Courage to Refuse

"Our soldiers are not evil. I don't blame the soldier, who hears his tank tread snapping, thinks it is a bomb or a shell, and fires at everything in sight, killing a mother and her two children. That sort of incident is going to happen. It is the situation that we have to change—not the people. I thought things over, discussed it with my friends, and decided I would not go back there again. When I got my call-up papers for January, I went to my battalion commander and told him I was not prepared to serve in the territories. It was a very personal decision, and I didn't want to make an ideology of it. I only signed the 'Courage to Refuse' manifesto later on."

Adi Eilat

A third-generation kibbutznik, Adi Eilat comes from the heartland of Zionist pioneering. An IDF captain and the son of an IDF colonel, he is from the left-of-center establishment that built the state of Israel. His grandparents founded Kfar Masaryk in 1933. A green jewel of a kibbutz, some three miles south of Acre in western Galilee, it is named after Czech president Tomas Masaryk. A community of the left-wing Kibbutz Artzi movement, it is famous for its avocados, harvesting the many different varieties for ten months of the year. It also has thriving dairy and poultry branches, and a factory for printing milk and fruit juice cartons. Not conspicuously wealthy, Kfar Masaryk has kept its head above water economically, and it is one of the few settlements preserving the traditional kibbutz way of life, with a large measure of cooperation and equality.

Short and stocky, prematurely bald, with a strong, expressive face, Adi inhabits a small kibbutz room of a starkly Spartan aspect. It is furnished with a simple divan, a table, and wooden chairs. There are no armchairs or carpets; the television set and stereo system appear to be his only material goods. A thirty-four-year-old bachelor, he is a teacher of math and physics at the local regional high school, where he tries to preserve the spirit of the Kibbutz Artzi *mossad* (boarding school), using projects wherever possible and insisting on first-name terms with his students. Sitting in his kibbutz room, he elaborates on his reasons for refusing to serve in the territories.

"As an individual soldier, I am powerless to change the situation. The Americans used to say that anyone who went to Vietnam was 'part of the problem.' Well, I don't want to be part of the problem of our occupation of the Palestinian territories. On the other hand, when you sit with three or four friends who have just received an emergency call-up and are due to go to Jenin, it is traumatic. Suddenly you realize you are 'outside the camp.' I've never had that experience before."

Kfar Masaryk, insists Adi Eilat, is "the best kibbutz in Israel." For the most part, he had a typical sheltered kibbutz upbringing, but, when he was in fifth grade, his parents spent a year at Samar, an unconventional kibbutz just north of Eilat. He claims that he came to Samar at age ten and left it a year later at age sixteen. Samar is different from other kibbutzim in that it has abandoned the formal kibbutz structure and put everything on a voluntary basis. Thus, there are no elected officers, only ad hoc committees; the members can turn up for work or not; and they can take as much money as they want from the communal purse.

"I grew up knowing just how a kibbutz should be run," he explains, "but suddenly, with no advance warning, I saw that there was an entirely different system that worked and didn't collapse. Furthermore, the members seemed perfectly content."

Prior to service in the IDF, Adi spent a year performing national service, something that many kibbutz children do. The exit from the "kibbutz bubble" can be traumatic, but Adi insists that, after his year in Samar, he was ready for anything. He worked as a youth leader in Ashkelon, on the southern Mediterranean coast, and enjoyed the experience.

Service in the IDF armored corps meant that Adi spent most of his conscript service instructing other soldiers how to operate a tank. He didn't serve many months in the territories, and nothing very traumatic happened when he did. By the time he found himself enforcing curfews and the like, he was an officer and was able to ensure that the soldiers under his command behaved with a modicum of decency. Certainly nothing that he experienced in his three years as a conscript made him think of refusing to serve.

Unlike many of his fellow soldiers, Adi did not feel the urge to go abroad immediately after his military service. He spent two years volunteering at a young kibbutz before returning to Kfar Masaryk and starting engineering studies at the Haifa Technion, Israel's premier institution for science and technology. When he realized that he aspired to a teaching career, he broke off his engineering studies and went to the Oranim Teachers' Training College, graduating two years later. Today, he is a member of Kfar Masaryk and teaches at the nearby mossad. Two of his grandparents and his parents are kibbutz members, as well as a brother and sister. Another brother became religious and lives in Jerusalem.

Because he was living and working at a young kibbutz after his conscript service, Adi Eilat was not called up too often. When he was mobilized, it was to service in the Jordan Rift and the Golan Heights, where he hardly encountered Palestinian civilians. He served once at Rafah in the southern Gaza strip, but that was after the Olso Accords had been signed, and the feeling was that there would not be much more service in the territories.

Eventually he did decide to travel abroad, and the second Intifada found him in New Zealand. Far from the reality of Israel, he was certain that the media reports of the violence were exaggerated. He returned to find a nation at war. Two mobilization orders awaited him: one for maneuvers and a second one for service in the Etzion Bloc southwest of Jerusalem.

Eilat was on maneuvers during the election, returning home to find that Ariel Sharon had been elected prime minister. His father, a battalion commander in the Lebanon War, had been highly critical of Sharon's performance as defense minister in that conflict. He told his son that his experiences in Lebanon finally confirmed to him that the end never justifies the means. Eilat had reached his own conclusion about Israel's situation.

"The difference between Left and Right is in the way they regard time," he asserts. "The Left tries to seize the window of opportunity when it appears; the Right thinks that time is on our side and does nothing."

Deeply distrustful of the new government and its prime minister, Eilat nevertheless reported for duty, resolving to be vigilant and to try to ensure that the men under his command behaved properly. Arriving at his unit, he was put in command of a checkpost on the former Green Line between Israel and the territories. The soldiers were engaged in almost continuous arguments, and he found himself in the minority, with only two of his fellow soldiers "speaking the same language."

In the end it was two incidents—neither of them particularly dramatic—that convinced Adi Eilat to refuse to go on serving in the territories. The first concerned the construction of a shower for a temporary checkpost three miles down the road into the territories. The tractor preparing the ground cut the water pipe to the Palestinian village of Jaba.

"I realized that it was a Thursday afternoon. Obviously nothing was going to be done until after the Sabbath. The pipe was eventually repaired on Monday. Not so terrible, you may think, but, in order that five soldiers could enjoy a shower without having to travel a couple of miles, five thousand people were deprived of running water for four days."

Only Eilat and his two "leftist" friends even noticed what had happened, and it set him thinking. Maybe he could have tried to organize a weekend water supply to Jaba, but it would not have changed the basic situation. What appalled him was the complete indifference of almost all his fellow soldiers.

The second incident concerned the trucks that transported gravel from a quarry in Israel to the Palestinian side. Some dozen trucks passed back and forth every day, each time presenting their permits at the check-post. One day they were visited by a detachment of police who were look-ing for Palestinians entering Israel without permits.

"There was this officer who claimed to have a 'nose' for illegals," recounts Eilat. "He singled out one of the truck drivers and decided that he was entering without the proper permit."

The policeman took the driver's papers and wrote up his report. He then contacted the police in Israel and requested a computer check. Within the hour, the answer came back: the driver's papers were in order, and he was entirely in the clear.

"You could see how annoyed he was," says Eilat. "His famous 'nose' had let him down."

The police officer looked at the truck and saw that the tires were worn, which is the normal state of affairs. He took the driver's papers, driving license, and vehicle license and told him that he was banning him from the road, because his truck was not road-worthy. It is the sort of thing that can happen anywhere with the police, admits Eilat. One hears about such incidents all the time, but, in Israel, the driver would soon receive a temporary license, along with an order to attend the local traffic court. The matter would be presented in court, argued over, and resolved. Justice would not be guaranteed, of course, but there would be a good chance of a fair trial. Because of the way things are run in the Palestinian territories, it would take at least two years for the driver, a fifty-year-old man with a family, to get his license back. During those two years, he would have no way of supporting his family. Adi Eilat speaks almost apologetically.

"I realize that these are trivial matters compared to the killing and de-struction that has happened these last two years. But I still found the sit-uation completely unacceptable. How can it be that five thousand people go without running water so that five can enjoy a shower? Why should a family man be deprived of his living because of the 'nose' of a police offi-cer?"

When he received his next call-up, Eilat told his commanding officer that he would not serve in the territories. He was not refusing military ser-vice, he stressed. He would serve anywhere he was sent, except in the oc-cupied territories. His commanding officer, like Eilat a kibbutz member, refused to accept his decision, arguing that it was officers of his type who were most needed for service in the territories. He probed to see whether his intention to refuse was really serious. When he realized that Eilat was in earnest, he warned him that he would go to jail.

"I told the [commanding officer] that I could find a dozen reasons to get out of service," he recalls. "I was just starting to teach. I had at least one valid medical reason, but my decision was final."

Eilat admits to an identity crisis. He feels torn. Again he returns to his basic premise: The problem is not the behavior of individual soldiers but the situation. Israel's occupation of the Palestinian territories is unacceptable, and he refuses to be a part of it. Initially he saw it as a very personal protest and for that reason hesitated to sign the "Courage to Refuse" manifesto, but after a few months he signed up.

The declaration reads in part:

> We, reserve combat officers and soldiers of the IDF, raised in the principles of Zionism, service, and contribution to the people and State of Israel, who have always served in the front lines, the first to carry out any mission to protect and strengthen Israel. . . .
>
> We, who have served for long weeks every year all over the Occupied Territories, have been issued with orders that have nothing to do with the security of our country, but have the sole purpose of perpetuating our control over the Palestinian people. . . .
>
> We, who have felt that the orders given us in the territories destroy all the values with which we have grown up in this country. . . .
>
> We hereby declare that we shall not continue to fight this War of the Settlements, we shall not continue to fight beyond the 1967 borders, in order to dominate, expel, starve, and humiliate an entire people.
>
> We hereby declare that we shall continue serving in the IDF in any mission that serves Israel's defense.

Of course, many of the signatories have far more dramatic stories to tell than those of Adi Eilat. Assaf writes:

> Without thinking, I turned into the perfect occupation enforcer. I settled accounts with "upstarts" who didn't show enough respect. I tore up the personal documents of men my father's age. I hit and harassed people in the town of Kalkilya, barely three miles from my grandparents' home. No, I was no "aberration." I was exactly the norm.

Daniel recalls, not without pride, a moment of humanity:

An ambulance arrives at the roadblock. Inside sits a silver haired Palestinian doctor. He could have been my father. He explains that he is required to attend to a woman in the village of Hable, but his license plates are the wrong color. I look around. My officer is not paying attention, and I let the ambulance slip past. I feel pleased, like a naughty child stealing cookies when his mother isn't looking. My upbeat mood is shattered by the arrival of the battalion commander. He is puffed up with rage. Apparently a certain soldier has allowed unauthorized vehicles to pass through the roadblock. He received this information from a Palestinian collaborator.

Perhaps the bitterest comment comes from Dan:

Just a few days ago a senior officer was quoted as saying that the IDF must learn the lessons of the German army in the Warsaw Ghetto battle. Technically this officer is ABSOLUTELY RIGHT. May every Hebrew mother know that she has put her children into the care of a commander who has learnt his lesson!

Eilat is convinced that the refusal is far wider than the four hundred or so who have signed the manifesto. Many soldiers find ways of avoiding reserve service, citing medical reasons, studies, or trips abroad. The overt refusenik fits a certain pattern, he suggests. Many of them are bachelors, because the family man can't afford to give up the National Insurance payment he gets during his military service. Quite a number are kibbutz members, who do not depend on others for their jobs, and who don't receive the National Insurance payments anyway.

Eilat admits he was very worried about how his father, a former battalion commander, would feel about his decision, and he was surprised by his reaction. First, he offered his son practical advice about the trial from his own experience as a senior officer. He then told his son about an experience of his own in the Six-Day War of 1967.

A senior officer in the Engineering Corps, he was checking over installations in Sinai after the Egyptian troops had retreated, when six soldiers and an officer, who had been left behind, came out with their hands up. The officer was lightly wounded in error, but they transported the seven to a temporary IDF base, pointing out that one of them was a wounded officer who should be cared for and treated with respect. He later inquired about the condition of the officer, only to learn that he had been gratuitously shot. He had resolved not to complain during the actual battles, and when the war was over, he lodged a complaint, but nothing ever came of it. Later, at one stage in the Lebanon War of 1982, his father considered walking out in protest, but he had resolved not to abandon his men.

"In a way, I feel my refusal is for him also," says Eilat. "Not that this was in my mind when I refused, but as an afterthought. He had a much tougher time in the army than I did, and he achieved higher rank."

He was favorably surprised by the reaction of his friends, "although, naturally, you hear from people who support you. The opponents don't say anything at first." Some of his fellow teachers did suggest he was not suitable to instruct high school children, but they soon appreciated that he made no attempt to propagate his views. He says that he overtly educates toward "humanism, the fulfillment of potential, and doubt." Doubt means questioning everything, and that means also querying a decision to refuse to serve in the territories. High school children are natural patriots, he suggests; they are fighters. He doesn't try to counter this.

In refusing to serve in the territories, isn't Eilat legitimizing in advance soldiers with right-wing views who may one day refuse military orders to evacuate settlements?

"Let them," he snaps. "There's nothing wrong in that sort of protest. It's absolutely legitimate. The problem with the Israeli Right is not passive resistance to obeying orders. It was a right-winger who assassinated Yitzhak Rabin. The problem with the Right is its activism—not its passive protest."

Isn't he leaving the field to soldiers less humane than himself?

"If I could have exerted the tiniest influence, I would have remained," he insists. "I couldn't change anything. My remaining would just afford legitimacy to what we are doing. I think that I am exerting much more influence by refusing."

The present Intifada, I point out, was launched after Prime Minister Ehud Barak made the most far-reaching offer ever made by Israel.

Eilat rejects the thesis that the Palestinians are entirely to blame for the breakdown of the peace process. He does not believe that Barak was really trying to achieve peace. In his view, the Israeli prime minister was looking for an alibi. He wanted to prove that there was no one to talk to and nothing to talk about. The only good thing Barak did was to get the IDF out of Lebanon. In Eilat's opinion, Israel should withdraw from the West Bank and Gaza also, before peace. Peace will come later. Israel is the stronger side and therefore the responsible party.

"We have been holding the Palestinians with their hands behind their backs, and we should stop doing this," he asserts. "The trouble is that we don't really want to give up the territories."

The traditional right-wing stance that they cannot be expected to negotiate while the violence continues sounds plausible enough, he allows. The problem is what a noted Israeli writer called "the second half." The whole sentence should state, "They cannot be expected to negotiate while the violence continues, and, when the violence stops, they don't *have* to negotiate."

He is confident, though, that eventually a majority of Israelis will support a compromise. A significant majority agrees that there should be a Palestinian state and withdrawal from most of the settlements, he says. Most of the population is prepared to divide Jerusalem.

"The stupid clichés no longer frighten the people because they know there is no other solution," he suggests. "It is only the politicians who are afraid of tackling the settlers. They are afraid of the confrontation because the settlers are prepared to kill for their beliefs."

Until now, he suggests, the agenda has been set by the settlers and the suicide bombers, because both of them are prepared to sacrifice their lives for their causes. The moderates have been prepared only to talk. Now those refusing to serve are making a sacrifice, albeit only a very small one. Perhaps it is the start of more action by the moderates, he suggests.

He notes that his father, a lifelong left-winger, quotes Menachem Begin, Israel's first right-wing prime minister:

"War can always be avoided—peace is unavoidable."

A few weeks after my visit, a well-known son of Kfar Masaryk, Tamir Masad, was killed trying to foil a suicide bomber in the West Bank town of Ariel. Tamir had been manifestly embarrassed by his moment of fame in the Lebanon War in 1982, as he stood atop the Beaufort Crusader fortress in Lebanon, answering questions posed by Prime Minister

Begin. Defense Minister Sharon, standing nearby, had said in front of the television cameras that the Beaufort had been taken without casualties. In fact, as he well knew, six of the IDF's finest soldiers had been killed in that completely unnecessary battle. Now, after Tamir Masad's death, the media called back the picture on the Beaufort and gave details of the many senior IDF officers, who were members of the kibbutz. At Tamir's funeral, several veterans of Kfar Masaryk demanded to know why their sons were again being sacrificed in an unnecessary conflict.

"What a tragedy," said one of them bitterly. "Tamir survived Sharon's war in Lebanon but fell in Sharon's war in the territories."

Living in a kibbutz that has such a strong tradition of military service, Adi Eilat finds it particularly difficult when his friends are mobilized and he is left behind. Although he is confident that he has made the right decision, his final statement discloses his doubts and inconsistencies.

"I am on the right road, and I am sure about it. I feel easier with myself. There is a lightening of the load. I don't get that sickness in the stomach every four months when the call-up papers arrive. I think that what I have done is right for me, but I am not a missionary on the subject.

"At the same time, I have not cut myself off. I am still a teacher. I talk to people, and people talk to me. I feel as if I am standing on the watershed between two possible courses of action. I am closer to the soldier who continues to serve with doubts than I am to the soldier who refuses to serve in the IDF altogether. There are friends here in Kfar Masaryk who come and tell me about their doubts, and I feel very close to them. They tell me about other soldiers who have gone to jail rather than serve. You could say that we exchange doubts.

"I don't feel I have changed or moved to the left. On the contrary, the nation has moved to the right. I don't understand how we have all been dragged into this mess. The situation has changed, and our task is to change it back to what it was before. I still believe in Zionism, in building the nation. I still have faith in the egalitarian kibbutz way of life. Absolutely!"

Captain Adi Eilat is not so different from his fellow high school teacher, Lieutenant Nir Shoshani, who continues to serve. Of course, many IDF soldiers serve in the territories with enthusiasm, totally convinced of the justice of Israel's cause. There are also extreme refuseniks, who compare

Israel and its army to the most immoral regimes in history. Most of the nation's soldiers, though, reject both extremes, finding themselves somewhere in the middle. They are Israel's reluctant warriors.

Jonathan Kuttab: The Nonviolent Militant

"Arabs, generally, and Palestinians, specifically, do not have a military culture or tradition. We have not contributed a single weapon, a single tactic, a single strategy, a single improvement, and we have proved ourselves singularly inept at armed struggle in all its forms. We have perfected the *language* of armed struggle, the slogans, and the poetry—the horse, the sword, the gun—but that is *all* we have perfected!

"On the other hand, since the 1930s, the Palestinians have been successful in organizing strikes, protests, demonstrations, economic boycotts, noncooperation, and appeals to the international community, albeit accompanied by the rhetoric of violence and armed struggle."

The speaker, Jonathan Kuttab, is a remarkably articulate man, intelligent, humane, and funny. With his jet-black hair and mustache, his forceful manner, and his wide-ranging discourse, he is a rewarding interviewee. You don't really have to interview him at all. Once you have located his east Jerusalem office, up several flights of stairs on the same street as Orient House (which served as the main Palestinian center in Jerusalem, until it was closed down by the Israeli minister of public security), all you have to do is march in, introduce yourself, and switch on the recording machine.

"We will never outviolence you Israelis. Israel has proved successful at warfare, imposing its will by force, pursuing a strategy of violence, and acquiring the most advanced weapons, while perfecting the rhetoric of peace. It is Shalom this, Shalom that, Shalom the other thing, while being one of the most militarized societies in the world!"

Jonathan Kuttab

In trying to put his ideas over to his fellow Palestinians, Kuttab's main problem is that they see nonviolence as submission. Even the Indian leader Mahatma Gandhi said that if the choice were between submission and violence, he would choose violence, he observes. Nonviolence doesn't translate well into Arabic, he concedes. *La-onf* places the emphasis on the *la*, the not doing, but you can do a great deal, he insists, adding that he doesn't like the term *passive resistance*.

"I am not passive at all," he declares. "I want to be extremely active."

Jonathan Kuttab was born in the Jordanian capital of Amman. His parents returned to Jerusalem when he was two years old. His father, George Mussa Kuttab, now retired, was an Anglican pastor, serving his Nazarene Church in both Jerusalem and Bethlehem. Jonathan was educated at St. George's School in Jerusalem, where Nasser Eddin Nashashibi had studied four decades earlier. After completing his matriculation, he went on to further studies at Messiah College in Grantham, Pennsylvania, majoring in history. Law school followed at the University of Virginia in Charlottesville, after which he worked on Wall Street for two years to pay off his tuition fees.

Kuttab returned to Jerusalem in 1980, where he has worked as an attorney ever since. Already a member of the New York Bar, he joined the Palestinian Bar (formerly the Arab Lawyer's Union) and qualified for the Israeli Bar, after studying Hebrew at the famous Ulpan Akiva in Netanya. Making his living chiefly from civil law, he has also been active in the field of human rights. He was part of the group that founded Al-Haq (Law in the Service of Man), the first Palestinian human rights organization, established to uphold the rule of law in the occupied territories. Al-Haq became affiliated with the International Commission of Jurists in Geneva. In 1982, Kuttab coauthored *The West Bank and the Rule of Law*, a study of Israeli legal policy in the occupied territories, with his friend Raja Shehadeh from Ramallah.

In its first decade, Al-Haq concentrated on combating civil rights abuses by the Israeli authorities, but, since the Palestinian Authority was established in 1993, the organization has worked hard to establish an independent Palestinian judiciary.

In his memoir *The Third Way*, published in 1982 (long before the term was made famous by U.S. president Bill Clinton and British prime minister Tony Blair), Raja Shehadeh spelled out his approach to life under the Israeli occupation. "Faced with two alternatives," he writes, "always choose the third. Between mute submission and blind hate, I chose the third way. I am *Samid*" (Arabic for steadfast or persevering).

Sumud, "perseverance," is okay, allows Kuttab, provided it has an active component. The word does perhaps have the implication of waiting for something to happen, whereas he stresses active resistance. He allows that his Christian identity has influenced his opinions, saying that his individual belief happens to coincide totally with the "perfect strategy" for his people. He insists, however, that the nonviolent movement is not a Christian affair. He is not promoting it because of his religious and philosophical background, but because of logic, common sense, and reason. Haider Abdel Shafi, the Gaza physician who headed the Palestinian delegation to the 1991 Middle East peace conference in Madrid, is sympathetic toward a strategy of nonviolence. So are lecturers Mustafa Barghouti and Hanan Ashrawi. Even Marwan Barghouti, the leader of the Fatah militia in the West Bank, who is currently imprisoned by Israel and on trial for promoting terrorist attacks, showed great interest in the idea.

Kuttab rejects the notion that the Palestinians are temperamentally unsuited to this type of action. He is sure that nonviolent resistance is more compatible with the Palestinian character than violence. Challenged that he represents a tiny minority of Palestinians, he snaps back that he knows more Palestinian pacifists than Israelis of that persuasion. He is fully aware of the extremely militant image that Arabs—and indeed all Muslims—have acquired in today's world, but he repudiates it firmly. At the height of their empire, the Arabs excelled in all fields of human endeavor except warfare, he asserts. They were great scientists, physicians, philosophers, authors, architects, engineers, and artists.

"Their greatest military leader was Sallah Eddin [Salladin], a Kurd," he points out. "Their most famous battle lasted half a day. Some Ethiopian told them that if you dig a trench, it is difficult for people to get past it, so they used it in a battle, known to this day as 'The Battle of the Trench.'"

Even the Palestinian resort to terrorism proves how inept they are at fighting, in his view. They don't have the talent to collect intelligence, plan, and hit serious targets, so they strike at random civilians. Apart from being morally repugnant and counterproductive, he asserts, terror is the easiest form of violence to carry out.

Despite his scathing description of Israel practicing violence while preaching peace, Kuttab shows an awareness of Jewish history. All the terrible things that happened to the Jews over the centuries, culminating in the pogroms and the Holocaust, happened because the Jews were nice and polite and accommodating. The Israeli reaction, he suggests, has been to swing to the other extreme and make a virtue out of being harsh, nasty, aggressive, and disdainful of public opinion. Even decent, humane Jews feel that Israel must live by the sword and cannot count on the goodwill of others. The Israelis need to have the military power to impose their survival on others.

This has brought Kuttab to the conclusion that it is futile to challenge the Israelis on the battlefield. He tells his fellow Palestinians that they are dealing with a superpower that is totally wedded to the concept of violence as a means of survival. The Palestinians cannot compete with this, so why bother? In taking up the gun, the Palestinians are also reinforcing the negative elements in the Israeli character. The struggle must be shifted to other fields: to law, ethics, decency, rationality. In taking this message to his fellow Palestinians, he insists that he has found a receptive ear.

"There is a huge thirst on the Palestinian side for alternative strategies," he declares. "There is a growing realization that the suicide bombings and other acts of violence have been harmful to the Palestinian cause."

It is true that frustration has grown so acute that hurting Israelis gives a momentary satisfaction to many Palestinians, he allows, but that is not going to bring them closer to their goal. Speaking against violence is difficult, because many Palestinians feel that they have received no real help from the Arab states, or anybody else. They see that all the United Nations resolutions have not gained them anything.

Kuttab thinks that the first Intifada was the supreme example of the success of nonviolence. He understands that most Israelis see throwing rocks as violent and agrees that, at close range, a rock can be destructive—even fatal—but most of the stones were thrown by youngsters at soldiers and police who were well out of range. The rock throwing was an act of defiance, rather than a real attempt to harm Israeli security personnel.

The rocks became the story, he concedes, and that is a shame. The media concentrated on the confrontation between stone-throwing youngsters and Israeli soldiers, ignoring other aspects of the struggle. The Arabic word *Intifada* means "shaking off," and the important thing about the first Intifada was the Palestinian attempt to shake off Israeli rule: exercising noncooperation, going on strike, closing stores, setting their own summertime daylight savings scheme, and, above all, boycotting Israeli goods. Although the boycott was only partly successful and caused the Palestinians economic hardship, local farmers, manufacturers, and entrepreneurs showed great resourcefulness in increasing local production.

Mubarak Awad, a Jerusalem-born American citizen, started trying to promote nonviolent resistance when he arrived in Jerusalem in 1983. His efforts were derided by many, but, when the Intifada broke out in December 1987, his ideas suddenly became popular. The Unified Leadership of the Uprising never adopted his philosophy of nonviolence, but most of his ideas on noncooperation and civil disobedience were implemented. Awad himself became such a celebrity that his residency permit was not renewed, and, in May 1988, he was hastily deported by the government of Israel.

The greatness of the first Intifada compared to the current struggle, says Kuttab, is that all sectors of Palestinian society participated—not just the armed few.

"It released the creative energies of the people in a beautifying, uplifting struggle, full of hope and promise," he declares. "Despite the suffering, the nonviolent struggle highlighted the justice of the Palestinian cause."

Not wanting to see the conflict spread from the territories into Israel, the Israeli authorities actually started to encourage local economic development, improving procedures and cutting red tape to boost local production. Most important, a number of Israeli political leaders became convinced that an agreement with the Palestinians and an end to the occupation was necessary. It was the first Intifada that led to the Oslo agreement of 1993, but Kuttab is not impressed with the Palestinian Authority, which was established in the wake of Oslo.

In his view, the Authority served Israeli interests. While supposedly negotiating peace, it permitted the expansion of the Jewish settlements and the continuation of the Israeli occupation of the West Bank and Gaza. In addition, Israel subcontracted some of the dirtier and more difficult tasks to the corrupt Palestinian leadership. The fact that he espouses

nonviolence doesn't mean that he is prepared to compromise over principles. As far as he is concerned, the Israeli occupation must end.

"We have to resist at all levels. We have to fight the battle of the closures by nonviolent means. We should ignore the checkpoints and go right
through. We should lie down in the streets. We should enter the settlements en masse and put them under siege. We must try to revive the Israeli peace camp, while, at the same time, campaigning against current
Israeli policy on the international scene."

Another Palestinian interviewee described an incident when members of Taayush, a group dedicated to Jewish–Arab cooperation, started
dismantling a barricade between Issawiya and Hebrew University. The
ramp of rocks and earth had been put in place by bulldozers,
and the attempts by the Taayush protesters to destroy it with picks and
hoes were futile. Nevertheless, the police attacked them with truncheons. Similar incidents have been reported in Ramallah, where stun
grenades were used against peaceful demonstrators by Israeli and Palestinian journalists.

In reaction to these stories, Kuttab responds that he expects nonviolence to be met with violence. He hopes that the contrast between the
nonviolence and the violence will create a dynamic that will make the violence counterproductive. The longer nonviolence is maintained in the
face of violence, the more effective it is, but, he stresses, it is not a "magic
bullet that defeats Satan in one go." Violence is like an explosion: Bang,
and it's over. Nonviolence is like a sapling. It has to be planted and nur-
tured so that it grows strong, like a tree. Thirty years of violence have not
brought freedom, so other methods must be tried.

He admits that he is concerned that, in the face of Israeli violence,
"some stupid Palestinian hothead will pick up a gun," but he believes
that it is possible to maintain discipline. In the 1980s, he had helped
Mubarak Awad organize several nonviolent campaigns. There were
several tree-planting operations, replacing olive trees uprooted by Israeli security forces. The planters were instructed to put down their
hoes and spades as soon as police or soldiers appeared, so that they
would not have an excuse to use violence. Discipline was maintained,
recalls Kuttab.

Our conversations took place during the Israeli incursions into the
Palestinian towns in the spring and early summer of 2002, and, under

continuous closure and curfew, there was no possibility of organizing classes in nonviolence or carrying out simulation exercises. He finds the topic absurd.

"How can you expect any activity of any sort while the military is occupying our towns? In the current situation, the name of the game is survival. The individual Palestinian uses all his time and energy to get food, to do the countless small tasks in the time available. Only Palestinians like me, living in Jerusalem, have the luxury of thinking about the strategy of resistance. The others have to deal with the tactics of daily existence."

For all that, some efforts are still being made. Noah Salameh, who (like Kuttab himself and Mubarak Awad) studied in the United States, runs the Center for Conflict Resolution and Conciliation in Bethlehem, at which he teaches parents and children the ethic of nonviolence in their relations with each other. He says his classes have caused the students to become more open. There is no tradition of class discussion in the Palestinian schools, he notes, but students have been stimulated by his ideas.

Two years ago, when relations between the two sides were still good, he ran a seminar for Israeli and Palestinian security officials, working together at the Allenby Bridge, the main crossing point between Jordan and the Palestinian territories. He claims that relations between the two groups improved after the course. Seeming to echo Kuttab, he was quoted in a recent article as saying, "Building a democratic nonviolent society is not a commando thing, but rather a long-term process requiring education" (*Ha'aretz*).

The first Arabic-language book on the subject, *Toward Non-Violence*, was written by Iraqi-born Khalid Kishtainy. He maintains that studying the Israeli–Arab conflict convinced him that the Arab side has consistently lost out by going to war. He insists that nonviolence is a more effective weapon. He agrees with Kuttab that *la-onf* doesn't sound good in Arabic. He advocates "civilian jihad," as a good Arab and Muslim label for the strategy. Justifying his choice, Kishtainy explains that when the Prophet Muhammad returned from a battle, he used to say he was returning from the minor jihad (the military conflict) to the major jihad (civilian work). Arguing that *jihad* is a much abused word, Kishtainy also emphasizes that nonviolence is not tantamount to surrender.

Returning to Jonathan Kuttab, I ask him how he sees the future. He thinks the two-state solution, Israel and Palestine side by side, is inevitable, although it is an inferior alternative to one state for both peoples in all of Palestine. In a nonperfect world, he suggests, it is "more doable." He doesn't see Israelis agreeing to anything other than a Jewish state, and it's not for him to oppose them.

"I don't want to say to the Israelis, 'I deny your hopes and dreams, your goals, your ideology, your legitimacy.' If that's what you want, you are entitled to it. Let there be a two-state solution. That is a practical and pragmatic compromise."

Sadly for both Palestinians and Israelis, Jonathan Kuttab does represent only a minority of his people, but the force of his logic is clearly demonstrated by the speed with which Israel hastened to deport Mubarak Awad, when he seemed to be achieving a measure of success. Clearly, the authorities saw his campaign of nonviolent resistance as a threat. It is much easier to mobilize Israeli public opinion to fight the Palestinians when Israelis are being blown to bits in their streets, shopping malls, restaurants, coffee bars, nightclubs, and pizza parlors. As Kuttab writes in a piece distributed by the Search for Common Ground website, "During the first Intifada, Palestinian unarmed tactics effectively neutralized the superiority of the Israeli military and split the Israeli public down the middle. At the present time the unprecedented degree of violence on both sides has created an atmosphere of hatred and fury that is hardly conducive to nonviolence."

At the same time, following the spring and summer incursions of the IDF into the Palestinian territories, and the subsequent siege of the Mukkata, Yasser Arafat's headquarters, more and more Palestinians are talking about replacing the armed struggle with a "popular resistance movement." Increasingly, leading Palestinians are saying out loud that it was a mistake to use weapons in the current Intifada. So perhaps, after all, Jonathan Kuttab and his friends represent the wave of the future.

Strangely enough, Kuttab the pacifist is probably not best termed a "reluctant warrior." He is more than reluctant to use violence. He is totally against it. He is bravely on record as labeling the use of force "immoral and counterproductive." At the same time, he is enthusiastic about nonviolent resistance. Rather than "reluctant warrior," Jonathan Kuttab should be described as a "nonviolent militant."

No one needs the confrontation between the two peoples. Nobody benefits from it—quite the reverse. In the next chapter, the dreadful cost of the conflict—physically, psychologically, economically—is conveyed by the stories of three Israelis and three Palestinians.

CHAPTER 5
THE PRICE

Yitzhak Frankenthal, Israeli Bereaved Parent

On the evening of Wednesday, July 6, 1994, nineteen-year-old private Arye Zvi Frankenthal was waiting for a lift to his moshav cooperative village, Gimzo, which is situated not far from Ben-Gurion International Airport in the center of the country. "Arik" had finished the first phase of his service in the Armored Corps of the Israel Defense Forces and was looking forward to a few days of home leave. He had hitchhiked home many times since his mobilization a year earlier, but this time he was not fated to arrive. His body, riddled with bullet holes and stab wounds, was found the following day, outside Kafr Akab, a Palestinian village near Ramallah, north of Jerusalem.

He was buried that Friday at the Holon Military Cemetery. At the funeral, Israel Lau, the chief rabbi of Israel, lamented "our upside-down world, where fathers mourn their children," and lauded the young soldier who had "filled his life with the love of the Torah."

Over the weekend, the Hamas fundamentalist Islamic movement faxed the Reuters news agency a copy of the young soldier's army identity card, with a statement claiming responsibility.

"If the Israeli government wants to stop the series of kidnappings," read the message, "it must release 7,000 Palestinian prisoners from Israeli prisons. Our land demands to be perfumed by more blood."

Four months later, twenty-year-old Ayman Abu-Hallil and nineteen-year-old Issam Kadmani, both members of the Hamas, would go on trial in an Israeli military court for the murder of the nineteen-year-old soldier.

After burying Arik, his eldest son, Yitzhak Frankenthal, a religious Jew, observed the *shiva*, the customary seven days of mourning. Then he

115

sat down and wrote letters to Prime Minister Yitzhak Rabin and Foreign Minister Shimon Peres, urging them to continue in their quest for peace with the Palestinians.

These were the early months of the Oslo agreement: Ten months earlier, Rabin had signed the Oslo Declaration of Principles with Palestinian leader Yasser Arafat in Washington. Less than two months earlier, Israel had carried out its first withdrawal from Palestinian territory, evacuating the IDF from most of the Gaza strip and a small area around Jericho in the Jordan Valley

Israel's prime minister Yitzhak Rabin often visited the parents of soldiers who had lost their lives in action, but at this time he was particularly sensitive to terrorist strikes being carried out by Palestinian groups opposed to the Oslo agreement. Hamas terrorists carried out a number of attacks on Israeli soldiers and civilians, which the Palestinian Authority either could not or would not control. In two particularly deadly suicide bomb attacks toward the end of 1994 and early in 1995, more than forty Israelis were killed, and scores were injured. In between, Rabin, Peres, and Arafat had been awarded the Nobel Peace Prize in Oslo, but back in Israel right-wing demonstrators opposed to the peace process labeled Rabin and Peres "traitors."

Yitzhak Frankenthal

Rabin's visit to the Frankenthal home went well. It was an exceptionally warm and emotional meeting, with the general-turned-peacemaker finding a common language with the religious Zionist, who was in the process of liquidating his private business to devote all his time to campaigning for peace. Frankenthal continued to meet with Rabin, and, on one visit to his apartment, he encountered a group of bereaved parents who were protesting that the Oslo agreement had increased the number of Israelis killed in terrorist operations.

"It's simply not true," Frankenthal told the Israeli leader. "There has not been an increase. I'm going to organize a group of bereaved parents who will support your quest for peace!"

"You won't find more than two or three," warned Rabin.

"No, I'm going to find at least ten families," promised Frankenthal. "Just give me a list of soldiers who have been killed over the past seventeen years."

Rabin did not give his new friend the list, as it would have violated the right to privacy of the parents, but Frankenthal was undeterred. He went to the public library and combed through the newspaper files. After three months he had the names of 422 bereaved families. He managed to find addresses for 350 of them and sent them letters, inviting them to join his "Parents' Circle." He did not send letters to those who were on record as holding hawkish views, but, despite this, two of the parents wrote back in anger. Forty-four joined the circle, which today has grown to over two hundred. There are also 140 Palestinian families, mostly from Gaza, in a parallel group.

Frankenthal accompanied Rabin and Peres to Oslo for the Nobel Prize ceremony, and he was also on the platform with them one year later at the large peace demonstration in Tel Aviv. He spoke as a religious Jew and a bereaved parent. After his speech, the prime minister embraced him warmly. Not long afterward Rabin was shot dead.

Almost the first thing a visitor notices on entering Yitzhak Frankenthal's home in the Jerusalem suburb of Beit Hakerem is a large color blowup of Arik in his khaki uniform. The picture of the handsome tow-haired youth dominates the living room—and indeed dominates Frankenthal's life. Since his son's death, the tall, burly, gray-haired man, with rimless glasses and a knitted skullcap, has maintained a single-minded focus on his peace campaigning. His entire existence is directed toward one purpose: changing Israeli public opinion in favor of peace with the Palestinians, based on territorial compromise, so that no more human beings on either side will be sacrificed to the national cause.

Nothing in his upbringing presaged Frankenthal's role as an untiring advocate of compromise with the Palestinians. His parents, immigrants from Germany, made their home in Bnai Brak, a religious suburb of Tel Aviv. His upbringing was standard National Religious, although he was a member of the ultra-Orthodox Ezra Youth Movement, rather than the mainstream Bnai Akiva. He joined the IDF Engineering Corps and served in Sinai during the Yom Kippur War of 1973.

"I witnessed the tragedies of that conflict," he says. "I felt that the war was unnecessary. Later disclosures convinced me that I had been right. Prime Minister Golda Meir rejected overtures by Egypt's prime minister Anwar Sadat. I also felt that the IDF was deliberately heating up the situation in the north. Even then I felt the army was being used for political purposes, and it angered me."

Frankenthal describes his mother as "very right-wing," but she respected his views. He concedes that he was almost unique in his environment. The National Religious Party, which for many years had been more dovish than the ruling Labor Party, its partner in all the coalition governments, had lurched sharply to the right after the Six-Day War of 1967, adopting an increasingly nationalist—even messianic—point of view. Young members of the National Religious Party led the drive to settle the territories captured in the war. After the Yom Kippur War, they were the core of Gush Emunim, spearheading settlement in the occupied territories. None of his friends at school or in the youth movement shared Frankenthal's dovish opinions, but he had always thought things out for himself, never accepting the consensus but questioning everything.

Although he was sharply critical of the Lebanon War, launched by Israel in 1982, Frankenthal did not become politically active at that time. After his army service, he had entered the family food products business, and, when that was bought out by a larger company, he went into business for himself, devoting all his time and energy to it.

It was his son Arik who persuaded him to enter the political fray. Like his father before him, Arik was a nonconformist in the National Religious environment. He attended high school at Kibbutz Alumim, where, after a terrorist strike, some of the boys started chanting, "Death to the Arabs!" Arik jumped up on a table, and shouted, "Heil Hitler!" His classmates were shocked, but Arik insisted, "That's how it happened in Germany: Hitler and his gang shouting, 'Death to the Jews!'"

While he was still at high school, Arik encouraged to his father to join Netivot Shalom (Paths of Peace), a dovish movement of religious Israelis. The Netivot Shalom people believed that the National Religious Party had taken a wrong turn. They opposed Gush Emunim's settlement drive, which was based on a fervent conviction that the people of Israel should settle the Land of Israel and live according to the Torah of Israel. The Gush, they maintained, had elevated the "land" above both the "people" and the "Torah." Netivot Shalom held that the fundamental principle of Judaism was *Pikuah Nefesh* (the sanctity of life), which superceded everything else. Thus, if lives could be saved by compromising with the Palestinians over the Land of Israel, it was the imperative of Judaism to support compromise.

In 1995, Frankenthal became the general secretary of Netivot Shalom, and he continues to identify with the movement, but after three years in the position, he decided to devote all his time to his Parents' Circle, and to the "Families' Forum," which he founded alongside the circle. Whereas the Parents' Circle espouses "tolerance, Judaism, and democracy," along the lines of Netivot Shalom, the Families' Forum, which also includes Arab and Druse bereaved parents and siblings, places "reconciliation, tolerance, peace, and democracy" on its bannerhead. Yitzhak Frankenthal is chairman of the Families' Forum and general manager of the Parents' Circle, which work together in close cooperation. He devotes all of his time to these activities.

"Since Arik's death," he explains, "I simply haven't had the head for business."

From the outset, Frankenthal was determined to reach out to the other side. His initial contacts were with Palestinian families in Gaza, which he visited more than a hundred times. His subsequent activities in the West Bank were limited by the difficulties of maintaining contacts between Israelis and Palestinians during the Intifada.

His contacts with Palestinian bereaved parents started with a couple of families, but the word spread, and today 140 families are members of a Palestinian Families' Forum. The Israeli group has visited a "peace tent" in

Gaza, and Palestinians have come to sit with the Israeli families in a similar tent in Tel Aviv's Rabin Square. Personal contacts are maintained wherever possible in face-to-face meetings or by phone.

The project has not been free of trouble. On one occasion, when visiting a Palestinian demonstration of some one thousand people in Gaza to protest Israel's failure to keep its promises about releasing Palestinian prisoners, Frankenthal addressed the gathering in Hebrew. Although he is not fluent in Arabic, he sensed that his message was not being conveyed to the crowd in its entirety. His admission that Israel did not keep its promises to release Palestinian prisoners was translated accurately. His observation that violence would not achieve anything was toned down. He asked the translator to give his words in full. Although he stressed that he was speaking about violence by both sides, some in the Palestinian audience objected vociferously to this thesis, and about fifty of them yelled abuse and tried to rush him. He was protected by the vast majority of those present, who sympathized with his views.

On another occasion, a bereaved Palestinian told him, "As a father, I sympathize with the loss of your son, but as a Palestinian, I have to say I am glad he was killed, because he was a soldier."

"As a father, I feel like picking up this desk and throwing it at you," replied Frankenthal, "but as an Israeli, I must tell you that, one week before he was killed, I asked Arik what he would do if he were a Palestinian. He replied that he would kill as many Israeli soldiers as possible."

On the Israeli side, Frankenthal has also had problems. An exhibit in Tel Aviv's Rabin Square, toward the end of 2001, was supposed to display nine hundred coffins, representing the seven hundred Palestinians and two hundred Israelis killed in the current violence. (The figures are of course higher by now.) The Palestinian coffins were to be draped with the red, black, and green Palestinian flag; the Israeli coffins with the blue and white Israeli flag. The police refused to permit such a "provocative" mass display of Palestinian flags in the heart of Tel Aviv, arguing that it would disturb public order. The display was held with one Israeli flag and one Palestinian flag. The "title" of the display was a phrase from Yitzhak Rabin's speech the night he was assassinated: "Better the pain of peace than the agony of war!"

Subsequently, the Families' Forum has displayed this slogan on billboards all over Israel. There was also a media campaign with large paid announcements in the main newspapers and radio broadcasts. After a few days, Israel Radio banned the announcements on the grounds they were controversial and contentious. It should be pointed out that the national radio regularly runs advertisements for settlement in the occupied territories.

The next phase of the campaign was discussed at a Families' Forum weekend at a hotel on the shores of the Dead Sea. A long session was conducted with a diplomat from the Egyptian embassy, who came specially from Tel Aviv. One of the bereaved parents, an Arab from Galilee, served as translator. The Egyptian emphasized that, despite the coldness of the peace between his country and Israel, his people really did want peace. He noted the current disappointment that the process had not expanded to other Middle East countries, but, when Anwar Sadat returned to Cairo after his first historic trip to Israel in 1977, two million people turned out to cheer him.

"I know many people think our regime can mobilize crowds," he admitted, "but nobody can bring two million people into the streets. It was overwhelming." He also tried to reassure his listeners that Egypt would not go back on the peace treaty.

"In the Cairo Museum, there is a treaty that we signed with the Hittites of Turkey four thousand years ago," he declared. "We have never broken it. We are a people that honors its signatures."

The diplomat stayed on to listen to the campaign briefing by Shmulik Cohen, who explained that the Families' Forum and Parents' Circle positioned themselves in the center, so as not to be written off as "extreme leftist." That was why they were associating themselves as closely as possible with the late Yitzhak Rabin, who is seen as a figure of Israel's political center. To coincide with the anniversary of Rabin's assassination, the Tel Aviv Museum would display two coffins draped in Israeli and Palestinian flags, which would later move on to New York and Washington.

The parents learned that the Rabin phrase "Better the pain of peace than the agony of war!" was being displayed in Arabic in the West Bank and Gaza, even during this time of violent confrontation. The campaign of the Parents' Circle and Families' Forum was the first peace campaign since the start of the second Intifada in the fall of 2000. The Left had been paralyzed by the outburst of horrendous violence, but, following their lead, the remainder of the Israeli "peace camp" was coming to life.

Relaxing in the lobby after the session, a woman from a kibbutz in the coastal plain, with a single steel-gray braid, discusses the loss of her son with an elderly Druze from Galilee, with a mustache of the same color as his companion's hair, who has lost two brothers and two nephews. (The Druze, a minority Muslim community, inhabit the hill regions of Israel, Syria, and Lebanon. Israeli Druze are obligated, as are the Jewish citizens of Israel, to serve in the IDF.) The kibbutz member is a pioneer of the prestate period; the Druze is from a family of warriors who have served the nation for three generations. The Druze, dressed in the traditional baggy trousers and white keffiye headscarf, is fatalistic, believing it all depends on God. The kibbutznik, in slacks and sweater, is militant, demanding the replacing of the current government by one that will make peace. The two very different personalities are united in a personal grief that fuels their passionate belief that war solves nothing and that the time has come for peace. Their presence together, along with that of several dozen Israeli Jews and Arabs, symbolizes what the Families' Forum is all about.

Other activities of the forum and the circle have been phone-ins and blood donations. In an unprecedented gesture, twenty bereaved Palestinian parents and family members came to Jerusalem from Ramalla to give blood for Jewish victims of Palestinian violence, and twenty bereaved Israeli relatives went to Ramalla to give blood for Palestinian victims of Israeli violence. Quizzed on Israeli television, Rami Elhanan, who lost his daughter in a terrorist action, denied that the Palestinians rejected peace and coexistence.

"I do not see any moral difference between the terrorist who killed my daughter," he declared, "and the IDF soldier who prevented a Palestinian mother from passing through a roadblock to give birth in hospital and lost her child as a result." He pleaded for a cessation of what he called "keeping accounts of who killed whom and why." The important thing, he stressed, was to stop the bloodshed on all sides.

"HELLO, SALAAM! HELLO, SHALOM!" appeared in full-page advertisements in Israeli and Palestinian newspapers stating, "Two years have passed without our speaking to each other . . . call, and you'll see that there's someone on the other side who wants a dialogue." Readers were invited to call a special number.

My test of the system was successful. After obeying several electronic instructions, I eventually got through to Gera, a Palestinian from Ramalla, who said that the time had come to stop the senseless destruction and make peace. It was definitely possible, he thought.

Frankenthal informed me that the special number was flooded with requests from both Israelis and Palestinians who wanted to speak to each other. The claim was that there had been some ten thousand calls in the first week of the line's operation.

Even before his encounter in Gaza, Frankenthal was acutely aware that the other side did not share his perception of his son's death.

"When my son Arik was murdered," he wrote in a magazine article, "the whole of the people of Israel wept with me and my family, and felt our pain. While we saw Arik's death as murder, the Palestinians saw in his murder a means to further the goal of a Palestinian state. These different approaches led me to an understanding that what is just in our eyes is not necessarily just in Palestinian eyes. In light of this, I seek a solution of intelligent logic rather than justice."

Frankenthal's "intelligent logic" is in line with a peace map produced by Netivot Shalom in 1995. It proposes a Palestinian state alongside Israel, based on the pre–June 1967 borders, with adjustments. Seven percent of the West Bank would be annexed to Israel, containing three-quarters of the Jewish settlers. The remaining setters would be free to live as citizens of Palestine, like all other Palestinian citizens. The Palestinian state would guarantee safety of its Jewish citizens, as Israel is committed to the safety of its Arab citizens. Jewish settlers wishing to move back to Israel would receive assistance.

Surprisingly, Frankenthal describes the Jewish settlers in the West Bank and Gaza as "the cream of the crop of contemporary Jewry." Queried on this comment, he responds that parents may disagree with, or disapprove of, their children, but they still love them.

"The settlers are me," he proclaims. "They are my people, and I have a great affection for them, even though I feel they are making the gravest of mistakes."

He concedes that the feeling is not mutual and that the settlers on the whole don't return the affection he feels for them.

Under the Netivot Shalom plan, 93 percent of the West Bank and all of the Gaza strip would be Palestine. The Palestinians would be compensated for the missing 7 percent with some land adjoining the Gaza strip and an elevated highway and railroad, linking the West Bank and Gaza.

Frankenthal has met with Palestinian leader Yasser Arafat on several occasions, and, even after the new Intifada, he still refers to him as "the Palestinian Ben-Gurion." He agrees that in permitting the Intifada to be launched in October 2000, Arafat made a grave mistake.

"He should have led a peaceful march of one hundred thousand Palestinians on Jerusalem," he suggests.

Nevertheless, he blames Israel for the failure to reach agreement in the fall of 2000. The outlines of an agreement were clear at Camp David and subsequently at Taba, he insists. The Clinton proposals were more or less acceptable to both sides. Israel would have agreed to take in one hundred thousand Palestinian refugees over ten years but would cede to Palestine an area around Jerusalem with more than double the number of Arab inhabitants, ending up with fewer Arab citizens. A large-scale international compensation fund would be established for resettling the remainder of the Arab refugees.

"Barak didn't understand the Palestinians' 'Red Line,' which is sovereignty over the Temple Mount," he maintains. "Following that, there was complete despair on the Palestinian side."

As a religious Jew, Frankenthal is prepared to cede sovereignty over Temple Mount to the Palestinians. He cites a presentation made by Professor Moshe Halbertal at the Parents' Circle tent in Rabin Square. Halbertal, a scholar and religious dove, argued that there is no connection between sanctity and sovereignty. On the contrary, a place that is *not* controlled becomes holy. For example, on the Sabbath, a holy day, people must not perform creative work or do anything to alter the surroundings. On regular days, people are free to govern and control, to create and conquer. On the Sabbath, people must treat nature as a gift that must not be modified. Thus, sovereignty and sanctity are contradictory terms.

"Those who demand ownership over holiness and want to reside in the House of the Lord for the rest of their days should know that the divine spirit abandoned the place in the past because of bloodshed," he stated, referring to the internecine strife that preceded the fall of the Temple of Jerusalem in 73 C.E.

Halbertal's sermon is included in a special *Guide to the Perplexed*, prepared by Frankenthal, in which he endeavors to answer some sixty questions, ranging from whether Israel has a real partner for peace to what is to prevent a Palestinian state from entering alliances with hostile states, such as Iraq. He offers the guide, he explains, "not as a scholar or a wise man, but as a man of experience, experience that every year runs deeper and deeper than the six feet of the grave of my dear departed son, Arik."

A few sample questions and answers from his *Guide* lay out the message that Frankenthal is trying to convey to the Israeli people:

Q: If we agree to evacuate settlements for the sake of peace, where do we draw the line? Why not leave Tel Aviv?

A: Some settlers have voiced this absurd argument. Our starting point, which we share with the international community and with the Palestinians, is that the 1967 borders are now the accepted compromise. In reality these borders give Israel fifty percent more land than it would have received had the UN resolution in 1947 been upheld. But yes, there are settlers whose pain makes them willing to give up Tel Aviv rather than Hebron.

Q: Even if we make peace with the Palestinians now, Israeli Arabs in the future will seek independence, and again we'll have problems with the Arab world.

A: There is no reason in the world why citizens, who have a good life in their country, would want national independence. Do the ultra-Orthodox Jews want autonomy in Jerusalem, or the Jews of New York want autonomy? Why would the Arabs of Israel want this unless their situation is inferior to that of their Jewish neighbors? We must therefore act fast to rectify the wrongs we have inflicted upon Israeli Arabs.

Q: Why not send the Palestinians to live in one of the other Arab states? After all there are twenty-two Arab states and only one Jewish state.

A: The Palestinians were here before the State of Israel was founded. There are several reasons why a population transfer is not possible:

1. The Palestinians don't want to be transferred—this is their home!
2. It is inhuman.
3. No country will accept them.

Q: Is peace with the Palestinians really possible?

A: The Palestinians are people just like you and me. We have also committed acts of terrorism in order to gain our independence. At this point in time, the Palestinians have nothing to lose. When they get their state, however, it will be in their interest to keep the peace and live alongside us with dignity. If they continue to have nothing to lose, the bloodshed will be horrific.

Despite his strenuous opposition to the current policies of the Israeli government, Frankenthal rejects the current movement of IDF officers and noncommissioned officers who are refusing to serve in the occupied territories. He is angry with these soldiers, who should serve in the army and behave morally.

"Illegal orders should be disobeyed," he agrees, "but the law defines what is illegal—not a private citizen. In a democracy, people cannot make their own rules. This movement is destructive."

He is also opposed to proposals, currently being floated by some opposition leaders, for "unilateral separation." These suggest withdrawing from much of the West Bank and Gaza, *without* an agreement with the Palestinians, and putting up physical barriers, such as walls, fences, buffer zones, electronic devices, and patrols, between Israel and the Palestinian entity. Frankenthal dismisses this idea as "a new Bar-Lev Line," after the fortifications along the Suez Canal, destroyed by the Egyptians in the 1973 war. There is, he insists, no substitute for a peace agreement between Israel and the Palestinians. This will require a change in Israeli public opinion, and that is what the Parents' Circle and Families' Forum are trying to achieve.

Frankenthal is certain that eventually peace will exist between Israel and the Palestinians. He thinks that eventually an Israeli government will agree to dismantle many settlements, because "that is the price that we have to pay." It will only happen when a majority of Israelis realize that there is no alternative.

"Unfortunately, it is going to take many more casualties on both sides," he opines, "and that makes me very sad."

Tariq Essawi, Palestinian Bereaved Parent

"Whatever happens in this country, you are going to be here tomorrow morning, and so am I!"

It was my first meeting with Tariq Essawi, a Palestinian bereaved parent who has come to believe in the inevitability of peace between Israelis and Palestinians. His position is especially significant because he comes from a long line of anti-Zionist fighters. His father, Ahmad Ali Essawi, was a comrade in arms of Abdel Kader Husseini, the legendary leader of the 1936–1939 Arab rebellion against the British mandatory authorities and the Zionist enterprise. In fact, Tariq insists, his father actually preceded Husseini in the struggle.

"When Abdel Kader left to fight the British, he was riding a horse and carrying a rifle that he received from my father," he relates proudly. "We don't think that the revolt was a mistake—even with the advantage of hindsight. It was the right thing to do at that time."

Essawi's father also fought with Abdel Kader Husseini against the Jewish forces in 1947, helping him to seize the Kastel, overlooking the main road to Jerusalem. When the commander was killed, he went with all the other fighters to his funeral on Temple Mount. After the burial, he begged the Palestinian warriors to return to the Kastel, but the sense of grief pervaded everything. There was no response to his call, and the Palestinians lost the Kastel and everything else.

Following our first encounter at the American Colony Hotel, I visited Issawiya, a Palestinian village northeast of Jerusalem that is today a suburb of the city. Driving down a potholed road, winding east toward the Judaean desert, past the mosque, with its tall minaret, I arrive at a squat building of cream Jerusalem stone.

"*Ahlan wesahlan*" (welcome to my family realm—the traditional Arab greeting). Tariq Essawi comes to the door, his thick white hair and a white mustache vivid against his brown face. A sturdy man in his early fifties, he wears an expression that shows something inherently good humored, and, despite the grimness of our subject, his conversation is punctuated with smiles and laughter. His sister, Dr. Rihab Essawi, an American-educated social worker employed by the Palestinian Authority, sits with us. Unlike Tariq's wife, who is dressed in the traditional long black dress and keffiye, Rihab wears modern clothes. We talk over sweet tea and a large bowl of fruit.

Tariq is the second son of ten children, several of whom live in the United States. One brother was killed in the 1982 Lebanon War. Their mother died after inhaling tear gas in 1991, during the first Intifada. Early in 1994, Tariq's son Fadi was shot and killed during a protest demonstration in the village.

"Fadi had been in prison," he recounts. "Two months earlier he came home from a year in jail. He wasn't a wild boy—not even a mischievous child. He just happened to be there, with the others. I can't say he suffered in prison, because he was there with a dozen of his friends, who were also sent to jail for stone throwing. They were all there together and weren't mixed up with criminals. Anyway, he missed most of the school year, so he was doing odd jobs to earn some money. Earlier on the day that he was killed, he was relaxing on our terrace, still savoring his freedom. I find it difficult to believe what happened."

Tariq Essawi

It was the day after Baruch Goldstein shot dead the twenty-nine Arab worshippers in the Ibrahimi Mosque. Fadi Essawi was one of the protesters killed in the riots that followed Goldstein's act of terrorism.

In Issawiya, the village youngsters put up a barrier to block the entrance to the village. A unit of the Israeli Border Police that approached was received with a hail of stones. Seventeen-year-old Fadi was in the crowd. He was wearing a red shirt, which probably made him conspicuous. Again, he was not a leader or an activist. He was simply there, with the other village children. Rihab Essawi takes up the narrative.

"It was right by my house. I heard shooting and rushed outside to see what had happened. Fadi had been shot in the neck—just one shot—and he was bleeding. We pushed him into my car, and I drove him to the Mukassed Hospital. There was so much blood, I knew he must be dead. One of the doctors, a Druze from the Golan, came out to me and said, 'God be merciful.' I fainted on the spot."

Hearing that his son had been wounded, Tariq drove to Mukassed Hospital as fast as he could, but he arrived too late to see his son alive. They brought the body back to the house, and Tariq summoned his aged father from prayer.

"I never saw my father crying before," he relates. "Even when his wife died after inhaling tear gas and one of his sons was killed in Lebanon, he simply said it was the will of God, but when I told him about Fadi, he cried."

The villagers spirited away Fadi's body to the cemetery, creating a diversion with more than a dozen vans and light trucks, to prevent the Israeli soldiers from taking him for a postmortem. At first Tariq was unable to tell his wife what had happened. He told her that Fadi had been wounded, but of course he had to tell her eventually.

The Essawi family has a long history of armed resistance, and some of the Issawiya villagers say that the history of Palestine would have been different if there had been more families like them. Ahmad Ali Essawi, Tariq's father, graduated from Terra Sancta College in Jerusalem. He was an exceptionally high achiever, and his Roman Catholic headmaster, Father Eugene, wanted to send him to England for further studies, but the family vetoed the idea. They were concerned that there might be attempts to convert him to Christianity.

Instead, he became a teacher, one of the founders of the Ibrahimi School in Jerusalem, and the deputy commander of the Muslim scouts. He soon joined up with Abdel Kader Husseini, participating with him in the first attack against British soldiers at Husan, near Bethlehem. Subsequently, he took part in numerous battles and was imprisoned many times. On one occasion, he was sentenced to death and donned the red tunic, worn by condemned prisoners. Granted a last wish, he asked for a beer, and, while he was drinking it, a British officer arrived with the message that he had been granted a reprieve. The reason for this has remained unclear, but Tariq thinks it was a case of mistaken identity. Ahmad fled to Iraq, but he was back in Palestine in the late 1940s and joined in the fighting against the Jewish forces.

"We were cheated by the Arab countries," says Tariq. "We were left to fight the Jews alone. It was not simply a case of the Israelis taking our land; the Egyptians, Syrians, and the Transjordanian Hashemites gave it to them."

"Come on, everybody knows that King Abdullah worked it all out with Golda Meir," intervenes Rihab. "They divided up Palestine."

"The Syrians still say we are southern Syria," adds Tariq. "Even they don't really recognize our rights as Palestinians."

Following the 1949 armistice between Israel and Transjordan, Issawiya became part of the Mount Scopus enclave, including Hebrew University, where Israel maintained a garrison, surrounded by Transjordanian—eventually Jordanian—territory. A United Nations flag flew over the village. The Jordanian authorities were in charge during the day, but at night an Israeli army patrol entered the village and set up a roadblock. If the villagers needed to leave during the night, they had to apply to the United Nations. Ahmad Essawi was appointed *mukhtar* (village headman) by the Jordanians. He did not want to be a part of the Jordanian administration, but he wanted to help his villagers any way he could. In fact, there were two mukhtars, with the second one coming from the Obeid family, another leading clan of Issawiya.

Following the Six-Day War of 1967, the village was annexed to Jerusalem. Immediately after the fighting stopped, Teddy Kollek, the Jerusalem mayor, came to Issawiya and offered payment to the local officials in an attempt to maintain continuity, but Ahmad Essawi refused the money. Subsequently, when land was confiscated for building a Jewish suburb and expanding the campus of Hebrew University, municipal officials offered money in compensation. Again Ahmad rejected the offer.

Eventually, the Jerusalem municipality announced that there was no need for a mukhtar anymore, as the village was part of Jerusalem, but in fact, another village leader, unofficially recognized by the Israelis, has cooperated with them ever since.

When the first Intifada broke out in 1987, the Essawis were in the thick of it. "All of us were involved in the first Intifada: mothers, fathers, sisters, brothers, children—everybody," recalls Tariq. "It was the first time that we Palestinians put our foot down and began to fight for ourselves. I was involved, my brothers, and my sons. We all took an active role. If I told you that I wasn't proud of what my sons did, I would be lying!"

Rihab adds, "Since 1968, there hasn't been a single day without one of our family being in jail. I personally participated in the hunger strike in Jerusalem. I managed to go thirteen days, just drinking water. I was transferred to hospital three times. We were members of many different groups. Some of the leaders, like Hanan Ashrawi, were with us in the strike. We set out three basic demands: the release of our prisoners, Palestinian self-determination, and the Right of Return."

Tariq is very upbeat about the first Intifada, which he thinks secured more for the Palestinians than the Oslo agreement. In Issawiya, unlike in some villages, they managed to keep the school open in the mornings, but in the afternoons, there were confrontations with the Israeli security forces. What did stop was Perah, a special program in which Hebrew University students coached schoolchildren. Issawiya children had benefited from the program, but the situation became so chaotic that the student tutors stopped coming. Instead, the border police were there, frequently using tear gas in their attempts to control the unruly crowds.

Rihab explains the effects of the gas.

"It burns your skin and your eyes. It is like pepper. You sneeze; your eyes water; you suffer terrible headaches. I was so sorry for the young children. They don't understand what is happening to them, and they are terrified. It's no good splashing water on yourself—that makes it worse. The pharmacists now sell an antidote in a capsule that you break open. I don't even know what it's called, but it does help a bit."

By the summer of 1991, the Intifada was running out of steam, but occasional flareups still occured. On June 21, an incident of stone throwing took place in Issawiya. Border police fired tear gas canisters, and one entered the Essawi home.

"My mother couldn't breathe," recalls Rihab. "Her lips were blue. I took her to Hadassah Hospital on Mount Scopus. It was no good. The doctor came out and told me she had died."

Enthusiastic about the first Intifada, the Essawis are less supportive of the current confrontation. Tariq feels that, in resorting to an armed struggle, the Palestinians have given the Israelis an excuse to shoot them. The casualty toll has been much higher than in the previous confrontation. Furthermore, whereas in the first Intifada bereaved families were able to console each other, today they are cut off by the earth barriers, concrete obstructions, roadblocks, and checkpoints established by the Israelis.

"We cannot even cry together," observes Rihab.

Despite the fury of the current clashes and the high death toll, Tariq agreed to sign up with the Palestinian Families' Forum. He does not see anything strange about striving for peace, despite the tragic death of Fadi.

"I lost my son and Yitzhak [Frankenthal] lost his son for nothing," he says emotionally. "I have joined Yitzhak, because I see that there are some Israelis looking for peace, like me. They want to lead a quiet life."

Rihab remembers sitting in Palo Alto, California, in the mid-1990s, five Israelis and five Palestinians, all of whom had lost somebody dear to them. It was before Fadi's death, but she had already lost her mother and brother. An American journalist, present at the meeting, asked her how she could seek a dialogue in view of her bereavement.

"I told him that I lost my brother and lost my mother, and things didn't get better—they got worse. Killing and making more misery is not going to solve the problem. We have been fighting for so many years. We are not going to leave, and neither are the Israelis. Surely we have reached the stage when we can think and behave more rationally."

Today, Rihab is even more convinced that violence is not a solution. She lives in Issawiya and travels to Ramallah to work every day. She used to take her son to attend a kindergarten near her work, but the half-hour drive can take four to five hours sometimes because of roadblocks set up by the Israeli security forces. Consequently, she has put him in a local kindergarten.

"A three-year-old boy, and he already knows what a *machsom* [Hebrew for roadblock] is," she emphasizes. "He tells me not to take him that way because it is dangerous!"

My plans to continue the dialogue with the Essawis were rudely interrupted when the Jerusalem municipality had nine houses in Issawiya demolished. I called the municipal spokesperson, who told me that the buildings violated the Jerusalem city plan and that everything had been carried out in accordance with the law.

Tariq told me that the destruction had come out of the blue. On Saturday night, demolition orders had not been properly delivered to the owners of the homes. They were apparently thrown down at random near the houses and were only discovered on Sunday morning. They were in Hebrew. The following morning, police and troops entered Issawiya in large numbers. After them came the bulldozers. One of the destroyed homes had been built by Tariq's son, who would now have to continue living with him. The Issawiya demolitions do not cause desperate hardship, like, for example, the houses destroyed by the army in the Gaza refugee camps, stresses Tariq. The people who built houses in the village all work and are relatively prosperous. It is simply a matter of severe overcrowding and of the failure of the authorities to provide adequate space for the Arabs of East Jerusalem.

The matter of housing demolition is a complex one. In East Jerusalem, which was annexed to Israel in 1967, houses built without permits are pulled down from time to time, as they are in the Arabs towns and villages in Israel. In theory, there is one law for Jews and Arabs, and Jewish houses are occasionally demolished, but the law is enforced much more strictly with regard to Arab illegal building.

In the West Bank and Gaza, houses are often destroyed if Palestinian gunmen have fired from them. During the recent conflict, whole streets, notably in Rafah in the southern Gaza strip, have been bulldozed for security reasons. In the early days of the Israeli occupation, demolitions were also used as a punitive measure: The homes of convicted or killed terrorists were destroyed. The policy was discontinued after appeals to the Israeli Supreme Court, but, during the recent confrontation, the court has given limited permission to the IDF to renew the policy of punitive demolitions.

Since Israel took over East Jerusalem in 1967, almost all the public housing construction has been for the Jewish residents of the city. Despite the fact that the average housing density in the Arab neighborhoods is twice that in the Jewish quarters, only 12 percent of the building has been for Arab residents, most of it private. Even in the time of Teddy Kollek, the mayor at the time of the unification of the city, the policy was to do everything possible to increase the proportion of Jews living in Jerusalem. Preference was given to their housing needs over those of the Arab residents.

It is entirely possible that several of the demolished houses were indeed built without permits, but the shortage of housing for Jerusalem's Arab residents is a known fact. Releasing land in the eastern part of the city that has been declared a "green" area would alleviate the situation. From the point of view of town planning, this strategy would be regrettable, but allowing the Arab neighborhoods the same building density as the Jewish neighborhoods would go some way toward solving the problem. Faced with the absence of any effort to solve their housing problem, many Arab residents do indeed take the law into their own hands and build without permits.

Court orders delaying demolition had been issued for two of the bulldozed houses, noted Tariq. The owners were making monthly payments to the Interior Ministry, pending final rulings as to whether the buildings were legal. That same Sunday morning, attorneys representing the villagers had endeavored to get new court orders to delay the operation.

Despite their efforts, those two buildings were also destroyed. In a radio interview, Jerusalem's mayor, Ehud Olmert, described the Issawiya home builders as "a criminal Mafia, deliberately building illegally." One of them, Bassam Elian, had attended a meeting with the mayor a month earlier to discuss the development of the industrial zone at Atarot, in the northern part of the city.

"If I'm a criminal, why did Olmert invite me to his office?" he demanded.

On the phone, Tariq told me that he was running around from the municipal offices to meetings with attorneys and to various court hearings. He had no time for another meeting with me. I wanted to visit him to see the destroyed houses and hear about what had happened, but then his telephone was disconnected and he was unavailable on his cell phone.

After attempting unsuccessfully to make contact, I called his sister, Rihab, who informed me that Tariq had suffered a heart attack and was in Hadassah Hospital on Mount Scopus. She told me that her brother was on the fourth floor, but I couldn't find him at first. The hospital was jam-packed with visitors of all types, including large numbers of Arab women visitors in their traditional long, black dresses. After asking several Jewish and Arab nurses, I eventually found Tariq, who was sitting up in bed, looking quite fit in his pale blue hospital pajamas. He smiled and thanked me for the small gift I brought him.

"To be perfectly honest with you, I am happy to be here, away from it all," he confesses. "I have had a good rest, and I'm glad I don't know what is going on outside."

On the following day, he was scheduled to move to the larger Hadassah Hospital to the west of the city to have an angioplasti performed. It would be his fourth operation of this type. He had undergone two at Hadassah and one at Bikkur Holim, in the center of town. The food was best at this Hadassah, he informs me, not bad at the other Hadassah, and worst at Bikkur Holim.

As a citizen of Jerusalem, Tariq has been able to become a member of the Israeli Clallit Health Fund, which will pay for the hospitalization and the operation. He is full of praise for his Health Fund doctor and for the doctors and nurses at the hospital. A young, blond nurse, whose accent indicates that she has arrived from Russia in the last few years, comes to remove his lunch tray and give him his pills. She and Tariq exchange friendly smiles.

"I am receiving the best possible care in here," he declares, gesturing around him. "There are Jewish doctors and Arab doctors, Jewish nurses and Arab nurses. They all work together to look after the Arab and Jewish patients. Why can't it be like this outside?"

The Jerusalem municipality has asked the Israeli government for a grant of US $2 million to pull down all the illegal houses, Tariq informs me, wondering how much positive construction could be carried out for this sum. I knew that two more houses in Issawiya had been pulled down a week later. Tariq tells me that, whereas the first nine houses were dismantled in broad daylight, in the presence of security forces, the other two had been bulldozed during the night. Several houses have also been destroyed in another Arab neighborhood of Jerusalem, and Mayor Olmert promised to dismantle "several houses every week."

It was some time before Tariq responded favorably to my proposal to visit him again to continue our conversation. This time he invited me to the home of his younger brother, Hani, a smaller version of Tariq, with black hair and a black mustache. Unlike his brother, who prefers English, Hani speaks fluent and articulate Hebrew.

"You learned it in prison," I guess.

"Of course," he replies with a smile. "I had nothing else to do there."

Hani was seventeen in 1970, when he joined the Popular Liberation Forces, a group that no longer exists. He can remember very precisely how and why he enlisted. He was riding his horse in a field of lentils owned by his family, when he saw bulldozers digging up the land for the extension of Hebrew University. He rode up to find out what was going on, but the tractor operator ignored him.

"Land is important to us," he explains. "We are always fighting among ourselves about land, and we take it very seriously. My father received it from his father, and nobody ever took it away before. Neither the Turks, not the British, nor the Jordanians took away our fields—only the Israelis. I joined the resistance group the same night."

The Issawiya group didn't operate for long. It was betrayed by a Palestinian collaborator, and Hani was sentenced to twelve years in prison, later reduced to ten. Subsequently, people found guilty on similar charges received far lighter sentences. The only Arabic reading matter available in jail was that approved by the Shin Bet security service, which Hani found boring when it was not subservient to Israeli propaganda. He learned Hebrew and was able to read accounts of the Zionist underground, as well as several books on Arab history and politics translated by the Truman Institute of Hebrew University. He was not permitted to read those same books in Arabic.

During his time in prison, Hani came to the conclusion that the state of Israel was not about to disappear. He did not change his opinion that the Jews were an alien implant from Europe and that Judaism was a religion, rather than a nationality, but he realized that Jews born in Israel would not pack their bags and return to Europe. He also became influenced by Marxism. He became convinced that the development from feudalism to capitalism, which had taken centuries in Europe, was now happening at a much faster rate all over the world. Nations, which formerly took hundreds of years to develop, could now be formed in a matter of decades.

Eventually released from prison, Hani made his living by translating from Hebrew into Arabic, mostly for the Arabic press. He agrees with Tariq's account that the entire population of Issawiya was involved in the first Intifada. He, himself, was imprisoned twice for periods of administrative detention.

Hani makes a clear distinction between the first Intifada and the current confrontation.

"The first uprising was one of hope," he suggests. "We really felt that we were going to get rid of the Israeli occupation. But the present outbreak of violence is the result of despair. We lost all our hopes of a free, democratic Palestinian state."

Hani thinks that the Oslo peace process was wrongly conceived from the outset. He believes in a negotiated settlement between Israel and the Palestinians that will lead to a Palestinian state living in peace and cooperation with both Israel and Jordan, but it should have all been negotiated at the outset. The idea of reaching agreement in stages was wrong. The *implementation* can be in stages, he suggests, but only after the overall agreement is finalized. Oslo created a contradictory situation: The leaders of the Palestinian Authority had to satisfy Israeli demands, while at the same time leading the struggle against Israeli occupation.

"It was clear that the main problems—land, occupation, refugees, water, Jerusalem—were all unresolved," he points out.

Hani believes that the PLO officials, who were living in Tunis, were prepared to do anything to get back to the West Bank and Gaza, which meant that Israel was pretty well able to dictate terms.

"That is why I blame the Israelis for the current situation," he explains. "You are the stronger side, and you hold all the cards."

Hani has no hesitation in describing the Palestinian Authority as "corrupt," but he ridicules the reforms currently being demanded by the Israelis and the Americans. They don't want real reform, declares Hani. They want them to be *more* corrupt, so that they can prevent terrorism against Israel. Having been imprisoned for ten years and subsequently under administrative detention, Hani is not exactly a fan of Israeli democracy, but he admits that "in Israel the law is the law." He had to be brought before a judge. His administrative detention had to be approved by the defense minister in person, and a judge reviewed it at regular intervals. On the other hand, the Palestinian Authority imprisoned people without trial, without charges, without even the pretense of a legal procedure.

"We dreamed that we would be the first democratic state in the Arab world," he affirms. "We still want that."

Hani hotly denies the current Israeli perception that the Palestinians have shown that they are not prepared to accept Israel. Most of them still are. He is certain of that. Given a fair deal, they will be only too happy to make peace with Israel. He thinks that the second Intifada erupted because the Israelis came to the conclusion that the Palestinians didn't have a choice because they were in such a weak position.

"I am not in favor of terror against civilians," he insists. "I don't approve of the suicide bombings, but we do have the right to resist the occupation. The current cycle of violence is self-perpetuating."

I tell Hani that most Israelis think that if the IDF stopped entering the Palestinian towns and villages to arrest would-be bombers and others, more Palestinian terror would ensue. He shakes his head. That is a misreading of the situation, he says. The bombers are people who have lost hope.

"If there were ten would-be suicide bombers in Jenin before the IDF went in," he asserts, "now there are a hundred."

Even today Hani is sure the problem can be solved by the existence of two states living alongside each other and cooperating. The settlers must go, because they are the big provocateurs, but peace and coexistence are possible. His father, the lifelong warrior, reached that conclusion before his death two years ago. From Hani's point of view, there can be one state, a democratic state for Jews and Arabs in all of Palestine. That would be the best solution, he thinks, but he is pragmatic. If the Jews want their state, he concedes, let there be two states.

He introduces me to Osama, his eldest son, who is finishing high school and planning to study law at Hebrew University. As a Jerusalem resident, he can probably study there, although they are now checking entrance requirements. Hani's children are too young to be involved in the current confrontation.

The paradox is manifest, as we sit together in the Essawi home: Tariq has three sons currently in detention, suspected of "hostile activity." They have still not been tried. Thirteen Issawiya homes have been demolished by the authorities in a manner that might have been illegal and was certainly ruthlessly insensitive. At the same time, all the family are members of the Israeli Clallit Health Fund, which paid for Tariq to have up-to-date hospital treatment. Hani's eldest son plans to study at Hebrew University. If he is accepted, he may benefit from the Perah special tuition scheme that assists students. They are only too aware of the contradictions.

"Not only can the problem be solved," concludes Hani, "it *will* be solved. There will be two states. That is what will happen in the end. It is just such a shame for all the people who are going to be killed on both sides."

His brother Tariq emphatically nods his head in agreement with these sentiments, which echo, almost exactly, the words of Yitzhak Frankenthal, another bereaved parent.

Mariet Khoury: Ubiquitous Trauma

"The terror, the trauma, is universal. No one feels safe anymore. We are haunted all the time by so much fear. Normal life has been completely disrupted. The soldiers enter an apartment at random, often smashing the furniture and fittings. They confine the family to one room, sleep on the sofas and in the beds, use the kitchens, the showers, and the lavatories. There is no certainty. You don't know what is coming a few hours from now. So we have to live our lives day by day."

Sitting under the vines in Mariet Khoury's peaceful garden, drinking fresh carrot juice and eating dates, it is difficult to absorb the reality of the situation that she is describing. She admits that she is privileged compared to most Palestinians. The Israeli soldiers don't enter her Jerusalem neighborhood, or, if they do, they target a specific house. The situation is not comparable to Ramalla, with tanks in the streets and soldiers occupying many of the apartments. Seeing it on television is very different from the real thing, she explains. The tanks are huge, dominating the street. Although she has not experienced this directly, Khoury has nightmares: Every week she has one or two dreams of the Israeli army thundering into her street, bursting into her house, "with great savagery."

Mariette Khoury

"I have these dreams without having personally experienced these actions," she points out. "Can you imagine what sort of fear people experience when the soldiers are actually living in their homes, robbing them of their privacy and dignity in such an unimaginable way?"

Dressed in a light summer blouse and slacks, the forty-two-year-old Khoury is a manifestly modern Arab woman. Her voice is soft, but her tone is indignant, even passionate. Her large brown eyes are full of anger and pain. Sometimes she seems almost surprised at what she is saying. At the start of our conversation, she is hesitant and somewhat brusque, but once she gets started the words flow in a continuous, unstoppable stream.

Beit Hanina, the up-market northern Jerusalem suburb, where Khoury lives, has a military checkpost on the main street. To reach her house, you have to negotiate your way carefully past the concrete barricades, under the watchful eyes of the Israeli Border Police. It is a minor inconvenience, though, only delaying the driver by some minutes. It is nothing like the checkposts between Israel and the territories, where the Palestinian travelers often wait for several hours to go through on foot.

Beit Hanina is, after all, part of Jerusalem—or is it? Officially it is, and the residents possess the blue Israeli identity cards that afford them relative freedom of movement, but garbage collection is irregular, and the roads are full of potholes. In general, municipal services are woefully inadequate, but in the summer of 2002, despite the Intifada and the IDF incursions into the territories, the Jerusalem municipality organized a two-month summer day camp for five hundred children. There were not so many day trips to Israeli destinations as in previous years, although a visit was arranged to a swimming pool in Rehovot, near Tel Aviv. Soccer was the most popular of the sporting and cultural activities. A municipal official was quoted as saying it is important for the children to unwind and let off steam in the present difficult situation. The visit of a professional clown, a new immigrant to Israel from Russia, was a notable success. The children were utterly delighted, and their traditionally garbed mothers joined in the laughter.

Understandably, Khoury sees an ironic contrast between these gestures and what she says is "normal IDF behavior" toward the Palestinians. She is more concerned with the negative aspects of the Palestinian relationship with the Israelis. An American-trained clinical psychologist, she has managed, after months of struggle, to establish a private clinic in Ramalla, despite the obstacles in her path. I spoke to her during the summer incursion of the IDF, when she was able to reach Ramalla only intermittently.

Until she left in the spring to set up her own clinic, Khoury was one of the two clinical supervisors at the Palestinian Counseling Center in Beit Hanina. The center serves several thousand people, particularly children and adolescents. Its emphasis is clearly on the Jerusalem area, but the center has tried to extend its activities to other Palestinian towns. Since the current crisis, there has been a telephone hotline twenty-four hours per day, and calls have come in from Ramalla, Jenin, Bethlehem, and Hebron, as well as from the Jerusalem area. Most of the calls come from mothers, asking how to deal with their children who have been traumatized by the latest Israeli incursions.

The center's staff appeared on local television and radio programs to discuss the mental health situation and provide advice. They also organized television and radio sessions with parents and children to suggest ways of helping in the current situation. The use of the local media for counseling, however, was subsequently disrupted, as, during the Israeli military's summer incursion, all the Palestinian radio and television stations were closed down. The center also recruited volunteer teachers to replace those who could not get to their schools because of roadblocks.

Other efforts by the Beit Hanina center include direct family counseling, workshops for parents, training schoolteachers in crisis intervention techniques, fun days for children, and publishing a "Simple Guide" for parents to help them deal with their children in a situation of crisis and trauma.

Khoury's childhood in Jerusalem was relatively sheltered. She lived within her Palestinian community, attending a local school. Her father, a tourist guide, used to take groups to visit Syria and Lebanon, but after the Six-Day War of 1967, the Arab states were cut off from the Palestinians, and he concentrated on visitors from abroad. Her first encounter with what she calls "the ramifications of the occupation" occurred on a trip to Italy. She recalls being singled out from the other passengers at a Rome airport and searched "in a humiliating manner." After her European vacation, she became aware of the significant difference between her life and the lives of most Europeans. Until then she had regarded the periodic intrusions of Israeli soldiers into her neighborhood, the checkposts, and the body searches when returning from a trips across the Jordan as normal. It was only when experiencing normalcy outside the territories that she came to appreciate "the pathology of the occupation."

"It was as if I had been in a deep sleep," she says now. "In fact, I think all of us Palestinians were asleep."

Khoury took a first degree in economics and business administration at Birzeit University, near Ramallah, the West Bank's most prestigious college. After winning a Fulbright scholarship, she went to the United States. She took her master's degree in social work at the University of Wisconsin and subsequently earned her doctorate at the Illinois School of Professional Psychology. While she was in America, many of her friends suggested that she remain there. Most people dreamed of the chance to live in the United States, they said, but the idea of staying never entered her head. Khoury describes herself as someone with a "universal sense of belonging," but she is a very self-aware Palestinian, and Jerusalem is her home. Anyway, she didn't particularly like American society and was alienated by the strong pro-Israel sentiments. She believes that a majority of Americans understand and support Israel because the United States was founded by people who invaded a country and took it away from its original inhabitants.

"If the Americans recognize the injustice done to us," she points out, "they are nullifying their own foundations."

She herself does not understand or sympathize with Zionism. A believing Christian, she rejects the idea that God can have promised any land to one people.

"God does not have favorites," she declares. "He loves all his children equally. It doesn't make any sense."

She believes in the Bible, but, in her view, Jesus came to reform Jewish exclusivity and create an all-inclusive religion. The persecution that the Jews have suffered over the centuries does not justify taking the land from another people, she insists. You cannot solve one problem by creating another one.

She characterizes the current Intifada as "much fiercer" than its predecessor. It is much harder on people, she states, with a massive impact on everybody, particularly children and adolescents. She finds a high incidence of trauma in almost everyone she encounters. She stresses that counseling services are very sparse, and many more facilities are urgently required. Following the March incursion of the IDF into the Palestinian cities, she ran several crisis intervention groups in Ramalla. She started work in Jenin also but was unable to return there because of the almost-continuous curfew. Listening to counselors, she found that they themselves were seriously traumatized.

"They were so damaged that they didn't think they could help others," she recounts. "They felt that they could not restore themselves, so they couldn't heal others."

The effect of the situation on the children, says Khoury, is particularly distressing. The Beit Hanina center has figures showing that in the first Israeli incursion during April and May, fifty-five children were killed, more than a third of them under twelve years old. Three hundred forty were reported wounded, but the actual figure is believed to be much higher. One hundred seventy children were held in detention for varying periods of time. More than a third of the families in contact with the center had other families living with them because of damage to homes. More than 70 percent of families said that at least one member was suffering from mental health problems. There is no doubt that the situation deteriorated even further during the summer incursion of the Israeli army, which was more wide-ranging and lasted longer.

Khoury herself received reports of bed wetting, nightmares, excessive attachment to parents, fears of leaving the house, shivering, crying, jumping at sounds, and exaggerated fears of all sorts, particularly fear of the dark.

"There is uncontrollable anger, and their play has become very violent," she reports.

All children hit each other sometimes, concedes Khoury, but the violence in their play has become excessive. Parents come to her in despair, saying that they don't know what to do with their children. How are they supposed to discipline them? How can they reassure them?

As a teacher, she has direct experience with adolescents. Most of her students found it almost impossible to concentrate; they could not study on a regular basis, they had a feeling of being adrift, and they suffered from nightmares. Many of her students spoke to her about being unable to sleep or said that their sleep was disrupted. They reported increasingly frequent family quarrels. In class she and her fellow teachers faced constant disciplinary problems. The degree of unruliness was unprecedented.

When the time had come for the twelfth graders to sit for the International Baccalaureate (IB), however, the teachers were pleasantly surprised. The results were almost universally good. During the March incursion, when the students were in the final stage of their preparations, the school did not know whether to go ahead with the examinations. There was talk of postponing the exams until the fall. However, with no guarantee that the situation would improve, it was decided to go ahead. There was a feeling that they just wanted to get it over and done with, explains Khoury.

Surprised and pleased with the results of the IB, Khoury warns against drawing overoptimistic conclusions. Her students in Ramallah are an elite, she points out. Many of them are now abroad, and a good number will attend university in Europe or North America. They may recover from the trauma of the past two years comparatively quickly; the other Palestinian children from the poor neighborhoods, the villages, and the refugee camps will take far longer. She is sure that the trauma is very deep and that it will have a long-term impact. It is not clear how long the situation will continue, and the Palestinians simply lack the necessary resources for helping the children and adolescents, let alone the adults.

The Beit Hanina center is the largest of its kind in the Palestinian territories. Khoury reiterates that there are not enough such centers. There is some counseling in the schools, but this is still comparatively rare. There is a lack of trained therapists and social workers. For example, in Jenin, which suffered a real trauma, there is only one counselor for the entire town.

The lack of services has been somewhat alleviated in Hebron and the Gaza strip by teams of the Médecins sans Frontières (MSF, Doctors without Borders) organization, whose members have been present in the Palestinian territories since 1993. The MSF's *Palestinian Chronicles* reports general symptoms among Palestinian children and adolescents similar to those described by Khoury. The report adds that, apart from the effects of stress caused by the current violence, the MSF teams have encountered recurring traumas in people who suffered in the first Intifada. The MSF teams endeavor to visit the homes of Palestinian families in the areas most exposed to violence in Hebron and Gaza.

The local Palestinian doctors, explain the MSF personnel, are exhausted, overwhelmed, and have lost motivation. In any case, there are very few Palestinian psychiatrists or psychologists. One of the main problems faced by the MSF teams, of course, is language. They rely on the good services of a number of interpreters. They also receive assistance from Israeli psychologists, who are not themselves able to enter the territories. The demand for their services is "almost unlimited," and their medical teams can deal with only the most extreme cases. Furthermore, notes the report, the care they provide is no substitute for regular psychotherapy.

Since the escalation of the violence over the past two years, Khoury has found herself becoming more extreme in her views. She and other Palestinians of her generation, who were not witnesses to the establishment of Israel in 1948, took the situation for granted. They were born into a world where Israel was an established fact. They had pushed the trauma of what older Palestinians called the Nakba (the "Disaster") to the back of their minds, but the recent violence has brought it to the fore. She speaks with some emotion. "The recent incursions have had the effect of awakening us to the terrible injustice we have suffered over the years. I have heard this recently from other people as well. The feeling of hostility is growing. So many people conspired against us, made us flee from our homeland. What right had another group of people to come here from Russia and America and Ethiopia and uproot us, take over our homes?"

Previously she had not felt so passionately. When the Oslo agreement was signed, Khoury was one of those who thought peace should be given a chance, but in retrospect she feels the agreement didn't do the Palestinians much good. She thinks that many Palestinians, particularly the middle classes in Jerusalem and Ramalla, started enjoying an "inappropriate lifestyle." She speaks scathingly of the nightclubs and bars, the big cars, the using of Israeli health clubs, and the trips to the seaside. The Palestinians still did not have a state, but they started behaving as if they did.

"It is like a person who is severely pathological," she suggests. "His relationships are sundered. He looks for a cure in all the wrong places. He makes friends, but he doesn't look within himself to examine the cause of the trouble and heal himself."

The Palestinians were living a lie, she insists. They were not confronting the truth, which was that they had been deprived of their liberty. They were stripped of everything that gives a person his dignity. They were negotiating with a government that didn't really want to give them anything.

"There is a feeling of madness deep down in every Palestinian psyche," she declares, "a feeling of rage, of fury, and this anger increases because so few people in the world seem to understand and support them."

This is the feeling that leads to bombing attacks, she explains. She does not justify the bombs, but she does understand the feelings that drive the bombers to their desperate actions. She sees the attacks as a cry for help by young people who feel that they have been abandoned and who want their just cause to be heard. In her view, it is wrong to blow up civilians, but she can see why some young people take that path, even though she prefers a strategy of nonviolence that she thinks would achieve much more for the Palestinians.

In Khoury's view, it is now vital for the Palestinians to try to achieve some sort of unity. She is aware of the divergence of views represented by the Hamas and Islamic Jihad fundamentalists on the one hand and the more secular population on the other, but she feels there has to be a democratic dialogue with all the opposing voices being given a chance to express themselves. The Palestinians, she insists, cannot rely on anybody else: not the Arab nations, not the Israeli peace camp (which in her view has let down the Palestinians), and certainly not on the United States.

She is in favor of reform and change. Other nations change their leaders every few years, she observes, and the Palestinians have no reason to continue with the same old leaders for so long. There is nothing bad about introducing new blood, but the Palestinians deeply resent being given orders by the Americans.

"In my work as a psychologist, I suspend value judgments. I try to understand my patient, and to work to heal him with love, to create a loving relationship that will help him, but successive American administrations have behaved like bad psychologists, without sensitivity or understanding. They keep telling the Palestinians that they are the problem and that they don't deserve a state. We are utterly fed up with this message!"

Khoury says that she is not in favor of talking peace at the present time. She is highly critical of her fellow Palestinians who still go to work out in Israeli health clubs and take vacations in the Red Sea resort of Eilat. When she studied in the United States, she had a few Israeli friends among her fellow students, but for the present she doesn't want any contacts. She feels it is shameful to talk peace in a situation of bloody conflict. Peaceful coexistence is for the long run. The Palestinians have to heal themselves first and only later think about "the troubled relationship with the stranger."

"For any reconciliation to be genuine, the Israelis must acknowledge and rectify their wrongdoing, and the Palestinians must be willing to forgive them," Khoury says. "Without this any peace will be on shaky grounds. People need time to heal, and this can only happen with the grace of God and the good intentions of all concerned. Every psychologist knows that you cannot begin to talk about healing with another person until you are healed yourself. When you are so terribly wounded, when you are filled with so much resentment and bitterness, you can't shake hands with your enemy."

Zehava Solomon: Selective Trauma

"An actual witness to a suicide bombing may be affected for the rest of his life, but there are enormous differences in the degree of trauma. Obviously, the highest price is paid by the person directly involved: someone who was wounded, or whose life was threatened, or who was close to somebody who was killed or seriously injured. Direct involvement destroys the basic assumption that 'it won't happen to me.' Despite the large number of violent terrorist incidents in recent years, however, most Israelis have not experienced terror directly. Consequently, Israel is not in a state of national trauma."

Israelis are involved, notes Zehava Solomon. They watch television, listen to the radio, and read the papers. There is more concern, more sensitivity, more awareness, but there are no waves of panic. People with emotional disorders are not being hospitalized on any scale. The country's doctors are not handing out vast quantities of antidepressants, nor are the psychiatrists and psychologists flooded with demands for help. Most Israelis are functioning more or less normally.

It is true that, following a concentrated spate of terror attacks, people become more nervous, more aggressive, less patient, less tolerant. Instead of going out to films, plays, concerts, or restaurants, they tend to rent videos and stay home. It is a behavioral change, but it doesn't last for long. It cannot be compared to the situation among the Palestinians, a high proportion of whom have felt the direct effect of Israeli retaliations and incursions. Residents of Jerusalem or Netanya, two of the Israeli locations hit most often by terrorists, are certainly worried, but an entirely different level of trauma exists in the Palestinian towns of Jenin or Ramalla.

In Solomon's view, Israelis have not experienced a similar situation since the War of Independence in 1948. At that time, she points out, the nation was far weaker, with far fewer resources. The population was smaller; the proportion of survivors of the Nazi Holocaust was larger. Today, despite pockets of poverty and unemployment, Israel is a relatively prosperous, well-organized country. Except for the minority of victims who have been directly exposed, the vast majority of Israelis are managing to live with the situation.

Informally dressed in slacks and a summer blouse, her hair gathered in a ponytail, Zehava Solomon, the director of Tel Aviv University's Adler Institute for Child Welfare and Protection, looks rather young to be a professor. She is extremely articulate, eager to talk and explain. Despite the grimness of the subject, she smiles a lot. The phone is always ringing in her Tel Aviv University office, and her incisive answers to queries demonstrate an impressive command of detail. Despite the interruptions, she keeps track of our conversation, immediately taking up the discussion where it left off.

Solomon was born half a century ago in Kfar Shmariyahu, a small farming village that has since become a suburb of Tel Aviv. Her family was atypical in that her father was a Sephardi immigrant from Salonika and her mother was a Polish Holocaust survivor. Most of their neighbors had immigrated from Germany in the 1930s. The culture was German, with classical music concerts and lectures on Friday nights. She had what she describes as "a really protected childhood in a red-roofed house, with a lot of pleasure and happiness. There was a feeling of turning a page and building a new life."

She was a member of the Noar Oved youth movement, dedicated to agricultural settlement and pioneering. She and her future husband joined a group destined for a kibbutz, first serving in the Nahal, a division of the army that combines military service with kibbutz life. It was in this group that her middle-class bubble was burst by her first encounter with children from poorer homes. Following her military service, she had been planning to study literature, but her meeting with children less fortunate than herself prompted her to change to social work. Her studies at Tel Aviv University were combined with work in a rehabilitation center for disadvantaged youth, where she felt overwhelmed by the magnitude of the social problems that had to be solved. When she and her husband traveled to the United States for further studies, she switched to psychiatric epidemiology, which she studied at the Pittsburgh School of Medicine. Two children were born to the couple during their time in the United States.

Paradoxically, Solomon, who grew up in Israel and lived through three wars there, had her first professional experience with trauma in the United States, following the nuclear mishap at Three Mile Island in 1979, when she was involved in a research project among mothers of young children exposed to the accident. Returning to Israel, she found that her most promising employment opportunity was in the military, and she returned to the IDF as a regular officer at the age of thirty. She was appointed as head of the research section of the IDF Mental Health Department. Less than two years after her mobilization, the Israelis invaded Lebanon.

"After my appointment, the army didn't really know what to do with me," she recounts, "but with the outbreak of the war, I realized that I was the right person in the right place at the right time."

"Shell shock" or "battle shock" had long been ignored in the macho society of Israel, a country intermittently at war. The nation and the army, with its mythology of heroism going back to the earliest years of the Zionist enterprise, through the War of Independence and the Six-Day War, had little patience for "cowards" or "shirkers." Despite this, the IDF had been forced to face up to the reality by the scale of the phenomenon after the Yom Kippur War of 1973. Attitudes changed only slowly, however, and the records were far from comprehensive. In 1982, for the first time in Israel, complete records of every soldier suffering from psychiatric disorder were kept. This work resulted in Solomon's first book, *Combat Stress Reaction*, in which she combines a brief personal description of her experience with an account of her research.

She begins by noting that, since its establishment, Israel has lived in the shadow of war. As a small girl, she remembers the Sinai Campaign of 1956, with her father mobilized and her mother taping the windows to protect against possible bombing. Her involvement in the Six-Day War of 1967 was more direct: She spent time in the shelters, and two slightly older school friends were in the army. By the time of the Yom Kippur War, Solomon was a married student, and her husband was mobilized. In the student dormitories, she repeatedly dreamed that her husband had been killed. When he came home for his first leave, her "formerly energetic" husband was a "tired, mentally exhausted, introverted, taciturn young man." He wasn't interested in his family and was not inclined to share his thoughts and feelings. When he was demobilized after eight months of service, he was emotionally withdrawn, his body temperature had dropped, and he had constant nightmares, which continued even after the couple went to study in the United States.

Returning from her studies abroad, Solomon was for a time the only officer in the research unit of the IDF Mental Health Department. Others joined her with the outbreak of war in 1982. The male officers of the department were treating soldiers with combat stress reaction (CSR) at forward bases. Solomon organized the female officers to collect and organize the data accumulated by their male colleagues. This information became the database that included every soldier who reached the IDF Mental Health Department in the Lebanon War because of emotional problems. It was later expanded, utilizing the IDF general database.

Following the initial stages of the war, Solomon and her colleagues carried out a wide-ranging research project, including follow-up interviews with a large sample of soldiers who had been treated for CSR. The research continued over the years, focusing on posttraumatic stress disorder (PTSD), as well as CSR. Whereas CSR is the direct reaction to battlefield events, PTSD is the aftereffect of any severe emotional experience. It is not exclusive to soldiers but is also experienced by victims of natural disasters, accidents, severe illnesses, personal violence, or rape.

Although her research was focused on the Lebanon War and its aftermath, Solomon expanded her study to deal with other matters. She and her team went back to the Yom Kippur War to assess the effect of repeated wars on the soldiers who fight them. The subtitle of her book is *The Enduring Toll of War*. She discovered that reactivated trauma is generally worse than the first disorder, as the soldier has to deal with two sets of memories. There is accumulated trauma from war to war—trauma leads to more and deeper trauma. Veterans from World War II or Vietnam, she points out, have less reason for continued fears than the IDF veterans, who live in a society where terrorist incidents occur and who are subject to periodic call-ups for reserve duty in the military.

She also looks at the influence of the Holocaust on soldiers who are the children of survivors, noting that the traumas have been transmitted to the later generations. She compares the PTSD of combat stress cases who had at least one parent who was a Holocaust survivor with others and finds their posttrauma is more severe. She observes that the Holocaust survivor syndrome includes both guilt and a determination to defend their parents from future peril. A son of parents who suffered in the Holocaust feels doubly guilty if he suffers CSR: He has failed his nation and his comrades, and he has also failed his survivor parents.

In her concluding chapter, she acknowledges the positive attitude of the Israeli government and public toward disabled war veterans, and the huge resources devoted to their rehabilitation. When it came to psychiatric injuries, however, she found that attitudes were more equivocal. Essentially, this was because a physical injury was recognized as being beyond the control of the casualty, whereas it was easy to believe that the emotional casualties were themselves at least partly responsible for their plight. The best way of avoiding CSR, observed Solomon, is to stop making war, but as human beings seem incapable of this, they should at least understand "those who have lost so much on behalf of the rest of us."

Her book was written more than a decade ago, and attitudes have changed. Whereas survivors of the Holocaust in Europe used to be despised in Israel for "going like sheep to the slaughter," today they are admired. Many Israelis wonder out loud whether they would have had the strength to survive the Nazi concentration camps. Solomon thinks that the change came with the Yom Kippur War, when the entire nation was in a state of shock, and the cult of the heroic IDF general was deflated.

Nevertheless, when Solomon began her work on emotional injuries from combat stress, people were still suspicious of the condition. Today, it is almost prestigious to be diagnosed CSR. It has become legitimate. Only a few years ago, an article on the subject was censored from the IDF journal *Bamachaneh*. Today, Solomon turns down requests for interviews from journalists who previously had shown a notable lack of interest in her work.

Returning to the current situation, Solomon points out that driving on the roads in Israel is still statistically much more dangerous than sitting in a café, shopping in a mall, or buying in a market. More people are killed in road accidents than in terror and war, but Israelis are not in stress over this. This is because terror has become the focus. A fatal traffic accident earns a small report toward the end of a television news bulletin or a few inches on an inside page of a newspaper. On the other hand, headlines about terrorism are blazoned across the front pages, and reports of terror attacks lead the radio and television news programs.

She is concerned about the influence of the media, believing that the sensational newspaper headlines and constant repetition of television news footage of terror strikes are harmful. She mentions the case of children brought in for treatment for shock or actual injuries watching television reports of the incidents in which they were harmed.

"It is crazy," she asserts. "The children should be supervised and not allowed to see too much."

Repeated exposure to the same scene is harmful to adults and children. Watching again and again reinforces helplessness. It doesn't afford empowerment. People become addicted but this knowledge weakens and doesn't help. She approves of people wanting to be involved. It is healthy to see a report of an incident once and then rush out and volunteer to help at a hospital or first aid station.

There are many other reactions to the terror that Solomon also finds normal and healthy. To think about the terror, to be aware and vigilant, to be cautious about where you are going—these are healthy reactions. This sort of behavior is not psychopathological. At the same time, it is natural and healthy to continue with normal life as far as possible, to go to the beach, the cinema, have parties, go to work. Some children play games, enacting terrorist incidents, throwing their toy cars in the air and shouting, "Explosion!" They do this to overcome their fears, and that is all right.

Another phenomenon is what Solomon calls "the geography of fear." Jerusalem, for example, is perceived as dangerous. A few days after a terrorist bomb exploded in Tel Aviv, she was scheduled to give a lecture in Jerusalem.

"Don't go," her children urged her. "It is dangerous there."

During the Gulf War of 1991, it was exactly the reverse in Israel. The perception was that Jerusalem was safe and the Tel Aviv region was the dangerous place to be. Even there, people made preparations in the evening, donning tracksuits and placing gas masks within reach, but they relaxed in the morning, "as if Saddam Hussein had signed an agreement with Israel not to fire rockets during the daylight hours." People like to make order out of chaos, she explains, taking another example from the Gulf War. More rockets fell on Sunday than on Monday, it was noticed, so people were far more relaxed on Monday.

"Then suddenly it was Purim" (a Jewish festival where people parade in fancy dress, have parties, and drink a lot), she recalls, "and people forgot all about the war.

She cites another example of the geography of fear: an IDF reserve soldier suffering from PTSD who felt very threatened everywhere in Israel but walked unafraid at night all over Spanish Harlem.

"I wouldn't go there at night," she stresses, "but his fear was associated with Israel. He wasn't in the least bit afraid in New York."

There is a big difference in the way Israelis perceive the first Intifada of 1987 and today's confrontation, suggests Solomon. The earlier uprising reversed the Israeli mythology of David versus Goliath. It was a complex situation, when children with slingshots confronted armed soldiers. Israel's existential concepts were stood on their heads. Today, because the Palestinians are using bombs and bullets, many more Israelis are being hurt, which makes them feel more justified in hitting back.

The more suicide bombs that go off, the less soldiers will refuse to serve in the army, she says. If there are fewer Palestinian attacks, and the IDF continues to operate in the territories, the refusals will grow.

After a recent series of suicide bombs, Solomon noticed that several of her researchers, who were mothers of young children, began talking in a fatalistic way. Their work involves research into stress and trauma, she notes, but they themselves were suffering from considerable tension. They started talking about making wills; they wondered aloud who would look after their children if they were killed. She felt there was a serious degree of disturbance, so she invited them to her apartment for an evening of discussion. She told them to bring friends in similar situations. About a dozen young women showed up and talked about their feelings. It was an evening of tension but also of laughter.

Motherhood, suggests Solomon, involves a lot of shock, tension, and stress, but the current situation in Israel adds other factors. Most people assume they are going to live forever and don't confront the question of what will happen if they die suddenly. In a situation where mothers of young children are being killed almost every week, though, all sorts of questions arise: What will happen if I am not there to look after them? Is this a country in which to raise children? If we go to the market or the mall, should we go together as a family, or should we separate, so at least some of us will survive? These are questions that don't arise in normal times.

"It was a remarkable evening," says Solomon. "It seemed to fulfill a real need. They talked and talked, and none of them wanted to leave."

With the whole of Israel transformed into a potential front line, the term *acute stress reaction* (ACR) is the domestic equivalent of CSR, and PTSD follows for both victims and observers in much the same way as it does for soldiers. It took Israeli society a long time to recognize the battlefield version, and it is only now coming to grips with the domestic equivalent. Those suffering only from shock are (naturally) the last to be evacuated to a hospital following a terror incident. The number of shock victims receiving assistance from the National Insurance Institute has doubled, but at 3,500, it is still relatively small.

In a survey yet to be published, Solomon found that PTSD, as indicated by repeated traumatic memories, general distress, and dysfunctional behavior, only appears to be affecting some 9 percent of Israel's population. This is roughly half the proportion of New Yorkers who suffered such reactions following the Twin Towers attack on September 11, 2001. On the other hand, some 60 percent of those questioned said they had "feelings of depression and sadness," and only half of the interviewees were optimistic about the future of Israel.

Other researchers confirm Solomon's findings regarding the effects of repeated exposure to terror. Psychologist Ilan Kutz has found that "people with previous traumas are much more susceptible." He has treated several victims who have been involved in more than one terror attack. Professor Aryeh Shalev, head of the Trauma Department at Jerusalem's Hadassah Hospital, has compared brain scans of people subjected to a traumatic incident one week after the accident and six months later. Brain activity increased in the later tests, indicating the delayed nature of posttraumatic stress disorder. Shalev's research shows that one-third of trauma victims experience PTSD, but only 10 percent become chronic victims. Shalev also notes that 60 percent of the physically injured also suffer from trauma.

Undoubtedly, the continuous violence that Israel has experienced in wars and terrorism has spilled over into everyday life, asserts Solomon. Anybody who thinks that violence experienced during military service, for example, can be isolated in some bubble is deceiving him- or herself and others. It leads to a blurring of sensitivity. Someone who has learned to solve problems by using force finds it difficult to be a loving spouse or parent. Violence is often an easy way out. It becomes a way of life, part of your personality.

"There is very little sublimation in Israeli society," she points out. "There is a lot of direct aggression: on the roads, in the shops, in conversation. Look at the way people talk in television discussions, for example. Or take our festivals—they are all to do with survival from catastrophe. Every Jewish child hears during the Passover Seder meal that the Israelites escaped from being massacred in Egypt. He learns at Purim that there was a plot to wipe out the Jews of Persia that was narrowly averted. He celebrates the victory of the few [Jews] over the many [Greeks] at Hanukkah."

Israeli culture is very liberated, very uninhibited, but also very contentious. Even humor is aggressive. Furthermore, in recent years, it has become worse. During the past year, two people have opened fire with their weapons because of road rage. This behavior is unprecedented in Israel, although there was a spate of murders after the Gulf War. Violence goes in circles, and victims become perpetrators.

The trauma is, of course, much greater in the Jewish settlements in the Palestinian territories, and greater still among the Palestinian residents of the territories. A study by one of Solomon's doctoral candidates confirmed her observations about the geography of fear. A study of over a thousand teenagers indicated that 30 percent of children in Jewish settlements in the territories and 70 percent of Palestinian children showed symptoms of PTSD.

Although Israeli society is coping relatively well, sums up Solomon, there is no reason for optimism, as trauma only causes more trauma. The healing has to come from somewhere else. Sometimes, her continual involvement with stress and trauma does have a toxic effect, she admits. It can be profoundly depressing. Nevertheless, Solomon describes herself as "an incorrigible optimist." She could not continue with her research if she weren't.

"We cannot cure the trauma with research," she concludes, "but we can help to change perceptions, make people more aware, improve treatment. Maybe it doesn't make a big difference, but on the whole I have a positive feeling about what I am doing."

Baiga Shochat: Peace Means Prosperity

"In 1992, Israel attracted some [US] $140 million in foreign investments. In 1996, the figure was $3 billion, an increase of twentyfold. Olso had an extraordinary effect on our status in the world. The fact that we signed an agreement and embarked on a peace process gave Israel a legitimacy that it had never before possessed."

Avraham Baiga Shochat, the finance minister in the Israeli governments of Yitzhak Rabin and Ehud Barak, is an enthusiastic supporter of the much-maligned Oslo peace process. In his judgment, it was not a process that failed. For several years it worked well, and both Israelis and Palestinians benefited from it. The Israeli economy grew by 6 percent every year for four years. The Palestinians started more slowly, but Shochat is certain that if the agreement had not collapsed because of the outbreak of violence, they would have doubled their gross national product (GNP), in a very short time.

Our conversations took place in Shochat's tiny office in the Knesset, Israel's parliament, where he serves as a Labor Party member. Widely popular, even among his political opponents, he is a good-humored, comfortable man who has been struggling with a weight problem for most of his adult life. He is very much the sabra, the second-generation Israeli: plain speaking and pragmatic, with none of the rhetorical frills of someone like Shimon Peres.

Shochat, who as finance minister negotiated the Economic Protocol with the Palestinians, is emphatic that Israel wanted the Palestinians to succeed economically. The agreement was conceived in an optimistic spirit. The Israelis saw the Palestinians as partners with the same aim: an increase in the standard of living. The Israeli negotiators were acutely aware that the serious economic gap between the two populations was not sustainable.

Baiga Shochat

"We wanted them to feel good," he emphasizes. "We wanted the Palestinian public to feel that peace was worthwhile."

At the same time, concedes Shochat, he was concerned to protect the Israeli economy. He didn't want the Palestinian territories to become a channel for the import of cheap goods from all over the world. He wanted a measure of control, but he was prepared to make concessions. He was aware that Israel had to pay a price for peace. The two sides had to work out an economic relationship between them. In the first stage, they agreed on a customs union; later they worked out an agreement for a free trade area (FTA) between Israel and the future independent Palestinian state.

There were, of course, differences of opinion, but they were resolved in the best possible spirit. Recognizing that they would require their laborers to continue working in Israel for some years, the Palestinian negotiators wanted the actual number to be written into the agreement. The Israelis were not prepared to accept this proposal, but they did agree to the principle of free movement of labor and agreed that "a large number" of Palestinians would be permitted to work in Israel. There were also disputes about the level of value added tax (VAT) and other matters, but, after five months of intensive negotiations, the Economic Protocol was hammered out.

A last-minute hitch concerned the independent status of the accord. The Palestinians wanted it to be separate from the political and security agreements; the Israelis insisted on interdependence. The matter was left open, with Prime Minister Rabin and Palestinian Authority chairman Arafat exchanging letters on the subject.

Shochat admits to being surprised by the high level of the Palestinian delegation.

"I don't want to sound patronizing," he says, "but our delegation consisted of officials from government ministries, first-class people with decades of experience in running an advanced economy. The Palestinian negotiators had never been in charge of anything like a national economy, but they were absolutely up to scratch. They understood everything, knew exactly what they wanted, and fought for their views."

Shochat formed a warm relationship with his Palestinian counterpart, Ahmad Qurei, better known as Abu-Ala, and got on well with the other officials. He was, he recalls, surprised at the degree of control that Chairman Arafat exercised over Abu-Ala and the other delegates. Rabin only intervened when there was a crisis, he maintains, but Abu-Ala needed Arafat's approval for every detail. Subsequent to the Paris talks, Shochat met Arafat several times and found him "very charming and friendly," but he blames him for the breakdown of the Oslo process.

"Arafat thought he could gain more by armed struggle," he states baldly. "I know that his inner circle were sorry he didn't reach an agreement with us. Look what he could have had today: 97 percent of the West Bank and Gaza, part of Jerusalem. In the event, he ensured the election of Arik Sharon as Israeli prime minister and caused the total collapse of the Palestinian society and economy."

Avraham Shochat was born in Tel Aviv in 1936. He was known by his childhood nickname "Baiga" for so many years, that he eventually had it written into his identity card and passport. Even his Palestinian interlocutors know him by that name. He had a typically Israeli childhood: membership in the Noar Oved youth movement, service in the IDF, membership in a kibbutz. Like so many Israeli Jews, Shochat's initial memories of Arabs are far from positive. He had family in the moshav cooperative village of Beer Tuvia, south of Tel Aviv, and one of his earliest memories is of hearing that the driver of the settlement's milk truck had been killed in the revolt of 1936–1939. He also remembers his father telling him to duck down in the car to avoid the stones thrown by Arab villagers on the way to visit his relatives.

At school during the War of Independence, he subsequently served in the IDF, before joining Kibbutz Nahal Oz, opposite Gaza, in 1955. At that time, the Egyptians still controlled the Gaza strip, with its teeming refugee camps. It was a volatile period, with infiltrators trying to penetrate the kibbutz, and sometimes succeeding. Frequent firing across the border was heard. At night, after a hard day's work, Shochat manned an ancient Czech machine gun. One evening, four weddings were scheduled at Nahal Oz, he recalls, but were canceled after a particularly horrible incident in which a kibbutz member was murdered and his body mutilated.

Things calmed down after the Sinai Campaign of 1956, and Shochat left the kibbutz to study engineering at the prestigious Haifa Technion, where he became chairman of the students' union. On completing his studies, he became a member of the design team planning the new town of Arad in the desert overlooking the Dead Sea. When the first residents of the new town arrived, Shochat was elected chairman of the residents' committee. Cutting his political teeth in a series of struggles between the town's inhabitants and the government-appointed director, he was in due course elected mayor of Arad. He was reelected four times, generally with majorities of 95 percent and more. His friends used to joke that the only other elections achieving similar results were those held in communist Albania.

Shochat maintains that relations between the town of Arad and the local Bedouin were good from the earliest days. The town was built to the east of the Bedouin encampments, not infringing on their grazing lands, and the establishment of Arad brought a road, water supply, and electricity lines to the region. When Israel withdrew from Sinai, following the Israel–Egypt peace agreement, a military airfield was needed west of Arad to replace those vacated in Sinai. As a member of the regional planning committee, Shochat was involved in the negotiations with the local Bedouin to build the airfield. Under the agreement, which involved special legislation, the Bedouin were granted compensation and also allocated alternative lands. That particular problem was solved in a satisfactory manner, but the overall problem of Bedouin land ownership in the Negev desert has still not been resolved.

Shochat was not directly involved with the Palestinian problem, but, as mayor of Arad and chairman of a committee representing Israel's new towns, built since 1948, he found himself competing for funds with the settlers of the West Bank and Gaza. He was strongly opposed to the channeling of vast sums of money to the settlement projects in the Palestinian territories, which he knew came at the expense of Israel's other new communities. He became an active member of the Labor Party, and his involvement in party politics brought him into contact with Yitzhak Rabin. He admired Rabin on a personal level, but in becoming one of his leading supporters, he faced a dilemma. Rabin was identified as hawkish on security issues, whereas Shochat, a critic of West Bank settlement, was generally dovish in his political views. A private conversation with Rabin convinced him that the former IDF chief of staff was prepared to make "very large concessions" to the Palestinians to achieve peace.

In 1988, Shochat was elected on the Labor ticket to the Knesset, where he chaired the powerful Finance Committee. In 1992, the Labor Party won the election. Rabin became prime minister and appointed

Shochat as finance minister. As soon as the Oslo peace process became public, Shochat suggested to Rabin that the economic issues between Israel and the Palestinians were very complex and should be handled separately.

The French government put extensive offices near the Arc de Triomphe in Paris at the disposal of the Israeli and Palestinian delegations, which numbered about fifteen each. The negotiations for the Economic Protocol were very complex, and specialist officials were called in as needed: the director-general of the Agriculture Ministry when farming was on the agenda, the head of the Tourism Ministry for relevant issues, and the director of the Antiquities Authority when they discussed ancient sites.

Shochat and Abu-Ala established an immediate rapport at dinner on the first night. They began with talk about their personal experiences, after which Shochat proposed the alternatives of a customs union or an FTA between Israel and the areas to be governed by the Palestinian Authority. In due course, the two sides agreed to a customs union in the original phase, with an FTA after five years, by which time a Palestinian state was to be established. Abu-Ala was optimistic, seeing the future state of Palestine as a Middle Eastern Hong Kong, attracting large investments, particularly from the Arab states.

The Paris negotiations were conducted over five months on Tuesdays, Wednesdays, and Thursdays, leaving the long weekends for each side to consult its leadership. The Palestinians wanted to import lamb from Saudi Arabia and cement from Jordan. The Israelis did not want to raise difficulties by saying that they were still formally at war with those nations; they were more concerned to prevent the Palestinians from underselling these products to Israeli suppliers. They agreed to imports that would be sufficient for Palestinian consumption. A gradual lowering of tariffs between Israel and the territories would permit the Palestinians to export their agricultural produce to Israel. Within three years, the Palestinian exports were to be unlimited, and the Israeli treasury agreed to pay its nation's farmers millions of dollars in compensation.

"It was a real concession, and it cost us," asserts Shochat, "but we wanted to give them a fair deal."

He concedes that Israel had previously exploited the Palestinian territories economically but insists that this was all going to be changed under the terms of the new protocol. He remembers arguing with Abu-Ala about the VAT. The latter wanted to lower the tax in the Palestinian territories, partly to show their independence but also to make it easier for their population. Shochat agreed but insisted there couldn't be too great a discrepancy. The Israelis helped the Palestinians plan their tax system and undertook to transfer taxes, pensions, national insurance, and other money collected in Israel to the Palestinian Authority. Special arrangements, supervised by an international consultant, were made to ensure that the money paid over would not be diverted and the Palestinian workers would receive their pensions and other allowances.

Shochat's team also proposed five industrial parks on the border between Israel and the Palestinian territories. Israeli entrepreneurs would invest in factories and workshops, where the Palestinians would find employment. He thinks the Palestinians failed to take advantage of that plan. This was a notable mistake, in his view. Both sides made mistakes, he admits, but it wasn't economic matters that destroyed Oslo.

Terrorist actions by the Hamas and the Islamic Jihad, the assassination of Yitzhak Rabin, the defeat of Shimon Peres by Benjamin Netanyahu in the subsequent election—all contributed to the breakdown of the arrangements. Shochat emphasizes, however, that the system continued to work even through the three years of the Netanyahu government, with the Israelis transferring money to the Palestinian Authority as agreed. A Joint Economic Committee, with representatives from both sides, was monitoring the agreement and continued to meet until January 1996.

Israel benefited hugely, and the Palestinian economy showed many positive signs. The Arab boycott, from which Israel had suffered since 1948, was quietly shelved. Prior to Oslo, Israel used to run after investors and try to persuade them that business with Israel would not hurt them in the Arab world; now businesses started to come to Israel. The German motor company Volkswagen had been selling its cars in Israel but never put anything back into the economy. Suddenly Volkswagen asked to invest half a billion dollars in a magnesium plant in the Dead Sea. Countries that had previously shunned Israel, such as China, India, South Korea—and even Muslim nations such as Malaysia and Indonesia—were suddenly eager to do business with the Jewish state.

For the first time in its half-century of existence, Israel received a rating from Standard and Poors and other financial institutions, starting with triple B, and increasing to A-minus. It meant that investing in Israel was worthwhile. With $10 billion in loan guarantees from the United States, it became easy to raise money. Despite the large-scale immigration of Jews from the former Soviet Union, unemployment was down and the economy grew. Shochat takes some personal credit for reordering economic priorities: Expenditure on the West Bank Jewish settlements was cut back, and important investments were made in Israel's infrastructure, roads, railroads, public transportation, education, and development of previously neglected regions.

In particular, tourism made spectacular gains. For years, despite its biblical sites, pretty beaches, modern services, sunny climate, and multilingual population, Israel had struggled to attract even one million tourists a year. In the years after Oslo, the number approached three million.

The whole process slowed considerably during the Netanyahu period, recalls Shochat. When he next met with Palestinian representatives, during the premiership of Ehud Barak, the atmosphere was far less cordial, but the arrangement could still have worked. Strongly rejecting the popular perception that the Oslo agreement was a mistake, Shochat emphasizes that Oslo was "not just economics, Area A, Area B, the Palestinian Authority, and a number of rifles supplied to the Palestinian police." It was, he insists, a genuine attempt to reach a compromise. On the Israeli side, it was the end of the dream of "Greater Israel," with even the right-wing Likud accepting the inevitability of a Palestinian state. On the Palestinian side, it was recognition of the reality of Israel. The 1994 version of Oslo might be dead, but, even today, the idea that Israel must withdraw from most of the West Bank and Gaza to facilitate the establishment of a Palestinian state still commands the support of most Israelis.

So why did Prime Minister Barak fail to honor withdrawals specified by the Oslo agreement and continue to build settlements in the West Bank? What Barak was offering was *much more* than Oslo, asserts Shochat. The Oslo agreement had left open such matters as the final borders, the status of Jerusalem, and the question of the rights of the Palestinian refugees. At Camp David, in the summer of 2000, Barak came forward with radical proposals to settle these issues.

Yasser Arafat turned him down, and the resulting confrontation has been extremely damaging to Israel and utterly catastrophic for the Palestinians. Clearly, the Palestinian economy, much smaller to start with, has suffered more. In fact, it has virtually been destroyed. The Israeli economy, though, has also been severely harmed. Understandably enough, tourism was the first casualty, and the fallout was felt everywhere. Israel's credit rating is threatened—in fact, the rating of its leading banks has already been reduced—and investments have dried up. Tax revenues are down; the economy has stopped growing, Moreover, despite the highest unemployment in decades, the rate of inflation has increased sharply.

"The whole situation is a disaster," pronounces Shochat. "Everyone loses!"

The former finance minister believed for a long time that his party should leave the government. He could not understand how it remained in partnership with Ariel Sharon for so long. Labor's Central Committee officially approved a peace policy, which embraced the Clinton Parameters and the Saudi plan. Its program called for dismantling isolated Jewish settlements in the West Bank and Gaza and restarting negotiations with the Palestinians on the basis of sharing Jerusalem and evacuating most of the West Bank. Challenged on what is meant by "isolated settlements," Shochat remains vague.

"It can be five settlements, or fifteen. Definitely Netzarim in the Gaza strip. It doesn't matter. The important thing is the principle."

Not only is the stated Labor Party policy a solution to the problem, he believes, but it is the *only* solution. It is not so difficult to work it out, he maintains. There can be settlement blocs, and the Palestinians can be compensated with land in Israel. Some 150 settlements exist, but they occupy only 4 percent of the West Bank. As far as he is concerned, Ariel (halfway between Nablus and Ramalla) can be abandoned; Maale Adumim, east of Jerusalem, approached by a tunnel. The Clinton Parameters are the basis.

Arafat is finished, says Shochat. Even the Europeans, Egyptians, and Saudis want him to go. He will be ousted one way or another. Barak was right to make the offers he did at Camp David, asserts Shochat. He offered far more than any Israeli leader before him had dared. It was courageous and honest. He doesn't think Barak made mistakes in his negotiations with the Palestinians. He believes that, had he achieved an agreement with Arafat, the Israeli people would have backed him in a referendum.

Possibly he made a mistake on the Syrian front, he concedes. If Barak had kept his nerve and allowed the Syrians to have part of the northern shore of Lake Kinneret, a settlement with Syria could have been achieved, and then the Palestinians would have had no choice but to agree to an arrangement.

Although he was instrumental in getting Barak elected to the leadership of Israel, and although he personally got on very well with him, Shochat admits, in retrospect, that the man should never have been prime minister. Barak has a problem getting on with people, he observes. He isn't cut out to be a political leader.

Shochat's hope for the future is that the Israeli public will eventually make the connection between the lack of progress on the peace front and the catastrophic economic situation. Outside pressure and the economy will ultimately force Israel to change direction and resume the diplomatic process. Having twice served as finance minister, effectively number three in the government hierarchy—some would argue number two—Shochat is keeping his future political options open. Closely identified with both Rabin and Barak, he is not particularly close to any of today's aspirants to the leadership of his party and is not fired by a personal ambition to be prime minister.

"You have to want that very much indeed," he remarked in a recent television interview. "I don't have a sufficiently fierce desire for the job."

In the current situation, it is difficult to see an obvious way ahead. The problems will remain formidable. Nevertheless, if Israel comes to adopt Baiga Shochat's sort of pragmatism, it will find a response on the Palestinian side. This is clear when the views of a man such as Samir Huleileh are examined. As one of Abu-Ala's senior advisers, Huleileh was across the table from Shochat in Paris, when the economic protocol was negotiated. He is the subject of the next section.

Samir Huleileh: Preventive Action Now

Samir Huleileh doesn't think that this is the time for comprehensive solutions of the Israeli–Palestinian problem. He has a clear sense of priorities, and, right now, he wants to find ways of minimizing the irreversible damage liable to be caused by the current tendency of both sides toward separation.

"If you want this fence, okay," he says, "but let's ensure that the need for security doesn't destroy the possibility of economic cooperation. Let's have six or seven gates in the fence, and let's make them efficient, so that the goods can pass through quickly in both directions."

Huleileh is referring to the ongoing construction of the so-called security fence between the West Bank and Israel. In view of the Intifada and the subsequent escalation, a majority Israelis would like to see an impenetrable barrier between them and the Palestinians. Many on the Palestinian side have similar ideas, but Huleileh strongly disagrees. At the start of the Intifada, he and his colleagues in Paltrade, an association representing 120 Palestinian exporting companies, came out openly against a call for a boycott of Israeli goods. He is certain that economic cooperation is vital for Israelis and Palestinians alike.

"We are being dragged into a situation where no one will benefit. The political conflict may take years to solve. Meanwhile, we need continuous dialogue and discussion to show the people that it is in their interest to have good economic relations, even if we have other problems at the present time. There has to be a wise voice explaining matters to the security people so that we can find a way of getting through the present until they find a solution."

Samir Huleileh knows what he is talking about. After helping to negotiate the Paris Protocol, he became marketing and export manager of Nassar Jerusalem Stone, the largest quarry and stone-processing factory in the Middle East. Despite its name, Nassar is situated in Bethlehem. It buys 40 percent of its raw materials from Israel, sells a third of its products to Israel, and exports to thirty-two countries via Israeli ports. Huleileh, then, has an understanding of both the public and the private aspects of the Palestinian economy.

Samir Huleileh

Our conversations are conducted in the shady courtyard of the American Colony Hotel, that perennial meeting place, even during the most difficult times. Tall, urbane, fluent and articulate in English, Huleileh knows at least half the people sitting there—Israelis and Palestinians—demonstrating an easy camaraderie with all of them. Before one meeting, I wait patiently while he pursues a detailed business negotiation with the manager of the Israeli company that transports Nassar's products to Israel and the ports. Afterward, the Israeli remarks to me in Hebrew, "These guys are amazing. With all the curfews and closures, they keep on operating. If there are only four available hours in a day, they will use them to the full. It's a pleasure to do business with them."

Samir Huleileh was born in Kuwait. His parents, both of them refugees from the 1948 war, met and married in the oil-rich Gulf state. His mother was from Jaffa; his father came from nearby Yazur. His father, a trained accountant, had opened his own business in Kuwait. Moving to Jericho in 1959, he purchased land, becoming one of the more important landlords in the area. It was only eleven years after the 1948 war, and the West Bank was part of Jordan. Many of his relatives were living in refugee camps nearby, and they regarded his land purchases as treachery to the Palestinian cause. As they saw it, he was giving up the right to his land in Yazur, but Huleileh senior was a practical man, and, even then, felt he had to build a new future that took current realities into account.

In 1971, he moved his wife and their six children to Ramalla to take advantage of the good schools there, still spending much of his time managing his land in the Jericho area. Samir studied at the Friends' School, graduating in 1975. From there, he went on to study medicine in Cairo but was expelled three years later with seven hundred other Palestinian students for demonstrating against the regime of President Anwar Sadat, who had signed a peace treaty with Israel.

"We didn't mind about Sadat's deal with Israel," explains Samir. "That was Egypt's business, but we did object to the subsequent talks on Palestinian autonomy, which we felt he was conducting behind our backs."

The Palestine Liberation Organization had started winning recognition in the early 1970s, he notes, climaxing with Yasser Arafat's address to the United Nations General Assembly in 1974. Now, suddenly, an Arab leader was presuming to speak on behalf of the Palestinians. It was this that led to the stormy protests and the subsequent expulsions. Many of Samir's fellow students continued their medical and engineering studies in Syria and Iraq, but they were required to join the Socialist Baath parties in those countries, which he was reluctant to do. As his mother died in

1978, and his elder siblings were studying in the United States, he decided to return to Ramalla to look after his younger brother and sister. He enrolled in Birzeit University, starting again from scratch, this time studying economics and sociology. Subsequently, Samir earned a master's degree at the American University of Beirut, before embarking on a doctorate at East Anglia University in England, which he never completed.

He returned to Birzeit as a lecturer and head of the Student Affairs Office. In 1986, he joined the Arab Thought Forum in Jerusalem, a nongovernmental organization (NGO) that specialized in economic research. Three years later, he was running the West Bank program of the Geneva-based Welfare Association. Established by rich Palestinians living abroad, the association provided between US $5 and $6 million annually for projects. From there it was a natural step to founding the Economic Development Group (EDG), with some colleagues. Starting as a small organization, financing Palestinian entrepreneurs, EDG has since become a bank with a capital of US $35 million, and Huleileh is still a member of the board.

Around that time, he also had his first serious encounter with Israelis. An Israeli organization called The Twenty-First Year sought to end Israel's occupation of the West Bank and Gaza and tried to foster discussions between the two peoples at grass-root levels. Huleileh, a young, pragmatic Palestinian involved in economic matters, was a natural contact.

"I looked over my diary recently," he remarks, "and I saw that I participated in fifty-four parlor meetings in the years after 1988. I visited Tel Aviv, Haifa, Herzliya, Ashdod, and Beersheba. I learned more from the Israelis than I expected to; I also learned about them."

In 1992, he joined the Palestinian team for the multilateral talks with Israel that took place after the Madrid Conference on Middle East Peace. In due course, he met with Abu-Ala, the man in charge of the PLO's finances, and traveled to Tunis for talks with other PLO officials. After Oslo, he was one of the team personally selected by Abu-Ala to negotiate the Paris Protocol with Israel.

Huleileh's account of the Paris talks interestingly parallels that of Baiga Shochat. He agrees that there was enormous goodwill on both sides and sees the agreement as "a good step forward." It was not a radical separation from the past, but considerably improved the economic prospects of the Palestinians. Told about Shochat's positive impression of the expertise of the nonexpert Palestinian negotiators, Huleileh offers this version.

"We were mostly people of academic background. There was a university lecturer from the Najah University of Nablus. I worked for an NGO. We had a professor who lectured in agriculture and economics. We had read a lot of books and held many discussions, but, to be honest, none of us had any experience of running a government. For example, we didn't have a clue how to operate a central bank.

"Abu-Ala told us to probe. We were not to take a position on anything. We were to ask, and ask, and ask. It was a learning process for us. Of course, we wanted to learn the Israeli positions, but, even more than that, we wanted to learn about the issues. This probing went on for almost three months, and I had the feeling that the Israelis were getting a bit fed up. The actual drafting of the protocol only started in February 1994."

The Palestinian negotiators were able to call on experts from other Arab countries and from the World Bank, he explains, but they wanted the Israelis to take them seriously. This meant they had to demonstrate a firm grasp of all the issues. Possibly it was this need for consultation that gave Shochat the impression that Abu-Ala needed Arafat's approval for every detail of the agreements. Among those giving advice to the Palestinians were the deputy director of the Jordanian Arab Bank, the biggest bank in the Arab world, and the governor of the Bank of Lebanon. Two senior financial officials from Egypt also lent their assistance.

Agreeing that the Paris Protocol was good for both Israel and the Palestinians, Huleileh maintains that the accord was later harmed by military elements, who were not there, did not understand the agreement, and had a different set of priorities.

"The Protocol was negotiated by civilians," he explains. "The only member of the military present in Paris was General Danny Rothschild, former coordinator of the occupied territories. Our experience shows that the other army commanders don't have much respect for their colleagues in administrative roles. The army men got in the way, when the time came to carry out the decisions."

He cites the example of the industrial parks. Shochat maintained that the Palestinians failed to take full advantage of the opportunities provided by the parks, but Huleileh insists they did as much as they could. In point of fact, he maintains, the idea of the industrial parks was not raised at all in Paris. It was a later idea, and he was personally involved in picking the sites. They had to be in Palestinian territory, near the Israeli–Palestinian border, not on top of an aquifer, not too near a Jewish settlement or too near the area earmarked for settlement expansion.

"We fulfilled all these conditions," he recalls, "but we were surprised that some twenty army commanders and settler representatives turned up to the meetings at the sites. We had the feeling that the settlers were angry about the parks."

The Israeli side rejected seven of the nine proposed sites, but in the end, three parks were established, and for a time things went very well. The Karni Industrial Park, just inside the Gaza strip, is still operating, with plants for clothing and electronic goods among others, but the violence of the past three years has reduced economic activity everywhere in Israel and the Palestinian areas, and the parks are no exception. All in all, charges Huleileh, nobody on the Israeli side spelled out the situation to the military; nobody balanced economic interests against security concerns. In that situation, security always won.

Nevertheless, he is sure that the Paris Protocol was starting to show positive results. Embarking on a brief description of the background to the negotiation, he notes that after the 1967 war, the Palestinian economy grew considerably. The Israelis assisted the Palestinians to modernize their agriculture, which became more productive. On the other hand, the traditional farming of olive trees, vineyards, goats, and poultry declined. Moreover, the Israeli authorities maintained a water quota of seventy cubic meters per person annually, which remained stable in the Palestinian areas. In other places, the quota was increased. In Jordan, the quota increased to around 140 cubic meters; in Israel, it is now around 300. The Jewish settlers on the West Bank consume even more than this: an estimated 400 cubic meters per person annually. Leaving the Palestinians with only seventy cubic meters annually means that, despite the increase in agricultural production per unit, the general growth slowed as time went on.

With regard to industry, the situation was worse. Israel, maintains Huleileh, deliberately held back industrial development in the Palestinian territories to protect Israeli manufacturers. This is generally acknowledged to be true, although there are different versions of the scale of Israeli obstruction.

In that period, though, the Palestinian economy benefited primarily from two external sources: Some 400,000 Palestinians moved to the Gulf states in the mid-1970s, sending back money to their Palestinian families. By 1989–1990, this accounted for US $1.1 billion. At the same time, some 140,000 Palestinians working in Israel contributed around US $800 million annually. The nearly US $2 billion coming from Israel and the Gulf amounted to almost half the GNP of the Palestinian economy. The Gulf War of 1991, however, showed how fragile these sources were. Annual revenues from Palestinians working in the Gulf dropped to US $400,000, after some 270,000 Palestinians were forced to leave Kuwait. At the same time, the closure imposed by Israel during the war caused a sharp decline in the income earned by Palestinians working there. This meant that the Oslo peace process was accompanied by a dramatic decline in income for the Palestinians. In addition to this, as its army withdrew from Palestinian areas, Israel became more security conscious, and every terrorist attack resulted in further closures. Huleileh points out that, until the Gulf War, there was completely free movement of people and goods between Israel, the West Bank, and Gaza. Through all the attacks by Palestinian gunmen and bombers—and even through the first Intifada—there were no restrictions on free movement. The first closure, preventing Palestinians from entering Israel, was implemented during the war. Subsequently, closures were increasingly used by Israel as security measures. In 1995, after a series of terrorist operations, the territories were completely closed off from Israel. A comparatively small number of Palestinians continued to receive permits to work in Israel, and many more entered illegally, but the resulting loss of income for the Palestinian economy has been severe.

Despite that, the post-Oslo situation was promising, says Huleileh. The loss in income from Palestinian workers in Israel and the Gulf was replaced by the international aid that started to flow in. Private investment also increased. Palestinian residents of the territories, who had kept their money abroad, started to invest in local concerns, and money began to come in from the Palestinian diaspora.

Huleileh points out that 1995 to 2000 are the relevant years. Oslo was negotiated in 1992. The subsequent agreement and the Paris Protocol were signed in 1993. The Gaza–Jericho withdrawal was in 1994, and in 1995, the Israelis withdrew from the major West Bank towns. Growth was not, of course, immediate. A World Bank report shows that serious growth occurred in 1998–1999, and the results began to be felt in 2000. At this point it became clear that, economically, things were going in the right direction.

True, unemployment was at 13 percent in the Palestinian economy, which sounds bad, but it must be compared with the 37 percent rate in 1995. It must also be stressed that, in the case of the West Bank, many derive income from their land, with olive trees, goats, cattle, and poultry. Huleileh quotes an Israeli survey of 1986, which showed that 64 percent of West Bankers working in Israel earned additional income from farming and other local activities. The official average unemployment rate of 13 percent is therefore not too bad in Palestinian terms.

Much has been made of the fact that the Palestinian Authority had some 140,000 on its payroll, but it should be noted that half of those came from outside, which meant that the Authority provided only 70,000 jobs locally, some 10 percent of the labor force. Private business was employing 18 percent more than previously. The Palestinian Authority was planning to limit public employment as of 2000, and there was every prospect of the private sector taking up the slack. Furthermore, the economy was now based on local enterprises, a far healthier situation than the previous dependence on employment in Israel and the Gulf. Despite the contention of many Palestinians that they had not benefited from the Oslo agreement, things had turned around and were starting to look promising. Economically speaking, it was manifestly not the right time for the Intifada to break out.

Huleileh "doesn't buy" the Israeli contention that Yasser Arafat deliberately launched the Intifada. In fact, he says, it started with massive stone-throwing demonstrations by the Palestinians. The Palestinian police failed to control the mobs, he admits, but they were frequently fired on by Israeli troops. The police were caught in the middle.

"We were not wise enough and the Israelis were not wise enough to control the situation," he says. "It escalated, and soon the confrontation was unstoppable."

In his opinion, the Israeli political leaders had no solution and quickly handed the problem to the military. The army stepped in with a large measure of brutality and tried to suppress the Palestinian uprising. Within a few months, the military campaign extended beyond countering riots and attacks, he contends, and targeted the Palestinian economy and society. He offers an example from his personal experience. The Nassar stone-processing plant is situated near Bethlehem's Dehaishe refugee camp, where there were frequent clashes between Palestinian fighters and Israeli troops. The company built a wall around the plant, erected strong lights, and employed a team of security guards to ensure that no hostile actions were launched from the area. Despite this, they were told by a friendly IDF reserve officer that they were an "economic target." Huleileh and Nassar Nassar, the owner, went to the military governor of Bethlehem to check out the information. The governor assured them that there was no such list.

Five months later, claims Huleileh, the Nassar plant was accurately shelled by an IDF tank, which deliberately knocked out all their machinery. The IDF spokesman said that the tank was responding to firing from the Dehaishe refugee camp. Huleileh emphatically denies this. When they returned to the military governor, he apologized, admitted there had been no shooting from Dehaishe, and said that "in the army one has to obey orders." He promised to try to ensure that it didn't happen again. In fact, it turned out to be a one-off incident. Nassar replaced its machinery—at a cost of US $600,000—and continues operating to this day. However, the incident confirmed the company's decision to move part of its operations to Jordan. The plant in Amman now has a turnover of US $9 million annually, about a third of that of the Bethlehem plant.

When Huleileh first told me this story, less than a year into the Intifada, I was convinced that he was being paranoid. I had no doubt that the Nassar plant had been shelled by mistake in the confusion of the battles between the IDF and Palestinian fighters. I rejected the concept that the army was engaged in a war of economic sabotage against the Palestinians. However, the destruction of computers, hard disks, administrative records, bank documents, educational equipment, and other such items during the Israeli incursions in the spring and summer of 2002 indicated that Huleileh might have a point.

Moreover, Huleileh's contention that he and his colleagues did not make a big fuss about the shelling of their plant but kept everything low-key rings true. The last thing they wanted was for their foreign customers to hear about the incident. Business always flees from a war zone, as proved by the current economic situation in Israel and the Palestinian territories.

Nassar has continued operating through all the closures and curfews. When there is a curfew, the Nassar workers sleep at the plant. If its trucks are held up at checkpoints and roadblocks, it causes unwanted delays, but stone products don't decay like fruit and vegetables. Business is down by 28 percent, but the company is big enough to ride out the storm.

Other businesses have been less fortunate. Unemployment increased to around 60 percent average in the Palestinian territories. Paltrade did a survey of 250 companies, finding that they had reduced their labor force by 56 percent on average, which is consistent with the unemployment figure cited earlier. The survey also found that most of the companies were operating at 30 percent capacity, meaning that they were keeping on more workers than their production justified. The big companies are surviving so far, but the smaller ones are in difficulty. Their most severe problems are transportation and the shrinking of the local market. Sometimes they can't transport their produce at all because of the closures. When they can, they have to transfer their goods from truck to truck, because of earth barriers and roadblocks, which doubles their transportation costs.

In addition, since the start of the Intifada, Israel has withheld payments of taxes collected in Israel, on the ground that the money was being used to finance terror operations. Recently some of this money was released to the Palestinians, under a system of supervision designed to prevent it falling into what Israel regards as the "wrong hands."

A World Bank report on the Palestinian economy in March 2003 pointed out that the gross national income of the Palestinians had fallen to nearly half of what it had been two years previously. Sixty percent of Palestinians were living on less than US $2 per day. The number of poor Palestinians had risen to two million. Over 50 percent of Palestinians were unemployed.

Lending and sharing, noted the report, were widespread, and families for the most part remained functional. Two other factors preventing total collapse were the efforts of the Palestinian Authority to continue delivering basic services, and international donations. Outside donations had increased to over a billion dollars, but even such a high level could not prevent further economic decline, if the confrontation and the closures

continued. The World Bank director for the West Bank and Gaza concluded:

> An agreed framework for political progress remains indispensable to
> reestablish the conditions for the resumption of economic development
> both in Israel and the Palestinian territories. This poses many challenges
> to the three main groups: the Palestinian Authority, the donors, and the
> Government of Israel. Closure remains the most significant factor af-
> fecting the Palestinian economy. The Government of Israel should find
> ways to ease closure in ways compatible with its security. The Bank wel-
> comes Israel's decision to resume the transfer of Palestinian Authority
> tax revenues and to issue more permits for Palestinians to work in Israel
> as positive steps.

The dire economic situation led to angry demonstrations of Palestinian workers against the Authority. Criticism grew of corruption by Palestinian officials, after the failure of the Authority to pay salaries. Huleileh,
himself a former Palestinian Authority official, admits that there is great
public disappointment with the Authority. He even goes so far as to say
that there might have been an uprising against it, if Israel had not placed
itself in the middle.

"Once Israel entered the towns and villages, people saw Israel as the
enemy," he explains. "The army ensured that the anger of the people was
deflected, and because Israel has tried to delegitimize the Palestinian Authority, the people now support it."

Huleileh is strongly in favor of reforming the Palestinian government,
"despite the fact that Israel and the United States are calling for it." He rejects the idea of a "deal," whereby the Palestinians will receive land in exchange for carrying out reforms. The private sector has been active in this
field and has been pressing for economic reforms for some time.

As noted earlier, Samir Huleileh is today mainly concerned with the tendency toward separation on both sides. He instances a recent meeting
with Dan Proper, the chairman of Ossem, the large Israel food products
company, which used to employ large numbers of Palestinians and sell its
products widely in the territories.

"He told us that he has not employed Palestinians for more than a
year," says Huleileh. "He doesn't want to sell to us or buy from us at the

present time. And Proper was one of those supporting economic relations between us. It is very worrying."

He points out that the two peoples have lived together in the past and must live together in the future. His own company, Nassar, which buys raw materials in Israel, sells its product to Israel, and exports via Israeli ports, is a case in point. Haifa and Ashdod ports are not in it for the charity, he points out. They benefit from the business, as does Nassar.

"We and our Israeli counterparts go to the international market together. We get much of our stone from the Negev; they get theirs from all over Israel and the West Bank, but we market it together as 'Jerusalem stone,' particularly in the United States. We don't wave our Israeli and Palestinian flags around. We work together, and all of us benefit from the business."

It is difficult to disagree with Huleileh's thesis. As he says, the crisis must be managed properly. A dialogue must be maintained so that a future agreement in the spirit of the Paris Protocol will maintain cooperation and openness. It is in the interest of both parties to work together economically for their common good—no matter what is happening on the political front. After the violence of the past two years, Huleileh fears that Israelis and Palestinians are moving into "a hysterical and paranoid situation." He is determined to play his part in rebuilding the mutual confidence that existed in the past, offering this bottom line:

"The economic situation must not be jeopardized by the myth that separation is the best solution."

Separation has, in fact, become impractical. In the following chapters, the full extent of the entanglement of Israelis and Palestinians will become clear. Whatever the ultimate solution, it has become impossible to detach the two peoples from each other entirely. The two peoples live within each other: Israel has more than a million Palestinian citizens; Palestine contains over two hundred thousand Israelis; and Jerusalem is an Israeli–Palestinian city, no matter how it is eventually divided up.

CHAPTER 6
THE ENTANGLEMENT

Meira Dolev and Amit Segal, Second-Generation Settlers

Benny Katzover and Haggai Segal made conscious decisions to settle in the West Bank, formerly part of the Kingdom of Jordan, conquered by Israel in the Six-Day War of 1967. Some Israelis called the new areas acquired by Israel (the Golan Heights, the Sinai Peninsula, the Gaza strip, and the West Bank) "the conquered territories." (The English term is usually "the occupied territories." Prime Minister Sharon recently caused a sensation when he referred to "the occupation.") Many preferred the more neutral term "the administered territories" or even, simply, "the territories." For Katzover and Segal, though, they were "the liberated territories." In their view, no area taken in that war deserved that label more than the West Bank, the biblical Judaea and Samaria. They and their friends believed in Israel's right to possess that land and in their own right—even their obligation—to settle there. Despite their total conviction, however, they could hardly have failed to realize that most of their fellow Israelis thought differently.

This was not the case with their children, who grew up with a natural feeling of belonging and only learned in their teens that the settlements where they lived were the subject of controversy. It never occurred to Amit Segal, Haggai's son, or Amira Dolev, Benny Katzover's daughter, that anyone doubted their rights to the territory of Samaria, where they both grew up. Jewish settlement in the entire Land of Israel was an axiom; they literally drank it in with their mothers' milk.

"It was entirely natural for me to live in Elon Moreh," recalls Meira Dolev. "I never asked why I was there. I heard people criticizing us in the media, but I didn't understand what they were talking about."

"We never had a feeling of being rebels," says Amit Segal. "On the contrary, we always felt that we were a part of the mainstream."

Neither of them is manifestly unsympathetic to the Palestinians, but they see the Palestinian problem as a secondary issue. As far as they are concerned, retaining the territories is not only an imperative but also an internal Jewish matter: The Jews have to decide what they want. Only after that is resolved should the Palestinian problem be addressed.

Meira Dolev's earliest memories are of visiting the Cave of the Machpela in Hebron, where tradition says the biblical patriarchs, Abraham, Isaac, and Jacob, and their wives are buried and where her parents had been married. When she was a small girl, the building seemed huge. Later she wondered why it had shrunk. She remembers walking freely in the Palestinian town, field trips to biblical sites, winter snow in the surrounding hills. She has very ordinary memories, she stresses, nothing dramatic.

She is a striking young lady, with the round hat and long skirt worn by most religious Jewish women. Self-confident, without being aggressive, articulate but not verbose, she projects serenity and inner certainty. As she talks, a smile frequently lights up her dark-complexioned face.

Our meeting took place in Psagot, a Jewish settlement about a mile south of the Palestinian city of Ramalla. Visiting Psagot, one is soon aware that the Palestinian territories have become a different world. Danger lurks all over Israel today, in towns and villages, shopping malls and pizza parlors, cinemas and supermarkets. A suicide bomber or gunman is liable to strike anytime anywhere, and all of us tread warily, but in the West Bank the tension is tangible—it has become a war zone.

The bus is crammed to bursting point with soldiers. I haven't seen so much khaki since I became too old for reserve military service, nearly twenty years ago. It is an armored bus, with thick double-glazed windows and steel-plated sides. South of Jerusalem, massive concrete walls line the roads, and the bus stops are fortified bunkers.

During the first two decades of Israel's existence, crossing the border into any Arab country, including the Jordanian West Bank, was inconceivable. After the Six-Day War of 1967, though, traveling through the occupied territories, including the West Bank, became routine. From Jerusalem, we would travel north to Galilee or south to the Negev desert without thinking twice about it. We would vacation on the beautiful Sinai coast, hike through the Golan Heights, and enjoy meals in the charming outdoor restaurants of Bethlehem and Jericho.

As a journalist in the 1970s and 1980s, I drove freely through the West Bank, reporting from Nablus, Ramalla, and Hebron or writing features about the Jewish settlements. All that changed in 1987, with the outbreak of the first Intifada, when it became prudent to stay away from the areas of conflict. Even then, we still used the eastern roads, north through the Jordan Valley, or south, via the Dead Sea. After the Oslo agreement in 1993, it again became possible for Israelis to travel through the West Bank, but, as territory was handed over to Palestinian control, most Israelis again tended to stick to the eastern roads.

Since the start of the new Intifada in the fall of 2000, it has been a different story: most of us have stopped traveling in the occupied territories. In fact, it is forbidden to enter Area A, the Palestinian-controlled territory. So-called bypass roads, many of them constructed after the Oslo agreement was signed, allow Israelis to drive through the area at top speed. Paradoxically, these roads, which were built to separate the Jewish settlements from the Palestinian territory and thus afford greater security, have made it easier for Palestinian gunmen to single out Israeli targets.

Meira Dolev works on the local paper of the Benjamin Regional Council, *Benjamin News*. The council is named after the ancient Israelite tribe of Benjamin, which purportedly inhabited the area north of Jerusalem in the biblical period. The Benjamin region has many Jewish settlements, some of which are urban style, with high-rise buildings. From Psagot, Ramalla looks almost close enough to touch, but in several places high concrete walls have been erected to protect the settlement from random shooting. In these locations the Palestinian town is invisible: out of sight, out of mind.

Meira's mother, Bina, was born in Dimona, a new immigrant town, established in the desert east of Beersheba in 1955. Bina's parents came to Israel from Morocco. She met Benny Katzover through his brother, who worked as a sports instructor in Dimona. The two brothers were born in the veteran town of Petah Tikva, near Tel Aviv, established in 1878 with assistance from Baron Edmond de Rothschild. The son of a Polish mother and a German father, Katzover received a conventional National Religious upbringing and attended the militantly Zionist Mercaz Harav yeshiva in Jerusalem. He was involved in the Hebron exploit of Rabbi Moshe

Levinger, which was one of the key events in West Bank settlement after the Six-Day War.

It is fair to say that the Israeli government and the Israeli people were in somewhat of a daze after that war—not a mood of power-drunk exhaltation, as has often been depicted. The overall sentiment was one of intense relief, mixed with some pride, but also with uncertainty and doubt. What do we do now? Where do we go from here? Is it possible that there might really be peace at last? These were the questions people asked each other. More than anything else, Israelis were certain that, as had happened after the Sinai Campaign of 1957, the IDF would be forced by the great powers to withdraw. There was a mad rush to visit, Sinai, the Golan Heights, and the West Bank, "before we give it back."

Of course, some saw it differently. One of them was Moshe Levinger, then still an obscure village rabbi. On the face of it unimpressive, near-sighted, slurred of speech, and with a deceptively hesitant manner, Levinger would become the charismatic leader of West Bank settlement. I interviewed him more than once and also saw him in action. When Henry Kissinger was negotiating the disengagement agreements on the Egyptian and Syrian fronts, after the 1973 war, Levinger could be relied on to stir things up. The demonstrations would be peaceful, until his scarecrow-like figure arrived. Then the rabbi would bellow incoherently, tear his clothes (literally), and lie down in the street in front of the prime minister's office. Hundreds of demonstrators, as if mesmerized, would do the same.

After hours of conversation with him, I have to confess that I find it difficult to understand his appeal. He is single-minded, determined, and sincere, but incredibly simplistic. His message is plain: The Jewish people has to settle in the entire Land of Israel because that is God's purpose; the entire world will benefit from this development.

Suiting action to belief, Levinger and some of his followers (including Benny Katzover) rented the Park Hotel in Hebron for the Passover Seder meal in the spring of 1968. They took it for ten days, with an option to extend their stay. They subsequently refused to move out until they were permitted to relocate to the military government headquarters in Hebron, where two huts were erected for them. In August that same year, Katzover, then a student, married his wife, Bina, at the Machpela cave. A thousand guests came from all over Israel, many of them not supporters of the settlement enterprise.

Meira was born while her parents were living in the military government compound. When she was one year old, they joined the first fifty families of the newly built suburb of Hebron, Kiryat Arba (Township of the Four—i.e., the three biblical patriarchs and Abraham's wife, Sarah).The establishment of the new suburb, which began as a private initiative by a group of religious men and women, was approved by Israel's government and parliament at a time when they were still led by the Labor Party. It was a pattern that would be frequently repeated in the years ahead.

Meira was not to remain in Kiryat Arba for long. Her parents and their friends calculated (correctly) that what had worked in Hebron could also work in the northern part of the West Bank, which they naturally called by its biblical name, Samaria. Their initiative, which started in the summer of 1973, was interrupted by the Yom Kippur War. With their husbands mobilized during that war, a group of women met with Prime Minister Golda Meir to offer to do "something positive for the country." The prime minister naively hoped that they would collect candies and cookies for the serving IDF soldiers or go to a border settlement to boost its morale. They suggested settling in the vicinity of Nablus, the largest Palestinian town in the West Bank, which they called by its biblical name, Shechem. As a result of the meeting, the settlers saw that they could not count on government support for their next project—at least not yet.

The Yom Kippur War trauma caused Israelis to solidify their opinions about the territories. The Left was more than ever determined to push for an agreement with the Arab nations on the basis of "territory for peace." The Right concluded that its thesis concerning the vital importance of retaining the areas for defense had been proved. The religious Right determined to continue with its attempts to colonize the territories; it formed a new organization, Gush Emunim (Movement of Believers). This movement set as its first priority the settlement of Samaria.

The project was two-pronged. While the "Elon Moreh" group attempted to settle in the vicinity of Nablus, the "Ofra" group settled in a deserted Jordanian military camp near Ramalla, some fifteen miles north of Jerusalem. The first group operated in a blaze of publicity; the second with quiet stealth. The Elon Moreh people settled in the area of Nablus no less than seven times. On each occasion, they were evicted by the army, amid extensive media coverage. A few Israeli political figures, including notably Ariel Sharon, encouraged them in their endeavors. On more than one occasion, the man who would later be Israel's defense minister and later still its prime minister told the young IDF soldiers to disobey their orders to evict the settlers. He termed such orders "immoral."

Each settlement attempt was accompanied by unprecedented behavior on the part of the settlers, including physical attacks against and verbal abuse of IDF personnel. Finally, after their eighth attempt, a "compromise" was worked out, whereby the settlers agreed to be evacuated to a nearby IDF base of Kaddum. The group next tried to settle near the Arab village of Rujeib, four kilometers from Nablus, but was forced to vacate the site, this time as a result of an order of Israel's Supreme Court, which ruled that the land was private and belonged to Palestinian families. Elon Moreh finally came to rest in 1975, at its present site five kilometers east of Nablus.

Meanwhile, some twenty miles to the south, the second group had quietly taken up residence in a deserted Jordanian military camp. When the army came to evict them, a settler leader managed to delay the matter until Shimon Peres, at that time defense minister, agreed to order the IDF not to interfere. Less than two years later, the right-wing Likud Party came to power and officially encouraged these and other settlement projects in the northern West Bank. Situated deep in Palestinian territory, surrounded by numerous Arab villages and towns, Elon Moreh and Ofra remain the models to which all West Bank settlers aspire.

The young Meira Katzover knew nothing of all this as she was growing up. She remembers moving home frequently, but always in the company of the same group of adults and children. For her it was a great adventure. She recalls the feeling of excitement, a sense of history being made, when the first public transportation bus arrived in the new village, the first running water, the first school building. She particularly remembers hikes and field trips as she was growing up.

"We never did anyone harm," she recalls. "There was no feeling of tension in those days. The Arabs weren't at all hostile. When we hiked to the biblical sites, we used to pass through Arab villages, and the atmosphere was friendly. We never had stones thrown at us or anything like that. I never sensed any bad feeling, even under the surface."

Meira was the first of seven brothers and sisters. She attended school in her own settlement and afterward the regional high school in the nearby settlement of Kedumim. It was in her high school years that she started to sense a change in the local atmosphere. The neighboring villagers and townspeople started throwing stones at the cars and buses of the Jewish settlers. Subsequent attacks were more serious, and a number of settlers were killed, notably in Hebron in 1980, but, Meira contends, it was difficult to change the feeling of tranquility in which she grew up, and it took time before the new situation sunk in. For her, the turning point came during a field trip she made in the eleventh grade, when one of her companions was shot to death. The settlers started equipping their cars with bulletproof windshields.

"I don't remember being frightened," she says, speaking carefully, "but we became very aware of a new reality. The rules of the game had changed."

Hikes and field trips became hazardous, but she was confident that the violence was only temporary. Around the same time, she became aware that Elon Moreh and its neighboring settlements were controversial. Through the media, she learned that some Israelis objected to the settlement project in the territories.

When she turned eighteen, she opted for national service instead of the army. The norm in her religious environment, the service involved working as a teacher and youth leader in the small town of Afula in the Jezreel plain. It was something of a revolution in her life. She admits that she grew up in a very sheltered environment but suggests her feelings were similar to those of a kibbutz child, encountering town life for the first time. After a year in Afula, she transferred to Sde Eliahu, a religious kibbutz in the Jordan Valley. There she found the same emphasis on education, dedication to a cause, and community service with which she had grown up.

After two years of national service, Meira decided to study for a first degree in social science at Bar Ilan, a religious university near Tel Aviv, and to take a parallel course in communications at Koteret College. At the same time, she began working for *Nekuda*, the settlers' journal. The college was her first experience of militant secularism, and she was rather shocked. Not all the residents of Afula were religiously observant, but in that community of predominantly Asian Jews, a strong feeling for tradition had prevailed. Now, for the first time, she came up against a different type of Israeli.

Following her studies, she married Yaacov Dolev, who had immigrated to Israel with his parents from the United States. Starting out in Jerusalem, the Dolev family later settled in Elon Moreh. Yaacov attended the same schools as Meira, but not in the same class. In National Religious schools classes are single-sex. After their marriage, the couple resolved to join a new settlement, deciding eventually on Talmon, west of Ramalla. Her husband's parents saw it as "a bit of a retreat." Elon Moreh, right next to Nablus, is seen as more of a spearhead of Samaria settlement. (The northern West Bank has been subdivided into two regional councils, Benjamin and Samaria.)

The Dolevs have four sons, two of them twins just over a year old. After the twins were born, Meira spent nine months at home, returning to work in 2002 at *Nekuda* and *Benjamin News*, but she soon gave up the former, which was too demanding. Today, she is in charge of communication between the regional council and the thirty-odd settlements of the Benjamin region. Her duties include working with the paper's editor and producing promotion leaflets about the settlements. The brochures, entitled *Benjamin Never Stops*, are unabashed propaganda. They have an identical format, with details of the individual settlements slotted in where appropriate. An upbeat introduction begins:

> Despite the uneasy period through which we are passing, life in Benjamin proceeds uninterrupted, even on the most difficult days. The residents of all the settlements have shown a phenomenal stamina, and we of the council are doing our utmost to provide answers to the challenges and difficulties, and to preserve and even intensify the pace of life and the strength of community. Whoever expected to see Benjamin residents depressed and exhausted, after a year of difficult security events, will be surprised to see that we have demonstrated a vital ability to meet the challenges and not be defeated by difficulties.

The next section, while again stressing the frequency of "security events," describes how the council's emergency services dealt with hundreds of incidents, "including, to our regret, those in which people were killed and dozens were wounded." The pamphlet goes on to give details of the educational services provided to more than ten thousand children in the thirty settlements, including schools, kindergartens, youth clubs, and child development centers. Other sections deal with investment, planning, construction of roads, building, health services, water supplies, and so forth.

In a final message, the council wishes its residents "continued building, population growth, development and prosperity." The Benjamin Regional Council also mounts publicity campaigns on radio and television, urging Israeli citizens to make their homes within its boundaries.

A recent edition of *Benjamin News* has a cover picture of the local children distributing packages to soldiers who took part in the "Defensive Shield" operation in the spring of 2002, in which the IDF temporarily reoccupied the major Palestinian cities for the first time. Inside there is a long interview with Yehuda Etzion, who is demanding that the government permit Israelis to visit Jerusalem's Temple Mount. It will be recalled that it was Ariel Sharon's visit to the mount in the fall of 2000 that triggered the current wave of Palestinian violence. Fewer people may recall that Yehuda Etzion was tried and imprisoned in 1985 for conspiring to blow up the Muslim shrines on Temple Mount. He and others were subsequently released under a presidential pardon, which was supposed to involve an expression of regret. In the current interview, Etzion declares, "I continue to believe that the Dome of the Rock and the Mosques on Temple Mount are the wrong buildings in the wrong place. They must be removed from there, so that the area can be prepared for our return to the mount and the building there of the Temple. That means that the current situation must change. The question is: whose responsibility is it? That, however, is a secondary question."

Although her settlement, Talmon, is only ten miles from Psagot, it takes Meira Dolev almost an hour to come to work in the morning. Since the recent violence started, the IDF has established countless checkpoints on the roads, and Palestinian residents of the territories are used to the fact that a one-hour journey can take as much as four hours. For the most part, the Jewish residents can move speedily along specially constructed bypass roads, but the Talmon–Psagot route is not yet one of them.

Meira says she drives by herself and does not carry a weapon. After the current violence started, she used to wait for another vehicle before setting off, but she no longer does. She maintains that stone throwing has been a perpetual threat to the settlers since the mid-1980s. The Oslo process, which was supposed to usher in peace, did not stop the stones. Of course, the current situation, with its often fatal drive-by shootings, is much more serious, she concedes, but she is not sure it is worse than the period following the Oslo agreement.

"We weren't being shot at after the Oslo process started, but we felt terribly threatened," she says. "There were some awful moments, moments of despair. We told ourselves that the Jewish people wouldn't allow the leaders to hand over our settlements to a foreign regime, but, particularly when Barak was prime minister, we were really terrified that this would happen."

The idea of evacuating Elon Moreh, Talmon, or Psagot is utterly unacceptable to Meira. She realizes that Israelis who call Judaea and Samaria "the territories" might be prepared to give up the settlements, but this is wrong. The past cannot be thrown away. For thousands of years, the Jews dreamed about Hebron, the Cave of the Machpela, Nablus, and Jerusalem—they didn't dream about Tel Aviv. It is inconceivable to surrender the heartland of Israel. Even from a pragmatic point of view, it is a mistake to withdraw, she maintains. The Palestinians only pretend to believe in peace to gain territory. They will take up arms as soon as they have it, and then Israel will be back with a "thin waist" of ten miles between the border and the sea.

Doesn't she realize that most of the world—and at least half of Israel—has differing opinions from hers? Yes, but she can't take the world seriously. It is not so long since the nations of the world allowed six million Jews to be killed. As for the Americans, they are Israel's greatest friends, but they are sitting on huge territories. How can they ask Israel to give up land from the miniscule area it occupies? She rejects the depiction of a strong Israel oppressing the unfortunate Palestinians. She sees a tiny Israel trying to stand firm against a gigantic Arab world.

The settlers were expecting the outbreak of violence that started in the fall of 2000, she observes; it was only a matter of time. She is convinced that Arafat and his colleagues never sought peace, and now their true faces have been exposed. She is relieved that it has happened now, before more territory was handed over to the Palestinians. All the settlers knew that Oslo was a swindle. They were frustrated that other Israelis didn't see it.

Does she have faith in the present leadership? Despite the criticism of Sharon by some of the settler leaders, she personally has great admiration for him. She realizes that he has to maneuver in the international arena and thinks he is doing well, but she is not prepared to follow anyone blindly and remains eternally watchful.

Meira's mother is from Dimona, I point out, a town in the Negev desert that suffers from unemployment. The textile factories built there in the 1950s and 1960s have mostly closed down, unable to compete with manufacturers from countries with cheaper labor forces. Dimona is not receiving the investment in new sources of employment that it so desperately needs. At the same time, billions of dollars are being invested in the settlements of Benjamin, in fortifications and bypass roads. How does she feel about that?

Meira rejects any suggestion that the Benjamin region is being developed at the expense of Dimona. All towns and villages need money for apartments, schools, clinics, and roads. There have to be investments everywhere, without discrimination. She doesn't recognize any difference between the territory acquired in 1967 and the rest of Israel.

What about the inequities between Jews and Arabs in the territories?

She does not enjoy the suffering of the Palestinians, she insists. It upsets her to see them queuing at checkpoints. They have a terrible life, and that is very wrong. They have a perfect right to live fulfilling lives, without fear, but they brought the present situation on themselves.

"I don't say it is easy for them," she emphasizes. "They should have full civil rights, but, when they attack us every day, the result is that we see each one as a potential terrorist, and we have to defend ourselves."

Israel is perfectly capable of dealing with terror, she says, provided it is determined. When Israel won an outright victory in 1967, the Arabs didn't dare think about killing Jews. The Six-Day War had deterred them from violence, and Israel must reestablish that deterrence.

Throughout her youth, Meira had contact with Palestinians. They built the settlements where she grew up. The contractors and local village leaders would visit them, and the settlers used to attend the weddings of their Palestinian neighbors. She knew many good people among them, "with real wisdom and a marvelous sense of humor."

"As individuals, they are not bad people," she stresses, "but they live in a murderous society. They send young people to murder women and children. They have to change their values, and it won't happen quickly."

Hasn't it occurred to her that they might be acting out of desperation, because they see that the Israelis are taking over more and more of their land?

"I'm sorry. I don't believe a Jew would become a suicide bomber. There is something basically wrong with a society that encourages suicide bombers!"

The pioneers who established Israel knew that it wouldn't be easy, she points out. Maybe it is even more difficult than they foresaw, but there is no cause for despair. If today's situation is compared to what it was fifty years ago, enormous progress has been made.

"Who knows where we can be fifty years from now?" she asks rhetorically. "Did anyone predict the collapse of the Soviet Union and the arrival of nearly a million Jews from there?"

The Arabs have the whole Middle East, she argues. If they want to live in an Arab state, they have plenty of choices. Her mother came to Israel from Morocco, and a Palestinian Arab can also migrate to another country. Nevertheless, she is not in favor of expelling the Palestinians. Provided they are not a threat, they can live in a Jewish state with full civil rights.

Can they have the vote?

Maybe, in certain circumstances. Or perhaps they should vote for their own assembly—she doesn't know. It is difficult to say. She cannot predict what will happen in the future.

"I am in favor of giving them a good, humane, satisfying life," she concludes, "as good a life as possible—provided it doesn't threaten us."

The first thing that strikes one about Amit Segal is his extreme youth. With the regulation knitted skullcap perched on his short, light brown hair, he looks as if he hasn't yet started shaving. Just under twenty years old, doing his military service as a reporter in the IDF radio station, Amit is fluent, even verbose. He talks in explosive bursts. No less assured than Meira, he appears to lack her inner calm. Possibly it is a function of his age, or maybe it is because he spends much of his life in the potentially hostile world outside the settlements. Then again, it might simply be the result of differences in personality.

Amit goes home on weekends to the settlement of Ofra, where he grew up. Like Meira, he is very conscious of living in one of the flagships of the Samaria settlement enterprise, and, like her, he has very conventional memories of growing up in his settlement. Early on, though, there was one dramatic difference: Amit's father, Haggai Segal, was arrested and put on trial for the attempted murder of the mayors of Ramalla and El-Bira. He is not sure that he actually remembers this or whether he has reconstructed the event from other people's descriptions.

In his memoir, *Dear Brothers*, Haggai recalls that when two plain-clothes police officers came to arrest him, he was allowed to say good-bye to his children. Two-year-old Amit blurted out, "Me, too! Me, too!" He was never one to be left out, observes Haggai.

Segal, a member of the "Jewish underground," was arrested for actions that even most of the settlers found unacceptable. True, he was not in-volved in the most bizarre conspiracy of that aberrant group: the plot to blow up the Muslim shrines on Temple Mount. He was, however, an ac-tive partner in the reprisal attack on Palestinian mayors, whom the settlers saw as supporting terror strikes against their comrades.

In 1976, the Israeli government had permitted municipal elections in the West Bank. Although held under a military government regime, the poll was generally accepted to be free and fair. It was, for example, the first time ever that women were given the vote, and they turned out in droves, as did other newly enfranchised voters. The result of this universal suffrage was an almost clean sweep for candidates openly supporting the PLO. These mayors soon formed a National Guidance Committee, which be-came a nationalist voice for the Palestinians and the bête noire of the set-tlers. The settlers charged that it was the incitement by the committee, and by the individual mayors, that caused the terror actions against them.

Although all the members of the Jewish underground subsequently were alleged to have expressed remorse for their actions—indeed, they re-ceived presidential pardons for this reason—Segal's account is entirely un-apologetic. His book, manifestly designed to explain and justify his actions and those of his fellow conspirators, starts with a dramatic account of the killing of six Jewish settlers, returning from Sabbath eve prayers in He-bron in the spring of 1980. He quotes Nablus mayor Bassam Shaka'a: "The Israeli policy and behavior will lead to further tension and a more tenacious struggle. If we, the mayors, do not speak and lead, our people will act on their own council. They are not afraid."

Thirty days after the murder of the six Israelis, Segal and some of his comrades resolved that they also "would not be afraid" and that "Bassam Shaka'a and Kerim Khallaf, the mayor of Ramallah, would have to pay per-sonally for their activity." The author does not present evidence that either man was involved in any violent actions, only that they opposed the Jewish settlements and supported the struggle against them.

Segal recounts how he left Ofra in the early hours of the morning and personally placed a bomb under the car used by Kerim Khallaf. That accomplished, he and his friend drove to nearby El-Bira and booby-trapped the garage door of Mayor Ibrahim Tawil. By two o'clock he was home in Ofra, and the following morning found him attending his statistics class at the Hebrew University of Jerusalem. Coming out of the lecture, he switched on his transistor radio in time to hear that Khallaf and Shaka'a had been seriously injured. Nothing was reported about the mayor of El-Bira. On his way back to Ofra, he heard "the horrifying report" that an IDF sapper had been injured while trying to dismantle the explosive charge on the garage door of Ibrahim Tawil.

The sapper, Suleiman Hirbawi, a member of Israel's minority Druze community, was permanently blinded by the explosion. Four years later, Yehuda Etzion, who was later also involved in the Temple Mount plot, wrote to the blinded sapper:

> You, Suleiman, lost your sight that day. And I, Yehuda, lost the privilege of knowing that I would never injure an innocent man. Since then, a heavy weight has been pressing on my heart. Both of us love the State of Israel. You set out to serve it in the army, and I too set out to serve it, both in the army, and in our decision to attack a group of murderers. We succeeded in injuring two of them. That was very important for the state. That you were injured, instead of the third murderer, was God's will. That's an onerous punishment for you, a punishment for life. For us too it is a punishment—a lifelong pain for having wounded a soldier of ours.

As a result of his injuries, Bassam Shaka'a had both legs amputated. Kerim Khallaf lost a foot. Nowhere in the book does Segal even hint at regret for these Palestinian injuries. Not long afterward, well before anyone had been arrested and charged for the attacks, Rabbi Levinger told me with some satisfaction, "We all feel safer after the attacks on the mayors."

Amit agrees that his father has no regrets about his part in the attacks, except about the blinding of Suleiman Hirbawi. In the book, Haggai claims that a warning was delivered to the IDF before the attacks in an attempt to prevent injury to army personnel. Amit thinks that the action would have been called off if his father and his friends thought there was even a 1 percent chance of a soldier being hurt. His father's book was not written to justify his actions, says Amit, but to set the record straight. It was a factual book. His father was not involved in the Temple Mount plot. He doesn't know whether his father was in favor of blowing up the Muslim shrines there, but he is sure he thinks they should not be there. He himself would be happy if the Dome of the Rock and the Aksa Mosque were not there, but he is not sure that blowing them up would be "a clever idea at this point in time."

He brushes aside the religious argument of Moshe Halbertal that sovereignty and holiness are contradictory and that Judaism has moved beyond Temple Mount.

"Whether or not one agrees that we should be allowed to set foot on the mountain," he declares, "everyone agrees it is the most important square kilometer in the Middle East."

He sees no contradiction between living a modern life working in a radio station and connecting to Temple Mount, although the link he feels is national rather than religious. He does not feel divorced from the people he meets in his daily work. He contends that, in his youth, his father, from the small town of Acre, was more divorced from the Israeli mainstream than he, Amit, coming from Ofra.

Like Meira, he thinks that the Arab views—or American or European views, for that matter—are irrelevant to the question of what Israel should do. Israel should decide itself on the basis of its own beliefs and interests. Everything depends on Israel's stamina; what the Palestinians do or don't do is relatively insignificant. Like Meira, he does not support deporting Palestinians. He is sure that "transfer," as it is called, is only a minority view among Israelis. The Moledet Party, which openly supports transfer, never got more than two or three seats in the Knesset, he notes. If there is peace, the Palestinians can stay, but if they go on attacking Israelis, there will be escalating conflict and many of them might be forced out. He has not seen any sign whatsoever that the Palestinians are prepared for peace and compromise. Where are the Palestinian demonstrations in favor of peace?

"Arafat is not a liar," insists Amit. "He always said the same thing. It was certain Israeli leaders who refused to see the warning signs."

Expelling Arafat won't help, he declares. In his view, Arafat faithfully represents the Palestinian people. Arafat and his colleagues are not a small clique that took over Palestinian society. They *are* Palestinian society. All the polls show that 90 percent of the Palestinians support suicide bombings.

Is his settlement, Ofra, not a barrier to a possible compromise and peace?

"No way!" Amit exclaims. "This is not a war for the settlements. The Palestinians were offered virtually all the West Bank and turned it down. I have far too much respect for the Palestinians to think that Sharon's visit to Temple Mount was the real reason for the Intifada. It would have broken out anyway. If they had accepted Ehud Barak's offer, the Palestinians would have got virtually everything except for the Jewish towns of Ariel and Maale Adumim. Are we supposed to believe that the Palestinians went to war for two small towns or for four caravans on a hilltop in Samaria? They went to war because they are not ready for peace. There has been no real Arab move toward peace. The Egyptian peace is in deepest freeze and even the Jordanian peace is not genuine. In the Middle East, one side [Israel] runs toward peace, while the other side [the Arabs] runs away from peace."

Does Amit really believe that it is so one-sided? What about Baruch Goldstein, who killed twenty-nine Palestinians while they were praying in a mosque? What about the children killed during the violence of the past two years? What about pregnant mothers who are stopped at roadblocks, with the result that they and their babies die?

"Does anyone really think that any Israeli soldier wants the pregnant mother to die? The roadblocks never existed twenty years ago. They were put up to prevent terrorism. If a soldier doesn't let an ambulance pass, it is because the Palestinians use ambulances to smuggle weapons and explosives. Even in the Jenin battle [in spring 2002], no soldier said to himself, 'There is a house with a child in it, so let's blow it up!'

"Maybe there is insensitivity, or even humiliation of Palestinians, but it is only because of their violence," he continues. "As for Goldstein, maybe 2 percent of Israelis thought that what he did was a good thing. On the other hand, when the Palestinians murder civilians, maybe 2 percent of their population disapproves."

What would he do, if he were a Palestinian?

"That is a hypothetical question, and it's not a fair one. It presumes equivalence. There is no equivalence. Israel has no choice. I don't agree that the incursion into the Palestinian towns was part of a cycle of violence. If the IDF is not sent in to respond to acts of terror, Israel will be perceived as weak, and there will be more terror—not less."

Nevertheless, Amit is more optimistic now than he was when the Oslo process was being implemented and talks with the Syrians were taking place. He envisages one state between the Mediterranean and the Jordan River. It cannot be divided territorially, and the same number of Jews and Arabs will live there, no matter what happens. He doesn't know whether it can be democratic in the normal sense of the word. It has to be a Jewish state. It can't be Switzerland.

Amit Segal and Meira Dolev have grown up in the settlement movement. Talking to them indicates that the message has been passed on successfully to the second generation. There are no indications of any serious rebellion among the settlement youth or any real dissent from the basic axioms of the settler community. Not one youthful settler appears even to be uncomfortable with the money poured into the Jewish settlements of the West Bank and Gaza at a time of increasing economic hardship in Israel and near starvation in the Palestinian communities that are visible from their homes.

Nobody has any idea of the cost of the West Bank settlement project, with its massive construction, its fortifications, tunnels, bypass roads, subsidized mortgages and loans, IDF defense, and salaried officials—to name only some of the expenses. The gigantic sums of money that have been spent have been buried in all sorts of hidden or disguised clauses of the budgets of government ministries. A conservative sum of US $50 billion has been suggested, but this seems to most observers to be an underestimate. It is evident that, if a fraction of the sum spent on the settlements had been invested in the rehabilitation of the Palestinian refugees living in the West Bank and Gaza, the miserable refugee camps would long have receded into history.

But the direct costs are only half the story. The losses to the Israeli economy caused by the continuing conflict—at least US $10 billion in the past two years alone—should be added. Defended by the IDF, heavily subsidized by their fellow citizens, the men and women of Ofra, Elon Moreh, and the other West Bank and Gaza strip settlements live in considerable luxury by any standards.

Meira Dolev and Amit Segal are attractive and articulate young people, with a burning belief in their cause, but their convictions have to be set against the reality of what has been going on in Israel and the territories over the last thirty-five years. Deception, ruthlessness, and moral blindness have characterized the settlement enterprise from the day that sixty people sat down to a Passover meal at the Park Hotel in Hebron and remained long after the celebration was over.

The settlements have necessitated an Israeli occupation of the Palestinian territories that has become more brutal year by year. The settlers argue that Nablus is the same as Nazareth or that Hebron is no different from Umm al-Fahm. The residents of the Israeli towns of Nazareth and Umm al-Fahm, however, have the vote. Ruling over more than three million people who have no civil rights is inherently immoral and corrupting. The disgusting use of Palestinian collaborators—either traitors to their own people or unfortunate victims of blackmail by Israeli security agents—is only one example. Many of these unfortunate people—men and women—have been tried and executed by the Palestinian Authority. Others have been murdered without trial.

The existence of the settlements has also forced decent young men, such as Lieutenant Nir Shoshani and Captain Adi Eilat, to perform duties that violate their consciences. Thousands of young Israeli soldiers have been compelled to fight and to face danger, not in defense of their nation but for the sake of a brutal colonialism in the guise of a messianic dream. Rarely has idealism been so blatantly perverted, and never before with such nauseating self-righteousness.

Shortly before the fall of the Sharon government, the Israeli media made a big fuss over the behavior of the so-called Hilltop Youth, who violently attacked the IDF troops who came to evacuate the so-called illegal outposts. The handwringing over their conduct is ludicrous; the distinction between "legal" settlements and "illegal" outposts is idiotic. There are even so-called settlement leaders, who pretend to deplore the violence of the Hilltop Youth, who subsequently distinguished themslves by stealing part of the Palestinian olive crop. No less an authority than a former chief rabbi of Israel ruled that olives grown in "the Land of Israel" belong to the Jews. It must be stated clearly: There has been no change whatsoever in the beliefs and actions of the Jewish settlers in the Palestinian territories. The youngsters of today are behaving exactly the same way that their parents behaved, when they settled Sebastia in defiance of the Israeli government and the Supreme Court. Despite the danger in which they live, the settlers are presently riding a triumphant wave of victory. Their presence effectively prevents the redivision of the land into two separate states. Their settlements in between Ramalla, Nablus, and Jenin, their suburbs and neighborhoods in and around Hebron and Bethlehem, their bypass roads and fortifications, entangle Israelis and Palestinians in a strangulating hug of death.

Their enterprise is the biggest obstacle to an agreement based on territorial compromise and division of the land. Their success must be acknowledged, but it is a vivid illustration of the term "Pyrrhic victory." The Hebrew version is no less apt: "Another victory like that and we are finished!"

At the same time, it must be acknowledged that the West Bank and Gaza are not the only parts of the land between the Jordan River and the Mediterranean where Jews and Arabs live side by side. The next section, which tells the story of an Israeli Arab, shows that the Israeli–Palestinian entanglement is also a reality within the borders of the state of Israel.

Sayed Kashu, the Invisible Man

For most of his twenty-six years, Sayed Kashu has tried to be inconspicuous. He doesn't travel on buses; only rarely hails a taxi; doesn't visit the cinema, theater, or concert hall; avoids speaking Arabic in public; and never initiates a conversation with a stranger. He has worked on disguising his appearance and his accent. His main purpose in life is to blend into the background, for Sayed is that contradiction in terms, an "Israeli Palestinian" or a "Palestinian Israeli," one of the million Palestinian Arabs who are Israeli citizens. Standing out in the crowd can lead to hurt feelings, humiliation, or worse.

Not all Israeli Arabs are as sensitive as Sayed, and most of them don't go to such great lengths to disguise their identity, but there is a distinct feeling of alienation, particularly among the young members of the community. This perception has become more acute since the recent eruption of violence between Israel and the Palestinians. Sayed spells it out bleakly.

"Before the war broke out, I was convinced that there was going to be peace. There was Oslo. It was clear to me that the Palestinians would

have their own state and that our task was to seek full equality as citizens in Israel. Suddenly it all blew up in my face. There is no halfway position anymore: Either you are a committed Zionist, or you are an enemy, a fifth column that wants to throw the Jews into the sea. I reject such a division. I'm not a Zionist, but I certainly don't want to massacre the Jews."

He deliberately says "war," rather than the generally used term *Intifada*.

Sayed Kashu

"With F-16 attack aircraft, tanks, and missile-firing helicopters, it is a war," he insists. "Such weapons were not deployed in the Intifada."

A talented writer of Hebrew, with a brutally direct style, Sayed Kashu saw his writing as a way to explain his position directly to his fellow Jewish citizens, man to man. His journalism was a means to this end, and he was glad to be writing in Hebrew. Among his best pieces is a savagely funny satire, "The Lexicon of the Good Arab." In it he portrays every Israeli's favorite Arab: the regular guy who sweeps your streets, builds your homes, tends your gardens, receives your slap on the back, asks you how you are in Arabic slang, and serves you delicious hummus with olive oil, accompanied by thick, sweet, black coffee with cardamom. The article was brilliantly crafted to make Israeli Jewish liberals squirm with embarrassment.

Sayed has just published his first book, *Arabs Dancing*, a fictionalized memoir of his life in Tira, a small town some fifteen miles northeast of Tel Aviv, and his subsequent experiences in Jerusalem, first in a Jewish boarding school and later at Hebrew University and in the suburb of Beit Safafa. The fictional narrator of *Arabs Dancing* attends boarding school, fails his matriculation, and goes on to work in a bar in Jerusalem's Old City while pursuing halfhearted part-time studies at the university.

The real-life Sayed is rather different. He took his studies seriously, although he didn't complete his degree. After a short flirtation with photography, he found his milieu as a journalist and writer. He worked for the local Jerusalem paper, *Kol Ha'ir* (All the Town), for five years, before transferring to its Tel Aviv counterpart, *Ha'ir* (The Town), where he has a regular weekly column and also writes features and television criticism.

His appearance is unremarkable: regular features, an open friendly face, close-cropped hair, sideburns, a stocky physique. He lives with his wife, Najat, and his three-year-old daughter, Na'i, in Beit Safafa, an Arab village-neighborhood of Jerusalem that was split down the middle until 1967—one half was in Israel, the other in Jordan. The Kashu family lives in what was formerly the Jordanian half. Na'i is a rosy-faced, plump, sweet toddler; Najat, tall, pretty, very modern, dressed in slacks and a sweater, makes no attempt whatsoever to disguise her identity. A social worker and doctoral student, also from Tira, she is manifestly at home in Jerusalem, talking Arabic freely in public, even as the security guard is inspecting her at the entrance to Jerusalem's largest shopping mall.

"It drives me crazy," says Sayed with an embarrassed smile. "She has none of my complexes. She doesn't agree with any of my views. She thinks I am irrelevant."

He humorously adopts the word *irrelevant*, used by Israeli prime minister Sharon to describe Palestinian leader Yasser Arafat. Apart from his literary talent, Sayed's sense of humor is the most noticeable thing about him. It permeates his conversation and his writing. Until September 2000, he knew exactly what he was doing, but now he isn't sure about his future path. He finds it difficult to write humorously in the current tragic situation, although he continues to do so. For some time now, he has been uncertain about his audience. His next book, he says, might be in Arabic.

In *Arabs Dancing* and in conversation, Sayed is harshly critical of the traditional rural Arab society in which he grew up, reserving his sharpest barbs for the school and its teaching methods. His picture of his teachers, with their verbal abuse and brutal physical punishments, is horrifying, but Sayed insists that he "didn't tell the half of it." Despite this, he describes his childhood in Tira as *sababa*, an Arabic word meaning "great fun." Initially, he didn't really know about anything outside the village, he explains, except that there was a nearby town called Kfar Sava, which was different and where you could get pizza. If he had never left Tira, he suggests, he would have been a happy man.

The Tira in which Sayed grew up was a village. Both his parents worked away from home, leaving him and his four brothers in the care of their grandmother. Illiterate but sharply intelligent, strong and proud, she is the most sympathetic character in his book and clearly had an enormous influence on his life. She lost her husband in the fighting between the Jews and Arabs in 1948. Left to bring up her children alone, she labored long and hard in the orchards and vegetable fields to put Sayed's father, Darwish, through school and university.

Sayed's depictions of his life with his grandmother are infused with warmth and love. When he is very young, he creeps into her bed at night, where she reassures him about his fears of the dark, his terror of thieves and monsters. Later he visits the village cemetery with her and goes on an expedition to the Dead Sea with her and her friend. They tell stories of the old days: how, during World War I, the young men would shoot themselves in the hand to avoid mobilization into the Turkish army, how his grandmother could ride a horse faster than any of the men, how young couples would exchange glances by the village well and meet secretly in the wheat fields. Most daring of all: how his grandfather dressed his grandmother in a tarboosh and male clothes and took her to the theater in Jaffa.

During his studies at the Hebrew University of Jerusalem, Sayed's father, Darwish, a political activist, soon found himself in trouble, spending nearly three years in administrative detention, under the same British Mandate law used against Abdulla Abu-Hadid and Hani Essawi. Darwish was a member of Rakah, a political alliance of communists and Arab nationalists, but he was suspected of belonging to the Popular Front for the Liberation of Palestine, a movement engaged in armed resistance to the Jewish state.

As he grew older, Sayed witnessed strikes, protests, and demonstrations. He remembers youngsters in the house, making flags and banners. He recalls his mother and grandmother worrying about his father. He was aware that there were problems, but he didn't really understand what it was all about.

"I knew there was some kind of a struggle going on," he relates. "I knew we were the good guys, but I didn't know whom we were against."

When he was in the fourth grade, his class exchanged visits with a class from a Jewish school in Kfar Sava, and he took his Jewish guest home. His mother prepared special dishes of *maklouba*, a sort of chicken risotto, and meat baked in *tehina*, sesame paste. The whole village went outside to welcome the Jewish children. Sayed's Jewish guest, Nadav Epstein, was a pleasant boy, although communication was limited by language. It took him some time to learn to pronounce "Epstein." Two weeks later, the Tira class went to Kfar Sava for a return visit. Sayed was amazed by the fact that a Jewish boy and girl, walking arm-in-arm in the school yard, were not even reprimanded—let alone beaten, as might be expected.

He was also offended: First, Nadav Epstein had been sent to Tira a second time by mistake; second, the Arab children were not invited to the Jewish homes but given lunch in the school. He was, however, compensated by the fact that, back in Tira, Nadav had burst into tears and refused to go to any house other than that of the Kashu family. Sayed was rushed back home in the headmaster's car to calm him down.

His contacts with Jews were limited to the school visits and to another occasion when his father invited a fellow employee home for dinner, but this changed dramatically when Sayed was selected for studies at an elite high school in Jerusalem. The School for Science and Arts aimed to gather together the most talented students from all over Israel. In the tenth grade there were two Arabs: Sayed and a girl from the western Galilee village of Kafr Yassif. Like all Israeli Arabs, Sayed had studied Hebrew in elementary and junior high school, but he had never read a Hebrew book or newspaper, nor had he been able to understand Hebrew television programs, unless they had Arabic subtitles. Suddenly he found himself in an entirely new world, where everything was unfamiliar: the language, the clothes, the food, and the music.

"I had never even heard of the Beatles," he confesses, "let alone classical music or jazz."

Today, Arabs attending the school undergo special preparatory courses to prepare them for their new environment, but Sayed was not so lucky. In his book, he calls the chapter about his first days at the school "The Most Difficult Week of My Life." He was utterly miserable, he recalls. After his first trip back home, he wanted to remain there, and only the shame of being a failure prompted his to return to Jerusalem. Despite his nationalist sentiments, his father was delighted with his son's selection for the elite school. Like any father anywhere, he wanted the best for his son, and the School for Science and Arts was "the best." He wasn't about to let his son miss this chance to get ahead in life.

Much of his book is pure fiction, says Sayed, but the description of his humiliating first journey home from Jerusalem was drawn from life. Some Jewish kids get on the bus, and he politely explains where he is from. They respond with mockery, imitating his accent and mispronouncing the name of his village. When the bus passes Ben-Gurion Airport, he is ordered off by a military police officer and permitted to rejoin the other passengers only when the bus leaves the airport area. He feels deeply insulted—all the more so as, when he finally arrives home, his father doesn't understand why he is making such a fuss.

Looking back today, is he glad he remained at the school?

He cannot answer the question. He doesn't know. Of course it was far superior to the Tira school. There was no corporal punishment or verbal abuse. You didn't even have to ask for permission to go to the toilet. There was a wonderful atmosphere of free inquiry, a good library, both for books and (another novelty for Sayed) for compact discs. He spent hours in the library, abandoning the physics and math that got him into the school and getting acquainted with Western culture, particularly literature and music.

"It was a good school, but it was a Zionist establishment," he emphasizes. "We learned Zionist history; we celebrated the Jewish festivals; we were not given time off for our Muslim holidays."

It wasn't until his second year that he made really good friends among the Jewish students, friends he still has today, but he also discovered the "red lines." He had a Jewish girlfriend, and that was "a nightmare" when her mother found out about it. He also became alienated from his family and his friends back in Tira. He no longer liked the Arab music to which they listened, preferring to listen to CDs of classical music and jazz on his Walkman. When his father gave him a lift to the bus stop in Kfar Sava, he asked him to turn down the volume of the Arab music on the car radio.

"I didn't live in two worlds. I adopted the Jewish world. I became ashamed of my Arab identity. I changed my clothes and my hairstyle. I did everything I could to become an 'ordinary Israeli.' When a fellow student told me that I didn't look 'all that much like an Arab,' I didn't see it as racist prejudice. I accepted it as a compliment."

Today he is frustrated that he is not more connected with the Arab world. He has read the classical Arabic literature but has little knowledge of the latest books being published in Cairo or Baghdad. Only one bookshop in Israel, in Haifa, sells modern Arabic books. Even in Jerusalem, in the Old City, they stock mainly textbooks.

When Ariel Sharon's visit to the Temple Mount in Jerusalem ignited the current conflict between Israelis and Palestinians, there were also violent clashes between Jews and Arabs inside Israel. After some prevarication, the government was forced to establish a State Commission of Inquiry to look into the killing of thirteen Arabs by the police. At the time of writing, the commission has not presented its conclusions. Sayed reported on the confrontation from the Israeli Arab town of Umm al-Fahm, where the clashes were extremely violent.

None of his customary mordant humor, sharp satire, or trenchant wit is evident in this report, which is spewed out with a rage that recalls the young James Baldwin. He took the title of a popular Israeli song for his scathing account, *Ain Li Eretz Aheret* (I Don't Have Another Country).

> It is so depressing to be an Arab. Give thanks to God that you are not one. This problem is much deeper than the shallow analyses that blame religion, or Sharon, or local Arab community leaders. It is a deep feeling of rejection, of anguish that affects everyone. This is a new generation that Israel should start understanding.

There follows a dramatic description of his trip from Jerusalem to Umm al-Fahm. Everybody tells him that Israel Radio reported the blockading of the main road outside the town long before it happened. It was only later that, following an internal protest march, some youngsters marched down to the main road, where they were met by the police. The police used truncheons, and the violence quickly escalated to the stage of shooting. Live ammunition was used from the start, claimed Sayed's informants, and more than sixty people, including children, were wounded.

There are different explanations concerning what started the protest. Some say it was the events on Temple Mount, others say it was the photograph of a young boy, lying dead in his father's arms in Gaza, shown repeatedly on television. Others cite poverty, unemployment, or discrimination. Above all, suggests Sayed, there was a general feeling of being in a dead end that left no alternative except to fight. It was all the worse because it was "our" state and "our" government that, apart from bombastic announcements, had done so little to look after the interests of the Arab community.

> We have accepted the expulsion of our people and the establishment of Jewish towns and villages on land that was ours, but we have reached breaking point. More than anything else it is the feeling that our state is telling us, a million Arab citizens: you are a pest, an irritation, you should get out. Every police bullet, fired at civilians, reinforces the message: you are not really citizens, you don't belong here, you are our enemies, you hate us, you are a hindrance to our Jewish state.

Sayed divides the Jewish citizens of Israel into two: One half is glad that the "real face of the Arabs" has been exposed and advocates hitting "them" with all available means; the other half is horrified by the way the "formerly loyal" Arabs are behaving.

"The first group sees us as wild animals," he writes, "the second sees us as pet animals, who are misbehaving. The first group sees us as enemies, the second as inferiors."

> Every Arab citizen knows that he can only gain attention by blocking main roads. The demonstrations are part of a battle for full equal citizenship. The Israeli Arabs are not fighting for control of Galilee, as some Jews claim, but crying out for freedom and equality. They don't want to destroy Israel, they don't want to live somewhere else, they want to live in their country, the State of Israel. What most infuriates the Arabs of Israel is that they are expected to be grateful to a state, where Jewish villages are established all the time on formerly Arab land, while the Arab villages are becoming intolerably overcrowded.

Sayed also protests at the Israeli media descriptions of Arab protesters as "masked," which immediately conjures up visions of armed guerrilla fighters. In fact, the demonstrators in question are schoolboys who have covered their faces with their shirts or headscarves, because they know that hundreds of them will subsequently be identified on the police video films and arrested.

Sayed quotes Israeli Jews as demanding to know why Israel's Arabs don't go and live in one of the twenty-two Arab states, if it is so bad for them in Israel, and he replies that none of the twenty-two states cares about the Palestinians. He concludes:

> It may be difficult for the Jews to understand this, but the Palestinians do not have another country. The Arabs in Israel have nowhere to go. The Arabs in Israel know very well what a refugee is, and all of them prefer to die from the bullets of [Northern District Police Commander] Alec Ron, than to leave their homes. Despite everything, we have no other country.

The reaction was not long in coming. Letters poured into the editorial offices of *Kol Ha'ir*. Over the phone, the threats were so specific that Sayed took his wife and daughter back to Tira for two weeks. The phone calls have stopped, but the letters are still coming in. He is genuinely worried about his future, unsure about what he wants to do or where he wants to live. He takes threats of "transferring" the Israeli Arabs out of Israel seriously. Whether it will take the form of expulsion, or of redrawing the map to include Tira in a Palestinian state, is not clear to him.

"I tell myself that it couldn't happen on such a large scale," he says, "but then I hear some Israeli politicians saying that, if transfer is wrong, Zionism is wrong. I cannot contradict that."

He would consider living in Western Europe or North America—anywhere his wife and daughter would be out of danger—but how would he earn a living? He has an Israeli passport, and his craft is writing in Hebrew. He would not consider living in another Arab country: Lebanon is unthinkable; Egypt, worse. If a Palestinian state were to be established, he would think about it. Despite his Israeli background, he feels that he has much more in common with a Palestinian of the same age in Ramalla or Nablus than with his Jewish fellow citizens. On the other hand, he is deeply disappointed in the way the Palestinians have been running their affairs.

"At least 90 percent of the current uprising is against the Palestinian Authority. Many of us hoped the Palestinians would create a democratic regime that would be different from the other Arab countries. Yasser Arafat was a symbol for us. We loved him and hung his picture in our rooms, but he came with a bunch of dishonest politicians who only wanted to make money. The police are corrupt; the courts are primitive; the ministers are robbing the public left and right."

Sayed does not attribute the outbreak of violence to the failure of the negotiations at Camp David. If an agreement had been reached, it would not have lasted. The uprising would only have been delayed. He is skeptical about a two-state solution. A single state for Arabs and Jews could have been the best idea, he suggests, but he doesn't see it happening. The Israeli Jews are not ready for a fair sharing of resources. They want a Jewish state without the "demographic threat," which really means without Arabs. On the Arab side, Muslim extremism is growing.

In his book, Sayed paints a remarkable portrait of his friend "Adel," who starts out as a communist but becomes a religious Muslim. Adel believes that Islam will conquer the world. The Mahdi, the Muslim leader, will come and freeze the atmosphere, and all the modern (Western) technology will seize up. The final battle will be fought with swords, and the Muslims will triumph over Israel and America. Adel is a composite figure, explains the author, made up of several of his friends who have become newly observant Muslims. They really think like that.

Sayed shares the feeling of despair that has prompted many of his friends to adopt extremist Islam, but he finds that he cannot accept it. The entire movement is a regression, he insists. All the images are a thousand years old: tents, campfires, horses, camels, swords. It's not realistic.

Sayed sharply rejects a suggestion that his rational perceptions were forged as a result of his attending the Jewish boarding school. True, the school was good in many ways. It encouraged him to think freely, but he reached his own conclusions in his own way. He does not admire Israel, he declares. The last thing he wants is a state with compulsory military service. Based as it is on power, Israel is in no way a model for him, he says testily, but he is incapable of sustained anger.

"France, perhaps—that could be a model," he says with a smile.

He is deeply pessimistic about the future and doesn't see how Israel and the Palestinians are going to emerge from the current mess. His family back in Tira has also lost hope, but they are in "a sort of ghetto." They don't come up against the Israeli reality as much as he does, and consequently they are less aware of the problems and less troubled. As a journalist, it is his job to chronicle the situation, which means he is forced to face the reality all the time.

Sayed's father liked *Arabs Dancing* and is very proud of it, but publication has brought unwelcome fame to the shy author, who devotes so much time and effort to being inconspicuous. He has been the subject of a cover story in the weekend magazine of *Yediot Aharonot*, Israel's best-selling newspaper, and has appeared on all the most important television talk shows. The publicity has generated reactions. In a recent debate on ynet, the website of *Yediot Aharonot*, there have been angry reactions from Arabs as well as Jews.

"You have a cheek," wrote an Arab from his hometown. "Tira belongs to all of us. You are a snob, who thinks he is superior, just because he wrote a book!"

"How do you explain the fact that all Arabs are rapists and murderers?" inquired a Jewish reader. Other comments were so violently anti-Arab that the editor of ynet deleted them.

The father of the narrator in *Arabs Dancing* angrily suggests that the best course for the Palestinians is to obtain Israeli identity cards and live under Israeli administration.

> It is better to be seventh grade citizens in the Zionist state, than first class citizens in an Arab state; better to be slaves of the enemy than slaves of your own people. We should blow up the Aksa Mosque and plow it under. That will be the revenge of the Palestinians against the other Arabs and Muslims who remain silent while we suffer. If the other Arab countries are so concerned about al-Aksa and Jerusalem, let them come and defend them.

His own father has never made such a suggestion, admits Sayed. He has put some of his own thoughts into the fictional father's mouth.

"In moments of anger, extreme thoughts do enter my mind," he confesses quietly, "but I don't really want to blow up anything."

Sayed's anger is not directed only against Israel. He is frustrated with the Arab world, which he sees as backward and corrupt. He wants to see the Arabs develop a democratic, progressive, fair, and equal society. If blowing up the Aksa Mosque would make that happen, he is not sure he would oppose the idea.

It should be stressed that Sayed is not a typical Arab citizen of Israel. He is far more complex and sensitive than most of his fellows. Other Israeli Arabs are doing their best to achieve something concrete in the current Israeli reality. In his book, Sayed depicts his fictional father as believing that, as a result of attending an elite school, his son will build the first Arab atomic bomb. This is his humorous way of pointing out that no Israeli Arabs are allowed near any science project that might have security implications.

Ibrahim Amer, a brilliant young Arab chemist from Kafr Kassem, is a case in point. Despite his talent, he has found his academic career blocked, failing to gain tenure at either Ben-Gurion University or Tel Aviv University. His response has been to launch an extremely successful program of science education in the country's Arab schools, starting with the most backward Bedouin schools in the Negev desert.

One of the schools where Amer's program has been taken up enthusiastically is the Arab Comprehensive High School in Ramle. This school is another example where the initiative of an Israeli Arab has had a positive impact. Nasser Abu-Safi took over a school where the illiteracy rate was high and where rivalry between local Arab families was fomenting gang warfare inside the school. He has turned it around, and it is fast becoming one of the better schools in the area, offering courses in physics, computers, business administration, and special classes for children with special needs. There are numerous examples of Arabs who have attained success, such as that of Dr. Muhammad Id, the only surgeon in Israel capable of performing a liver transplant. And, of course, there are the Arab members of the Knesset, Israeli's parliament, and the mayors of Arab towns.

When all is said and done, Israel, apart from the occupied territories, is a democracy, where the Arab citizens, as well as the Jewish, can advance by their own efforts. Like any democracy, it works on the basis of pressure groups. The reason that the Arab towns and villages have been neglected—and they have been badly neglected—is not racism. It is partly because Israel was founded to advance the interests of the Jews— Zionism is a sort of national affirmative action—but it is also because the Arab members of the Knesset have not managed to get their act together. There are ten of them, and if their public was not so riven by petty rivalries, they could have almost double that number. In Israel's system of proportional representation and coalition government, the Arabs can certainly attain a great deal more. They must learn to work together, to demand what is rightly theirs.

Adel Ka'anan is an interesting example of an Israeli Arab who *has* demanded his rights. Ka'anan wants to live in the Jewish village of Katzir, situated in the coastal plain, very near Umm al-Fahm. Most Israeli Arabs prefer to live in their own communities, but Ka'anan, a male nurse, decided that he preferred the superior services and education for his children available in a Jewish community. Katzir is a village of the type known in Israel as a "community settlement," which means it has a committee that determines residency. This committee has consistently denied the Ka'anan family the right to build a home there. Ka'anan took his problem to Israel's Supreme Court. After years of prevarication, the court ruled in Ka'anan's favor and ordered the Katzir committee to permit him to build a house.

The ruling created a storm, with residents of Katzir explaining that the presence of the Ka'anan family would "alter the character of the village." Shortly after the court's ruling, some right-wing Knesset members attempted to introduce legislation that would bypass the court and make excluding the Ka'anans from Katzir legal. Their attempt, which was even supported briefly by the government, was eventually shelved, but the story does not reflect much credit on either the government or the upper-middle-class Israelis of Katzir, who should, in theory, be among the most enlightened and liberal of Israel's Jewish citizens.

The situation of Israeli Arabs has become immeasurably more difficult in the current conflict. A particularly poignant example has been provided by IDF major Ashraf Mazariv of the Bedouin village of Zarzir in Galilee. The twenty-five-year-old officer was killed early in 2002, in a shoot-out with Palestinian gunmen in the Gaza strip. At Mazariv's funeral, the mayor of Zarzir, Hassan Hayeb, told IDF chief of staff Shaul Mofaz, "We don't want revenge for the attack; we want peace. Don't go to war."

Two days later, Bedouin troops who had been under Mazariv's command were dispatched to escort bulldozers that demolished dozens of homes in Rafah, an Arab town in the Gaza strip. The homes, announced the army spokesman, had "provided cover for the terrorists who killed Mazariv."

After the raid, Ashraf's brother, Asri Mazariv, was quoted in a newspaper article: "We kill, we liquidate people, but does anyone think that solves anything? The opposite; it only makes the other side stronger. When you leave a Palestinian family without a home, its desire to attack us becomes greater."

No less dramatic is the story of Rami Mahmeed, a seventeen-year-old carpenter from Umm al-Fahm, Israel's second-largest Arab town, after Nazareth.

One evening in September 2002, when waiting for a bus, he saw a West Bank resident who aroused his suspicion. Rami asked the man if he could borrow his mobile phone. He went some distance away and phoned the police, telling them to come quickly. Then he returned the mobile phone to its owner and waited. When the police arrived, the West Banker detonated his explosive belt. One policeman was killed, and Rami was seriously wounded, but the bomber's plan to get on a bus and blow himself up was foiled. Many lives were saved, and Rami Mahmeed was hailed as a hero—eventually.

In fact, for four days, the badly injured Israeli Arab citizen was chained to his bed in the hospital, suspected of being an accomplice to the bomber. While security agents grilled him, several police officers cursed and insulted his worried parents. In due course, the security men cleared Rami, and the police commended his bravery and responsibility. Now, however, the hero to the Jews is a villain to some of his fellow Arabs. Even many who do not support suicide bombings feel that Rami was unnecessarily helpful to "the Jews." His father, Mahmoud Mahmeed, turned out to be one of those rare cases, an Arab whose first wife was Jewish, and all sorts of rumors circulated in Umm al-Fahm concerning the family's alleged links with the police. In fact, Mahmoud was furious at the behavior of the police.

"When he was a suspect, they guarded him like bin Laden," says Mahmoud sarcastically. "Once they found he had told the truth, they left him alone. Anyone could get in: an Arab from Umm al-Fahm with a present, or an Arab from the territories with a knife!"

The case of Rami Mahmeed encapsulates the dilemma of the Israeli Arabs. They represent another part of the Israeli–Palestinian jigsaw puzzle. Distrusted and discriminated against by many of their Jewish fellow citizens, despised and suspected by their fellow Palestinians in the West Bank and Gaza, their situation is far from easy. As the tension mounts, their predicament becomes ever more complex. The irony is that, for many years, the Israeli Arabs were seen as a possible future "bridge" between Israel and its neighbors.

"We don't want to be a bridge," said Azmi Bishara, an Arab Knesset member, recently. "We don't want people walking all over us, which is the main function of a bridge."

Bishara's cynical remark eloquently illustrates a certain loss of innocence in the relationship between Palestinian Israelis and well-intentioned Jewish Israelis. Despite all the problems, a sort of romance existed between those two groups. There was even a political alliance—albeit rarely openly acknowledged. Today, both sides are far more hard-nosed about their relationship. Any solution to the Israeli–Palestinian riddle will have to take into account Azmi Bishara, Adel Ka'anan, Asri Mazariv, Rami Mahmeed, and Sayed Kashu. They aren't going anywhere, and they are becoming increasingly visible.

Menahem Froman, the Maverick Settler

If a novelist were to create a personality like Menahem Froman, he would be told by his publisher that he was being overly imaginative. One can see the editor shaking his or her head and pronouncing: "Sorry, he lacks credibility; he's just not a convincing character."

A Jewish settler in the occupied territories, on friendly terms with his Arab neighbors, Froman is also a passionate Zionist who thinks that the Jews should give up the conventional concept of national sovereignty. A founding member of the militant religious-nationalist Gush Emunim movement, he favors a Palestinian Arab state in all of Palestine. A rabbi, whose sons don't always wear the head covering regarded as mandatory by all religious Jews, he is strongly opposed to religious legislation. A liberal humanist in every sense of the word, he is striving to bring religion to center stage in the Israeli–Palestinian confrontation.

He is on excellent terms with Israeli prime minister Ariel Sharon, Palestinian Authority chairman Yasser Arafat, Egyptian president Hosni Mubarak, Archbishop of Canterbury George Carey, and Sheikh Muhammed Sayed Tantawi of Cairo's Al-Azhar Islamic College.

Twelve years ago, Froman was one of the first Israelis to meet openly with the late Faisal Husseini, then the leading PLO figure in Jerusalem.

He was going well beyond the Israeli consensus of the time, possibly even breaking the law. His fellow West Bank settlers were outraged and held protest demonstrations against his "treachery." Two of those demonstrating against Froman were his own children.

Born fifty-six years ago in the moshav cooperative of Kfar Hassidim, near Haifa, to parents who immigrated from Poland, Menahem Froman served in the IDF paratroops before going on to philosophy studies at Hebrew University. He received his *smiha* rabbinical qualification at Jerusalem's Mercaz Harav yeshiva, the breeding ground of the Jewish settlement movement in the West Bank and Gaza. When he was invited to become the rabbi of Tekoa, his wife, Hadass, became head of the kindergarten, where religious and nonobservant children learn side by side.

On one occasion, a visiting supervisor for religious education objected to the fact that some of the boys in the kindergarten were not wearing skullcaps, but Hadass took her stand on religious freedom. Jewish tradition must be respected, she allowed, but without compulsion. In fact, two of the Froman children were among those without head covering, "because they didn't want to wear them."

To visit Froman's home in the Jewish settlement of Tekoa, southeast of Bethlehem, I travel for the first time in many months via the "tunnels road." Several shooting incidents have occurred on this road, which connects Jerusalem directly with the settlements of the Etzion Bloc to the south. As in my visit to Psagot to meet with Meira Dolev, I find the bus crammed with soldiers. When the bus emerges from the tunnels, which have been dug through the Judaean hills to shorten the distance to the settlements south of Jerusalem, the road is protected by a continuous concrete wall. To reach Tekoa, however, the bus travels eastward through the Judaean desert, leaving the protection of the wall and winding through the dun-colored Palestinian villages. It is deceptively peaceful and pastoral. (Three weeks after my visit, two Israelis were killed in a drive-by shooting on the road between Tekoa and the nearby settlement of Nokdim.)

Tekoa, with its red-roofed houses and green lawns, is manifestly different from the dusty Arab villages nearby. The ancient hill fortress of Herodium, built by Herod the Great some two millennia ago, looms over the village. In a different era, before violence became so prevalent in the West Bank, we used to visit the ancient ruins and explore the caves that honeycomb the fortress carved out of the bulbous-shaped hill.

Froman, whose long hair and beard have turned white in the years since we first met, is leading midday prayers in the *beit midrash* (house of study). In Tekoa, as in many of the settlements, there are Yeshivot Hesder colleges, where Orthodox youngsters sandwich their military service between periods of religious study. Like many such institutions, the beit midrash has a shabby ambience, but the prayers are loud and fervent, accompanied by the vigorous traditional swaying of the body. Young men arrive all the time, and—a nod to modernity—they recharge their cell phones, plugging them into sockets located among the heavy tomes of Talmud (biblical commentary) and Midrash (sermons) before joining in the worship.

The prayers over, I am invited to lunch in the communal dining room nearby, during which Froman gives a *shiur* (religious lesson). He expounds a dispute between two rabbis in the Talmud over the question of whether one should devote all one's life to study, or whether earning a living by the sweat of one's brow is also important. Some rabbis threw students out of class, he notes, and ordered them to go and work. The lesson is conducted in high good humor, with lots of joking back and forth.

After the meal, we walk to his home, where Yehuda Lev Arye, his eight-year-old son, is waiting.

"My children were tardy about settling down and marrying," he remarks with a smile, "so we made our own 'grandchild.' After that, of course, we got some real grandchildren."

Interrupted by the youngster and by frequent phone calls, we resume our discussion of a dozen years previously. At that time, Froman explained to me his view that the campaign of the Left in Israel against the settlement project in Judaea and Samaria (the West Bank) was a campaign against Zionism itself. The settlers were genuinely appalled to be criticized by the Left, he insisted, because they were continuing in the tradition of settlement of the land, originally carried out by the kibbutzim and moshavim. This always involved injustice to the Arabs of Palestine, noted Froman, but more Arabs were driven off their land when Jews settled Galilee and the Jezreel plain in the 1920s and 1930s than when Jews settled in Judaea and Samaria in the 1970s and 1980s.

Nevertheless, the questioning of "the sacred cow of Zionism" was perfectly legitimate, said Froman. He had also asked himself whether Zionism could not be replaced with something better, whether Judaism could not be raised to a higher level. All over the world, a drive toward individualism was evident, and, although it was sometimes selfish and egotistical, it also had validity. He was not talking about internationalism, he emphasized, but about the withering away of the power of the state. He foresaw a new entity, which he called the "humane state," an improvement on the nation-state, which would permit greater cultural development for the individual and for society as a whole. Israelis and Palestinians, he said, could have parallel frameworks in a humane state in the whole area of Israel, the West Bank, and Gaza.

Our conversation took place in 1989, after the Palestine Liberation Organization had officially accepted a two-state solution. After many years during which the organization ostensibly supported "a secular state of Muslims, Christians, and Jews" instead of Israel, the PLO had come around to the concept of Israel and Palestine existing side by side. At that time, I suggested to Froman that, in espousing the humane state, he actually was putting the clock back. Now that the Palestinians had at last given up some of their dreams, why did he choose to repudiate them? His reply was unequivocal.

"No one need give up his dreams. Under my scheme, we have a complete Land of Israel, they have a complete Palestine: two flags, two anthems, two names, two capitals, two governments, two police forces, two judiciaries—all existing on the same territory: Palestine inside Israel; Israel in Palestine. The only thing that we both give up is a little of our national egos."

All human beings possess two conflicting aspirations, suggested Froman, to be free and to belong. These aspirations had to be balanced. He acknowledged that many Jews expressed their love of their land and people by hating the Arabs, and vice versa. In the humane state, only positive expressions of patriotism would be permitted.

Take Islam. It means submission. Some Muslims believe it means the submission of non-Muslims to the sword of Islam, but many believe it means the submission of all human beings to the will of Allah. Surely we should do all we can to encourage the second interpretation.

Froman conceded that he was asking a lot of the Palestinians in requiring them to bypass the normal trappings of sovereignty but maintained his ideas contained real advantages for them. He was suggesting a Palestinian president, anthem, flag, and nation, "tomorrow morning." Furthermore, they would be living in an advanced Western-style state. His proposed humane state would create a new international entity, a center of coexistence and tolerance in the spirit of the biblical prophets.

At the time, he strongly opposed partition of the Land of Israel into two separate states. He was sure that the Palestinians would not be satisfied with a state in the West Bank and Gaza. He was opposed to the transfer of populations, whether Arab or Jewish. The expulsion of the Arabs of Palestine was unthinkable, but so was the transfer of Jews out of Judaea and Samaria. The existence of two territorial states would encourage the negative tendencies of both peoples, he insisted.

Sitting in his house twelve years later, I challenge his previous thesis. I point out that I have come to visit him in an armored bus, along roads protected by concrete walls. Less than a year ago, two young Jewish boys from Tekoa, exploring a cave in the vicinity, were brutally murdered by Arab boys scarcely older than themselves. How can there be peace and coexistence in this reality? His reply is unequivocal.

"With superhuman effort. We have to strive continuously for it. One of the things that I have discovered is that age doesn't bring greater knowledge. You learn new things, but you forget other things that you used to know, so maybe it balances out. But perhaps experience brings understanding—or rather acceptance of a lack of understanding. The longer I live, the more I realize how little I understand."

As the rabbi of Tekoa, he is sometimes called on to reconcile a quarreling husband and wife, he notes. Sometimes he manages to achieve such resolution, but often it doesn't work out. The same rules that govern domestic quarrels apply to national disputes. It is true that the two Tekoa children were killed, and even more recently a woman was shot dead at the entrance to the village, but many Palestinians have also been killed. In the past eighteen months, they have suffered even more than the Jews. It is possible to request, demand, and pursue peace, but ultimately it is in the hands of God.

"We are commanded to try," he emphasizes. "We must continue the dialogue with the Palestinians, but it doesn't mean we'll succeed."

Less than two years ago, I point out, Israel and the Palestinians were on the verge of peace, but it didn't work out. Since then, there has been unprecedented violence. Surely now he must admit that there is no alternative to separation. Froman professes surprise.

"The idea that separation will being peace was the Oslo theory," he protests. "You have to admit that the partition model has turned out to be impractical. I never believed that it would work, and it didn't."

"It wasn't actually tried," I argue. "We talked about separation, but in fact we went on living among each other. If we had implemented genuine partition, it might have worked."

Froman insists that the Palestinians don't really want separation. He sees the whole question in an entirely different way. The Israeli–Palestinian problem is only part of the confrontation between the West and the Muslim world, he says.

"If Jewish settlement in the West Bank is the problem, why don't the Palestinians call their uprising 'the Settlements Intifada'?" he demands. "They call it the 'Aksa Intifada,' after the Aksa Mosque in Jerusalem."

The problem is one of honor and respect, he insists. When Europe was still comparatively primitive, the Muslims were the intellectual elite. It was the Muslims who preserved ancient Greek philosophy for the world. Furthermore, all the great medieval Jewish philosophers existed in an Islamic culture and wrote in Arabic. He rattles off the names: the Rambam, the Ramban, Yehuda Halevi, Ibn Gvirol, Saadia Gaon.

"Those great Jewish religious authorities existed in an Arab milieu," he says. "Islam is a great civilization, but today the West regards the Muslims as retarded, primitive, and pitiable! I genuinely respect Islamic and Arab religion and culture—that's why Yasser Arafat calls me his friend. I have spent hours in conversation with Arafat. He's an intensely religious man."

Froman has established a mixed religious–secular settlement at Tekoa, with observant and nonobservant Jews coexisting amicably side by side. He is certain that Israelis and Palestinians—Jews and Muslims—can similarly live together. He sees religious tradition as a bridge between ancient and modern. His mentor, Rabbi Kook, believed in coexistence between modernity and tradition. Osama bin Laden uses Western technology, he points out, but rejects Western values. Froman is certain that values such as freedom, democracy, and love can be reconciled with tradition. He thinks that the main reason the Palestinians and other Arabs dislike Israel is that the Jewish state has brought the West to the Middle East. The traditional Muslim Arab of Hebron is far more offended by the Tel Aviv beachfront, with its bikini-clad girls, than he is by Jewish settlements in the West Bank and Gaza, he insists.

On the other hand, Froman claims to know a leading resident of Hebron who wants Jews to stay there—although he would never say so publicly—to bring modernity to the town. The Palestinians, notes Froman, are by far the most modern of the Arabs. So the answer is to find a way of bringing modernity to the Palestinians and to the Arabs in general, without offending their sense of honor and tradition. It is important to stress that modernity doesn't mean just prosperity and technology, but modern concepts of human rights and human relations, the relationship between man and woman, citizens and the police, the juridical system, and that sort of thing. Freedom, equality, and healthy personal relationships can be reconciled with traditional Judaism and traditional Islam.

Israel can be a laboratory for this approach, he maintains. The West Bank settlements can be laboratories for different peoples living together. If this coexistence can be achieved, says Froman, other problems will fit into place. First you have to achieve peace, but then you need compromise and coexistence. This demands an enormous amount of hard work. It also requires humility.

Jerusalem is too big for either Israel or Palestine. It can be the religious and cultural capital of the world. It can be a pilot plant for coexistence. Why not raise it above national conflicts and make it an extraterritorial bridge between East and West? The United Nations can establish the headquarters of all its cultural organizations there.

Because he is convinced that religion is at the heart of the hostility in the region, Froman is devoting much of his time to interfaith meetings, the most recent of which took place in Alexandria at the beginning of 2002. Dr. George Carey, the archbishop of Canterbury, convened the meeting, with the full support of Egyptian president Hosni Mubarak. Froman helped to compose the manifesto that was signed by Carey, leader of the world's Anglicans; Sheikh Muhammed Sayed Tantawi, the head of Cairo's Al-Azhar Islamic College and Egypt's leading Muslim cleric; and Israeli chief rabbi Eliahu Bakshi-Doron. Part of the manifesto reads as follows:

> According to our faith, killing innocents in the name of God is a desecration of His Holy Name, and defames religion in the world. The violence

in the Holy Land is an evil that must be opposed by all persons of good faith. We seek to live together as neighbors, respecting the integrity of each other's historical and religious inheritance. We call upon all to oppose incitement, hatred and a misrepresentation of the other.

Other Israeli and Palestinian religious leaders—Jews, Muslims, and Christians—also signed the document in Alexandria on the same day that Israelis and Palestinians continued fighting each other. That day a Hamas gunman went on a shooting spree in the center of Jerusalem, killing an old man and wounding forty civilians, and the IDF raided a bomb factory in the Palestinian city of Nablus, killing four members of Hamas.

A plan for Froman to spend several weeks at Cairo's Al-Azhar to work with his Muslim colleagues on a detailed formula for peace did not come off, but he is pressing ahead with his interfaith dialogue. He continues to travel abroad and meet with Muslim and Christian leaders. Even after all that has happened, he continues to receive "warm greetings" from Yasser Arafat. Today, his primary aim is to secure "the religious acceptance of Israel in the Muslim world," which he thinks is even more important than a Muslim condemnation of terror. Froman rejects the generally accepted thesis that a religious dialogue depends on a political solution. On the contrary, he insists, the political dialogue will be insignificant if there is no religious reconciliation. Israel cannot be accepted in the Middle East unless there is an Islamic legitimization.

The settler rabbi likes to use the biblical story of Esau and Jacob to illustrate the possibility of Jewish–Arab reconciliation. After the dispute about their birthright, the two brothers meet many years later. They are full of fear and trepidation about the encounter, but, when they meet, they fall on each other's necks and embrace. There are differing interpretations of the story in the Talmud biblical commentary. Some rabbis have suggested that the reconciliation was insincere. Some have even suggested that Esau bit Jacob rather than kissed him. Others have suggested that Esau accepted Jacob only after he realized his brother's power. Froman favors the interpretation of Shimon Bar-Yochai, a teacher of the period of the Second Temple, whose house of study is thought to have been in Tekoa, where Froman now lives: "It is clear that Esau hates Jacob, but his love was aroused at that moment and he kissed Jacob with all his heart."

Froman interprets this to mean that, despite the bloodshed and destruction of the past hundred years, there can be a sincere reconciliation between Jew and Arab in the Promised Land.

While there is no reason to doubt Menahem Froman's sincerity, his ideas seem wildly impractical. The humane state is a marvelous vision, but its implementation is impossible to visualize. The idea of two separate frameworks existing side by side is "messianic" in the positive sense of the word, but what can it possibly mean in real terms?

Moreover, it has to be stressed that Froman is part of the settler enterprise, today the largest single obstacle to peace and reconciliation between Arabs and Israelis. As we have seen, it was the establishment of Tekoa in the 1970s that started Palestinians such as Abdulla Abu-Hadid on the path of violent resistance to the Israeli occupation of the territories. Furthermore, Froman's settler colleagues have stepped up their harassment of their Palestinian neighbors, although Froman joined other Israelis of goodwill in picking olives together with the Palestinian villagers in defiance of the settler thugs.

Despite these contradictions, it is an intriguing thought that the eccentric rabbi might have come up with the germ of an idea for solving the problem that he and his fellow settlers have considerably aggravated by their actions. Can a solution emerge from the very epicenter of the problem? In the final chapter of this book, a solution that has something in common with Menahem Froman's humane state is put forward.

Part III
TOMORROW

CHAPTER 7
THE IMPOSSIBLE SOLUTION
Partition

Of the four possible solutions to the Israeli–Palestinian problem, two can be dismissed out of hand: the expulsion of the Jews, resulting in a purely Arab Palestine, or the deportation of the Palestinians, leading to an exclusively Jewish Israel. Without considering the moral aspects of the so-called transfer, it can be stated with a fair measure of confidence that neither scenario will come to pass.

The diplomatic initiative in the summer of 2003, led by President Bush following the American victory in Iraq, was based on the principle of partition. Since 1937, when it was first put forward by the British, partition, dividing Palestine between the Jews and the Arabs, has increasingly been accepted as the most practical solution. Partition was an established fact between 1948 and 1967. It came very near to being ratified in a peace agreement after the Oslo Accords.

The idea was initially put forward by Reginald Coupland, a senior British civil servant and a member of the Royal Commission of Inquiry, chaired by Lord Peel, which was appointed by the British in the wake of the Arab Revolt of 1936. Coupland had served in India, and it is probable that his experience there prompted him to suggest separating the two warring communities in Palestine. It is worth noting that Britain initiated the partition schemes in Ireland, India, and Palestine, none of which has proved very successful. India and Pakistan have fought three wars since they were partitioned in 1947, and they continue to skirmish in Kashmir. Israel has been involved in three wars, two major campaigns, and a long series of armed conflicts since its establishment in 1948, based on the United Nations partition plan of the previous year. The Irish conflict still festers poisonously, more than eight decades after the six counties were separated from the Irish Republic. Partition is a logical and persuasive solution for

221

communal conflicts, but its record of success is hardly reassuring. In all fairness, however, it should be admitted that it is impossible to determine whether alternative models would have been any more successful.

As recorded in chapter 1, the 1947 UN Palestine partition plan was accepted by the Jews and rejected by the Palestinians and their Arab allies. In the subsequent fighting, the Jews succeeded in expanding the fourteen thousand square kilometers awarded them under the plan to some twenty-one thousand. In this area, they established their state and signed armistice agreements with the neighboring Arab nations. The Palestinian state was not established. In other words, an amended version of the UN partition plan worked for Israel—at least for nineteen years—but it didn't work for the Palestinians.

Since June 1967, numerous United Nations resolutions have called on Israel to withdraw from the territories it captured in exchange for peace. As we have seen, Israel withdrew from all of Sinai in the context of a peace treaty with Egypt. A similar solution for the Golan Heights, captured from Syria, has yet to be reached. With regard to the Palestinian territories, formerly held by Jordan and Egypt, the situation is more complicated.

Ever since the Six-Day War, a majority of Israelis have favored withdrawing from the West Bank and Gaza in return for peace. For several years, Israeli governments were opposed to the creation of an independent Palestinian state and hoped that the Kingdom of Jordan would be prepared to take back the West Bank and take over Gaza. By the time that King Hussein was ready to do this and agreed on a formula with Israel's foreign minister Shimon Peres in London in 1987, Israel had a coalition government that torpedoed it.

At the American-brokered Madrid Conference in 1991, the Palestinians were still represented in a Jordanian–Palestinian delegation. However, in the Oslo agreement two years later, Israel accepted the idea of a Palestinian state in the West Bank and Gaza, with mutually agreed changes in the 1967 borders, that is, the borders that existed on June 4, 1967, before the outbreak of the Six-Day War.

For their part, the Palestinians have also passed through several stages in their aims and aspirations. For several years, it was official Arab policy to deny the legitimacy of the Jewish state, and to advocate that all the Jews in Palestine should be driven into the sea, or at least returned to their "countries of origin." After 1967, when the PLO became the generally recognized representative of the Palestinians, it came to espouse a "secular state for Muslims, Christians, and Jews." However, the PLO's policy was also enshrined in the Palestine National Covenant, which stated that only "Jews who were living in Palestine before the start of the Zionist invasion will be considered Palestinians." In his speech before the UN General Assembly in 1974, Yasser Arafat stated that this "invasion" began in 1881. Despite this, the PLO gradually moved toward the concept of "two states for two peoples," albeit demanding that the borders correspond to the UN partition plan of 1947. Returning to those borders would mean that Israel would surrender some seven thousand square kilometers of land. In Oslo, however, the PLO officially accepted the existence of Israel in the 1967 borders.

The collapse of the Oslo process has been described earlier. Here let us examine the various current ideas for a solution based on partition. The official Palestinian position remains that Israel must withdraw to the 1967 borders, with only minor adjustments. The Israeli Labor Party has formally adopted the principle of the establishment of a Palestinian state in the West Bank and Gaza according to the Clinton Parameters. This would involve adjustments to the 1967 borders to facilitate the retention by Israel of "settlement blocs," in exchange for equivalent areas in Israel to be given to the Palestinians. Jerusalem would be functionally—but not physically—divided between the two peoples.

Most Israelis who favor an agreement more or less support this position. In recent months, however, as a result of the escalating violence of the past two years, many Israelis—possibly a majority—have despaired of negotiations with the Palestinians. They propose that Israel withdraw to the 1967 borders, except for blocs of settlements that would continue to be defended by the IDF. To this end, they support the construction of a border fence between Israel and the West Bank, like the one that already exists between Israel and the Gaza strip.

This seemingly pragmatic solution is complicated by the fact that the Sharon government, well aware of the popularity of a fortified barrier "to keep out the terrorists," actually started building such a fence. Sharon, who has an exact knowledge of the situation on the ground, is well aware that most of the supporters of the fence have only a very vague idea of the concrete meaning of "blocs of settlements." Consequently, the fence under construction appears to run along the 1967 borders; in fact, it is mostly situated to the east of the former boundary. It takes in many of the West Bank Jewish settlements, deprives the Palestinians of considerable amounts of land, separates hundreds of villagers from their fields, leaves many Palestinians in a "no-man's land" between it and the former border, and closes off Jerusalem from the West Bank. Estimates vary, but at least two dozen Palestinian villages will be adversely affected, and thousands of acres of land will be utilized for the construction. In addition to this, the fence notably fails to solve the problem of Jerusalem itself, where some two hundred thousand Palestinians live, partially entwined with double that number of Jews. In Jerusalem, the fence is termed "the Jerusalem envelope," and it is manifestly permeable, which surely makes it pointless.

This so-called separation fence has already prompted serious discussions among the Palestinian leaders, questioning whether it does not make a two-state solution impossible. Apart from any political or security considerations, the fence is an obscenely ugly construction of high walls—in some places twenty-five feet high—steel bars, ditches, earth ramps, concrete cubes, razor wire, and electronic devices that violates this tiny land. Even if this monstrosity were relocated along the 1967 border, it would prompt revulsion. The "unilateral fence" is the solution of despair. The fence's proponents claim that it will block direct shooting, hide Israeli activities from prying eyes, and afford a sense of security and protection. Critics have pointed out that shells and explosive devices can be lobbed over it, that it can be easily climbed, that the electronic devices can be vandalized, that it prevents observation of the Palestinian side and provides cover for ambushes. If the fence does manage to seal off the Israelis from terror—which is doubtful, to say the least—it will leave Israel as a pathetic ghetto state, cauterized from its neighbors, claustrophobically shut off between the sea and the wall.

It is difficult to persuade most Israelis that they have someone to talk to on the Palestinian side, and well nigh impossible to convince a majority of Palestinians that any Israeli government is prepared to negotiate in good faith. Despite this, people of goodwill on both sides, such as Ami Ayalon and Sari Nusseiba, have been making an effort. Sari Nusseiba, the president of Jerusalem's Al-Kuds University and the official Palestinian representative in Jerusalem, is a well-known intellectual and political moderate. Ami Ayalon was the commander of the Israel navy and later headed the Shin Bet security service. The two men have met and worked out a reasonable formula, based on two states for two peoples.

Their plan envisions that the border between the two states will be based on the 1967 lines, with territorial changes on a one-to-one basis. Jerusalem will be an open city and the capital of two states. No one will have sovereignty over the Holy Sites. Palestine will be the "Guardian of the Temple Mount"; Israel will be the "Guardian of the Western Wall." International compensation will be made for the Palestinian refugees, who will have Right of Return only to Palestine. The two states will recognize each other and declare an end to the conflict.

Observers have suggested that it will be very difficult for the Israelis to give up their claim to the Temple Mount, where the First and Second Temples once stood. For the Palestinians, the big concession is waiving their right to return to Haifa, Jaffa, and other towns and villages in what is now Israel. No doubt the observers are right on these two points, although the Israelis have permitted the Muslim authorities effectively to control the Temple Mount since 1967, but the major barrier is the existence of the Jewish settlements in the West Bank and Gaza. It is not just a matter of the settlements themselves but also of the network of roads, tunnels, and fortifications that link and defend them. No Israeli government has ever dared to face this problem head-on.

Maps have been drawn that permit Israel to retain the settlement blocs, but the problems become evident as soon as the mapmakers start to draw their lines. The 1967 borders are not exactly ideal. Add the settlement blocs, and they become surreal. The dovish religious Netivot Shalom movement has produced a map that envisions Israel taking over 7 percent of the territories. This would permit 75 percent of the settlers to continue living in their settlements within the new borders that this would give Israel. The Palestinians would be compensated by an extraterritorial link between the West Bank and Gaza. The actual map is a weird piece of cartography, producing a border unlike any that has ever existed between neighboring states anywhere in the world.

Yosef (Yossi) Alpher, formerly the director of Tel Aviv University's Jaffee Center for Strategic Studies, has probably spent as much time as anyone poring over maps of Israel and the territories. The American-born Alpher has produced a number of maps setting out the various border options, dealing with everything from security and water resources to the issue of demography. His key map for "moderate territorial compromise," published by the Jaffee Center, was first drawn in 1994. Although not as surreal as the Netivot Shalom map, it does indicate how tortuous a newly drawn border that takes in the settlement blocs would be.

(The precise details of the proposals that Ehud Barak brought to Camp David in the summer of 2000 have never been published. Although it is not certain that actual maps were on the table, it is fair to state that Barak's far-ranging proposals were along the lines of the Alpher "moderate territorial compromise" map.)

It can certainly be argued that the Jewish settlements have made it virtually impossible to separate Israel from the West Bank. In *Israel after Begin*, published in 1984, I wrote:

> Visiting the Jewish settlements in the West Bank with Matti Drobless, head of the World Zionist Organization settlement department, is an almost surrealistic experience. One can spend a whole day in the West Bank, without realizing that Arabs live there. Drobless points proudly to the red-roofed villas, set among the beautiful hills of Samaria, and says that the government has pre-empted any return of the area to foreign rule.

"He may be a little premature," I concluded. It was a reasonable conclusion in 1984. Partition still had the almost unanimous approval of Israeli doves, although Meron Benvenisti, a former deputy mayor of Jerusalem and an acute observer of the Israeli–Palestinian entanglement, argued even then that it was too late for separation. Today, nearly two decades later, there are many more settlements and settlers, and it is much more difficult to disentangle the West Bank from Israel.

In a recent study on territory in the West Bank, Israeli architect Eyal Weizman discusses what he calls the "Politics of Verticality." Developing a thesis originally put forward by Benvenisti, Weizman argues that the West Bank can no longer be viewed as a two-dimensional surface but has to be seen as a three-dimensional volume, "layered with strategic, religious, and political strata." The Jewish settlements in the West Bank are mostly situated on the hilltops above the Arab towns and villages, and they exercise effective control from above.

Moreover, under the terms of the Oslo Accords, Israel retains control of the water under the ground of the West Bank and the air above it. With regard to the water, a joint committee with an equal number of Israeli and Palestinian members makes all decisions by consensus, giving Israel an effective veto. The airspace above the West Bank is completely controlled by the Israel air force.

Weizman suggests that the system of bypass roads, bridges, and tunnels, linking the Jewish settlements to each other and to Israel, makes it almost impossible to detach the West Bank from Israel. There is also the question of the link between the West Bank and Gaza, which is supposed to include a road, a railroad, a power cable, and an oil pipeline.

Weizman's thesis, which has been sketched only briefly here, may not be correct in every detail, but it does demonstrate how complex the task of dividing the land has become. Furthermore, no Israeli government has yet dared to take on the settlers and their supporters, who are determined, unscrupulous, and fired by total conviction. The one Israeli leader who came near to confronting them, Yitzhak Rabin, paid for it with his life. It will take a very determined leader to follow Rabin's path and face the consequent incitement, threats, and real danger from these extremist elements. It has been suggested that Ariel Sharon might be another Rabin, but his record belies this. He has a long way to go before his views approximate those of the slain leader.

Although Sharon and Palestinian prime minister Mahmoud Abbas agreed to implement important moves when they attended a summit in the Jordanian town of Akaba under the chairmanship of President Bush in June 2003, enormous differences remain in their visions of the future. Sharon agreed to dismantle "unauthorized outposts," but he did not repudiate his frequently stated position that the vast majority of Jewish settlements in the West Bank and Gaza will remain in place. Abbas promised to find a way to stop Palestinian violence against Israeli targets, but he sees a Palestinian state, based on the 1967 borders, with all the settlements removed. Sharon believes that a united Jerusalem will be the capital of Israel forever; Abbas envisages East Jerusalem as the capital of Palestine. The two positions are notably farther apart than were the positions of the two sides at Camp David. It is therefore legitimate to suggest that partition has become the "impossible solution."

Let us be optimistic, however, and fly in the face of all precedents. Let us postulate that powerful American and international pressure on Israel and the Palestinians will somehow propel the sides toward a compromise.

Let us hypothesize that ingenious Israeli and Palestinian negotiators, utilizing the expertise and hard work of people such as Yossi Alpher, manage to hammer out the map of a new partition agreement. This map will be based on the principle of readjusted borders and land swaps, acceptable to the Palestinians, to permit the settlement blocs to remain in Israel. Even if this were to happen—and, let's face it, this is a gigantic "if"—an enormous amount of mutual confidence and trust between the Israelis and the Palestinians would be necessary for such tortuous lines to function as national borders. The degree of trust necessary for this would seem to make those borders superfluous. In other words, if Israelis and Palestinians can cooperate so effectively as to make even the Alpher border work, why have a border at all?

CHAPTER 8
THE IMPROBABLE SOLUTION
The State of Jerusalem

When you have eliminated the impossible, whatever remains, however improbable, must be the truth.

—Sherlock Holmes

Having reached the conclusion that the territory between the Mediterranean and the Jordan River must be shared but cannot be sensibly partitioned, we are left with only one alternative: Israeli–Palestinian coexistence in one nation. When it was put forward by Judah Magnes and his friends in the 1930s, it was called a "binational state." In modern parlance, we can describe it as a "multicultural nation." This is the improbable solution that remains after eliminating the impossible.

Perhaps the first thing that should be said about this proposal is that we Jews have been there before, because such an entity is similar to what existed here in the time of the Bible and the period of the Second Temple.

The latest theories of the archeologists and biblical scholars have been interpreted by some modern Israelis as "anti-Zionist." In questioning the Bible, it is averred, the scholars are undermining Israel's national epic. This is wrong: The consensus of most archaeologists and biblical scholars is that Israel originated in Canaan, the strip of land between the Mediterranean and the River Jordan. This consensus regards the stories of the patriarchs of the Bible and the accounts of Moses and Joshua as legends. The ancient Israelites did not originate in Ur of the Chaldees (Iraq), the purported home of Abraham. Nor did they "return" from Egypt under Moses and Joshua, as the Bible relates. The first Israelites were Canaanites, forced by superior forces—probably Egyptians—to flee to the desert fringes in the fourteenth and thirteenth centuries B.C.E., and starting to resettle in the hills of Galilee, Samaria, and Judaea around 1200 B.C.E. This narrative is more consistent with the Zionist idea than is the biblical story, which depicts the Israelites as nomadic interlopers and, later, as invaders.

The archaeological evidence supports the existence of an Israelite entity that evolved into a kingdom. King Saul may well have been a real person, suggests this modern consensus; David and Solomon most probably existed; the later kings of Israel and Judah are definitely historical figures. The Bible, the first books of which are composed of legendary material, becomes more of a historical document as it goes along. Both the Bible and the archaeology make it clear that ancient Israel contained many tribes and clans apart from the Israelites. Groups originating in Mesopotamia, Anatolia, and Egypt made up the population, along with the natives. Apart from the Israelites and their Canaanite cousins, there were the Jebusites and the Hittites and, in the coastal plain, the Philistines and the Phoenicians. King David, if the Bible is to be believed, conquered Jerusalem from the Jebusites and then shared the city with them. He even insisted on paying cash to a Jebusite leader for the threshing floor that eventually became the Temple. He made use of Canaanite officials, had a Hittite general, enjoyed good relations with the Phoenicians, and (after some bloody conflicts with them) deployed Philistine units, the Cherethites and Pelethites, in his army.

During the period of the Second Temple, Judaea (which included much of what had formerly been Israel) also had a mixed population. The Samaritans may have been ethnically similar to the Jews, but the population also included those who had immigrated after the Assyrian conquest of Israel and the exile of much of its population. There were also large numbers of Helenist colonizers, notably in Samaria and in the coastal plain, who arrived continuously from the time of Alexander the Great onward. The Nabataeans inhabited the Negev. The Herodian dynasty, it should be noted, originated in Edom (the Kingdom of Jordan).

One can argue, then, that the establishment of a multicultural nation, rather than a specifically Jewish state, is a true expression of Zionism in that it is reconstructing a model similar to the historical entities of ancient Israel and Judaea. It is, in the memorable phrase of Ronald Storrs, the British governor of Jerusalem, "something stranger than history—the past summoned back and made to live again." Indeed, an examination of modern Zionism can provide justification for such a model. It is true that the founder of modern political Zionism, Theodor Herzl, called his groundbreaking pamphlet *The Jewish State*, but, when he envisages this state in his prophetic novel, *Altneuland*, he describes an entity with a Jewish president and an Arab vice president. Moreover, Herzl has his hero, David Littwak, declare, "We have no state, you see, as Europe had in your time. We are an association of citizens, who are trying to find happiness in work and cultural activities."

Even David Ben-Gurion, the Zionist leader who was Israel's first prime minister, did not envision an entirely Jewish state. When he first heard about the Peel partition plan, which involved a transfer of the Arab population out of the Jewish areas, he wrote in his diary, "This could give us something that we never had, even when we stood on our own during the days of the First and Second Temples . . . an opportunity that we never dared to dream in our wildest imaginings."

It is wrong to depict Ben-Gurion as an advocate of binationalism. He was certainly one of its strongest opponents. He led the drive for a Jewish state, but the passage quoted here does indicate that the idea of a future state that would contain a mixed population was not foreign to his thinking. In this context, it can be pointed out that Kibbutz Meuchad, the largest of the kibbutz movements that laid the foundations for the state of Israel, aspired to create "Jewish communes in the Land of Israel," rather than a sovereign Jewish state. This movement was not prepared to pay the price of abandoning parts of the land in favor of creating a Jewish state with an overwhelming Jewish majority. It is a matter of record that, when the state was established, the kibbutzniks of Kibbutz Meuchad refused to celebrate.

We have already noted that the Nationalist Religious settlers in the West Bank and Gaza have made the achievement of partition almost impossible. Although their project never had the support of the Israeli majority, it was never resolutely opposed by any government. Furthermore, it generated sufficient popular backing to ensure its success. The conclusion must be that Jewish support for partition has been insufficient to guarantee its implementation.

As for the Palestinians, we have seen that, despite their current demand for an independent Palestinian state, they reacted with something approaching panic whenever they got close to achieving it. In 1937, their leader, Haj Amin Husseini, categorically rejected the Peel partition proposals and launched a full-scale revolt against the British Mandate. In 1947, the Palestinian side rejected the UN partition plan and initiated a war against the embryo Jewish state. In 1967, after the Six-Day War when Israel was looking for someone who would take back the territories it had conquered, the Palestinian response was a futile and counterproductive series of terrorist actions. In 1977, when Anwar Sadat implored the Palestinians to join him in his peace initiative, they scornfully turned him down. In 2000 at Camp David, the Palestinian negotiating team failed to come up with a counterproposal to Ehud Barak's unprecedented suggestions for a settlement that offered them an independent state. So, if the Jews have not been sufficiently enthusiastic about an independent state, the Palestinians have been almost pathological in their rejection of one.

It is almost universally acknowledged—not least by the Palestinians themselves—that the Palestinian Authority has been inefficient, corrupt, and largely ineffective. It failed abysmally to transform itself into something that could become an independent state. This was not only because it did not exercise control over the Hamas and the Islamic Jihad but also because it did not manage to build a working model, with an efficient administration. More than one Palestinian is on record in this book as saying that the current Intifada is "as much against the Palestinian Authority as it is against Israel."

Israel's faults are less glaring, and its achievements have been enormous, but many Israelis will admit to a tremendous sense of disappointment with the way their state has turned out. This is not only because of the failure to achieve peace, for which a majority of Israelis blame the other side. The prevalence of public corruption (which has reached the most senior figures in the nation), the decline of the national ethic, the increase in violence and lawlessness, the ubiquitous vulgarity and boorishness, the deterioration of the public services, and the huge growth in inequality are all reasons for profound dissatisfaction. Maybe, after all, Israelis and Palestinians can do better together than they have done apart.

Israel is already in full control of the West Bank and in command of the Gaza strip. This reality should be honestly recognized by Israel's immediate annexation of the West Bank and Gaza. However, the takeover must

be accompanied by a pledge of full equality for all the residents of the en-
larged state. Within three months, democratic elections should be held.
These elections, conducted on the principle of one person, one vote, are
likely to produce a parliament where at least 40 of the 120 members would
be Arabs. This parliament would form a coalition government for the day-
to-day running of the country and establish a number of committees to
work out a constitution for the new nation.

The Jewish settlements could remain where they are for the most part,
but on the basis of strict equality. From now on, they would have propor-
tionately the same land reserves for their expansion and the same per
capita running expenses, development budgets, and water allocations as
the Arab towns and villages. The new government would decide whether
some settlements—notably those in the Gaza strip—should be transferred
to Arab residents, but there would need be no wholesale dismantling of
communities.

One of the first pieces of legislation to be discussed should concern
the Israeli Law of Return and the Palestinian Right of Return. Various
ideas can be suggested, but the simplest and most logical is to abolish both
the law and the right. Those in residence at the time of annexation would
be citizens. Anyone else—Jewish or Arab—who wants to become a citizen of the new state would have to be naturalized in a process similar to
that in any other country.

Both Israelis and Palestinians will be horrified at this suggestion. Israel enacted the Law of Return following the trauma of the Holocaust,
when the mortally endangered Jews had nowhere to go. Today, however,
Jews are not threatened anywhere as Jews. Many populations are in distress, but there is no specific Jewish misfortune. There is no need for the
new state to give a home to Russians who cannot gain entry to Western
Europe or the United States. Nor is there any necessity for admitting obscure African and Asian tribes, whose dubious Jewish roots are constantly
being searched out by eccentric rabbis.

The Palestinians are still full of pain at what they see as the gross injustice of Israel's establishment and the turning of so many of their people into refugees. Nevertheless, they will surely realize that the
admission of hundreds of thousands of former residents is simply not
practical. Self-interest should encourage them to accept a pragmatic solution to the problem of the refugees. This should involve a combination

of repatriation, compensation, and resettlement outside the borders of the new state. Some sort of affirmative action, both for Palestinian refugees and for Jews in danger, could be included in the new legislation.

The name of the new state and its language would have to be rethought. The Palestinians will surely be reluctant to accept "Israel" as the name of the new state or to recognize Hebrew as its official language. Israelis will certainly reject "Palestine." The suggestion of "Canaan" might appeal to some Israelis and Palestinians, but not to the majority. My own proposal is to call the new entity the "state of Jerusalem," *Yerushalayim* in Hebrew, *Ursalim el-Kuds* in Arabic. It is not unprecedented for a nation and its capital to have the same name, and this one should be acceptable to both Israelis and Palestinians. English—the language in which most Israeli–Palestinian dialogues are held—Hebrew, and Arabic can all be official languages.

In the past, a number of proposals have been made for a binational state that would guarantee the rights and identities of the two nations that live in it. These ideas include separate voting rolls for Jews and Arabs, a constitution that guarantees equal rights to the minority, and autonomous regions. There is no need, however, to replace complicated borders with an unworkably complex system of government. The best guarantee possible is that of true democracy. Some Jews may argue in favor of depriving the Arab residents of the right to vote or at least limiting that right in certain ways. It must be firmly stated that a state cannot be partly democratic, anymore than a woman can be partly pregnant. There can be no compromise on this, and it makes sense for the Jews to set the democratic rules from the outset. The idea, put forward by some Israelis, that the Palestinians be given the right to vote in Jordan verges on the grotesque. Would anyone suggest that Mexicans vote for the U.S. Senate or that citizens of the United States help elect Canada's parliament?

While Menahem Froman's "humane state," with two independent entities coexisting inside each other, is impractical, it does point in an interesting direction. The state of Jerusalem would be well advised to work out an innovative structure, with the maximum possible ethnic, historical, religious, cultural, and educational autonomy for its various communities. Apart from the Muslim Arabs and the secular Jews, this autonomy could be granted to communities, such as the ultra-Orthodox Jews with their special requirements. It would also solve the problems of the various Christian communities in the country. These include the Arab Christians, the significant number of Christians who have arrived from the former Soviet Union in the past decade, and the large community of foreign workers who have come in the same period.

If the state of Jerusalem is established, the Palestinians will be required to give up their independent Palestinian state, even before experiencing it. Paradoxically, they might be the first to welcome the proposal, provided it brings them genuine equality. Many Palestinians have told me that they would prefer a single state but accept a two-state solution because that is what the Jews want.

We Israeli Jews will have to relinquish our dream of a Jewish state, only fifty-four years after its coming into being. Many Israelis, and other Jews, will argue that historical justice demands a Jewish state. They will insist that, particularly after centuries of horrendous Jewish suffering culminating in the Holocaust, there should be one place on Earth where the Jews can exercise their natural right to sovereignty. They are absolutely right, but, unfortunately, given the choice between sovereignty and land, we chose land. We have manifestly preferred settlement in the whole Land of Israel to a state of Israel in *part* of the land. It is irrelevant that the settlers are a small minority. The rest of us have permitted them to do what they wanted. Their conviction and determination have overcome our apathy.

Other Israelis will say that they want to live in a Jewish state and have no desire to live in some multiethnic framework. To them, I say that the state of Jerusalem can fulfill all the aspirations of Jewish history, religion, and culture. The Jews will be able to observe their national and religious festivals in their ancient homeland. The Israelis will be able to continue to create their unique Hebrew culture, including literature, theater, and music. The ultra-Orthodox will continue to obey the *mitzvot* (religious commandments) in freedom.

The advantage of the state of Jerusalem for the Palestinians is that they gain immediate access to a relatively modern, free, democratic state. The advantage for the Israelis is that, as the current majority, they get to set the rules. Many Jews are currently in a panic about the so-called demographic threat. They are concerned that the faster Arab birthrate will make them a minority, even in today's state of Israel. The prospect of becoming a minority in the proposed state of Jerusalem, which would include the West Bank and Gaza, is certainly greater.

If we Israeli Jews use our initial majority to run the new state of Jerusalem solely for our own benefit, we will deservedly lose out, if the Arabs eventually become a majority. On the other hand, if we conduct ourselves in a wise manner, there is no reason for concern. The Israeli Council for Demography has estimated that within eighteen years an Arab majority will exist between the Mediterranean and the Jordan River. The response of the council is to propose all sorts of schemes for "increasing Jewish fertility." Even if the various programs worked, the effect would be to start a grotesque competition between Jewish and Arab wombs, resulting in the overpopulation of our tiny country. The proper answer to the "demographic threat" is to prevent it from becoming a threat: Democracy is the answer—not an increased birthrate. If the council's estimate is correct, the current Jewish majority has almost two decades to establish a free, fair, just, and democratic state.

In its early years, the new state will be dominated by the Israeli Jews. We will form a majority of its parliament, run its government, lead its army, head its judiciary, and administer its educational system. The Palestinians should not be too apprehensive about this. We may not have behaved perfectly toward our Israeli Arab citizens, but we certainly relate to them better than we relate to the other Palestinians. Since the outbreak of the Intifada, we have reacted with equanimity to the more than two thousand Palestinian deaths—largely because of our own seven hundred fatalities. On the other hand, we have taken the shooting of thirteen Arabs in Israel very seriously indeed, establishing a three-man State Commission of Inquiry, including an Arab judge, which has conducted itself with manifest fairness and transparency.

If the presence of forty to fifty Arab members in the new parliament forces us to take even more notice of our Arab citizens, so much the better. The democratic system works by means of pressure groups and self-interest. In the state of Jerusalem, the social and economic status of the Israeli Arabs and the West Bank and Gaza Palestinians will be guaranteed by the reality of Arab political power. This will ensure that they receive adequate budgets and a fair allocation of available resources.

In any case, there is absolutely no certainty that the Arabs will become a majority. Higher living standards and better education bring the birthrate down. The Israeli Arab birthrate has already declined, and the Christians among them have an even lower rate of natural increase. Against this, some Jewish communities—the ultra-Orthodox and the National Religious—have maintained high rates of birth. If the new state of Jerusalem prospers, which it should, and invests a large proportion of its resources in education, which it must, there is every chance that the Arabs will remain a minority. The other possibilities are that there will be equality or a small Arab majority.

Abrogation of the Law of Return and the Right of Return, coupled with the fair and full application of democratic rules, should ensure a secure and safe life for all of us. If we, the Jews, the current majority, play the game fairly, we have no reason to fear the emergence of a vast Arab majority, composed of fanatical Muslims, who will murder us, expel us, or even discriminate against us. Zionism was supposed to abolish the cringing, frightened, impotent Jew. In a large measure it has done so in the state of Israel, but traces of the ghetto unhappily remain.

"It is easier to take the Jews out of the *galut* [the diaspora]," observed David Ben-Gurion, "than it is to take the galut out of the Jews."

The panic about the demographic threat is indeed a remnant of the galut and the ghetto. It is unworthy of the new Jews of Israel. Rather, we should adopt the motto of Franklin D. Roosevelt, when he quoted to Americans in the dark days of the Depression the words of naturalist Henry David Thoreau: "There is nothing to fear but fear itself."

This is not to disregard the fear—or the hatred and distrust. Recent events have taken their toll and increased the bitter resentment on both sides. It is enormously difficult to envisage a united nation after what has happened since the fall of 2000. Nevertheless, there is no alternative to coexisting somehow in this small land, and *any* model is going to be very difficult to implement after the latest confrontation. All possible solutions—except the obscene concept of transfer or the pathetic delusion of the fence—will involve interaction between Israelis and Palestinians. The mutual fear and hatred cannot be denied, but the despair and nihilism that have gripped so many Israelis and Palestinians are self-indulgent and futile.

Despite the deep distrust, a large reservoir of goodwill still exists. In the recent past, Jews and Arabs lived together amicably in Jerusalem and other locations. The relationship between Israelis and Palestinians has not been exclusively one of conflict and confrontation. Businessmen and scientists, doctors and nurses, teachers and researchers have all cooperated to their mutual benefit. Even Israeli and Palestinian criminals have often contrived to collaborate.

In chapter 5, we saw how Bethlehem's Nassar company cooperates with its Israeli counterparts, and that is only one example. Many other areas of business cooperation are possible. Despite the bursting of the high-tech bubble, there is still plenty of scope for the development of science-based industries. The Israelis have earned a justifiably good reputation for inventiveness and ingenuity, and, before the recent destruction in the West Bank, the Palestinians produced most of the world's Arabic computer software. Prospects for joint projects in this field are almost unlimited.

Although it is the bombs and bullets that capture the headlines, numerous examples exist of friendly cooperation between Israelis and Palestinians. When gangs of Jewish settlers on the West Bank started stealing the olive crops of their Palestinian neighbors, dozens of Israelis crossed through the IDF roadblocks to help the Palestinians pick their own olives and to interpose themselves between the villagers and the settlers, who were harassing them. Among the groups sponsoring such activities were the Rabbis for Human Rights, Peace Now, the Taayush Group, and other coexistence movements. Israeli participants reported a warm welcome on the Palestinian side.

Israeli groups have organized vigils at the army roadblocks, in an attempt to ensure decent conduct by the soldiers on guard there. Others have been organizing parcels of food and clothing for the Palestinians in their present dire straits. Israeli human rights groups such as the Association for Civil Rights in Israel, Moked for the Defense of the Individual, and Betzelem have been assisting Palestinians for years. The mutual blood donations of the Israeli and Palestinian Parents' Circle and Families' Forum have been reported in chapter 5.

Numerous joint Israeli–Palestinian organizations continue to operate even in the current situation, albeit on a reduced scale. The Israel–Palestine Center for Research and Information (IPCRI) continues with many of its activities, notably in the field of environmental protection, which is in the interests of both peoples. When it cannot meet in Israel or the territories, it holds its conferences in nearby Cyprus, Turkey, and Greece. *Palestine-*

Israel Journal, a quarterly with Israeli and Palestinian editors and equal numbers of Israelis and Palestinians on the editorial board, continues to be published in East Jerusalem, despite the difficulties that its Palestinian participants encounter when trying to enter the city.

Of particular significance are the various youth projects, such as Seeds for Peace, which takes Israeli, Palestinian, and Jordanian teenagers to the Maine countryside in the United States for joint camps, where lasting friendships are forged. *Crossing Borders* is a bimonthly regional youth newspaper, published in English in Jerusalem for Israeli, Palestinian, and Jordanian readers of high school age. It has Israeli, Palestinian, and Jordanian editors.

Windows, a magazine for junior high school readers, is published in Tel Aviv in Hebrew and Arabic. Since the Intifada, much of the consultation between its young Israeli and Palestinian editors and writers has been conducted via phone, fax, and e-mail, but sometimes they manage to get together physically. Recently, after continuous applications to the IDF, a "day of fun" was set up in the Israeli–Arab village of Kalanswa, just across from the Palestinian town of Tulkarm. The communication between the Israelis and their Palestinian counterparts at *Windows* is facilitated by Israeli Arab children, who translate from Arabic to Hebrew and vice versa. The exchanges are frank and open, with no holds barred.

In Israel, despite the bad feelings of the Arab citizens, particularly after the events in the fall of 2000, a large amount of coexistence prevails. The Olive Branch Festival "promotes coexistence in Galilee through a celebration of music, art, food and ecology" in Jewish, Arab, and Druze towns and villages. Jews and Arabs live side by side in Haifa, Lod, Ramla, and Jaffa. The experimental Jewish–Arab village of Neve Shalom continues to provide an example of cooperation and mutual respect. The Israel Tennis Center has just opened a branch in the Israeli Arab town of Jizr el-Zarka, and Jewish and Arab children play tennis together there, as well as in Haifa, Furdeis, Caesaria, and many other locations.

We Israelis and Palestinians are much more similar to each other than many of us would like to admit. The Palestinians often describe themselves as "the Jews of the Arab world." We are not identical twins, but we *are* twins, born of the same parents, sharing similar beliefs and traditions, fated to live in the same country. The time has come to translate this resemblance into a new political reality. In 1984, I wrote in *Israel after Begin:*

> The initial moves toward reconciliation with our neighbors will lead to the establishment of a Palestinian state, but withdrawal from the West Bank and Gaza does not mean cutting ourselves off from them. Having agreed on our boundaries, we will strive to make them irrelevant. Israelis and Palestinians will live, trade, and work in each others' countries.

Now, twenty years later, we have the choice of sinking back self-indulgently into our despair or opting for radical action. I am proposing to leapfrog over the interim period. I am stating that the borders are *already* irrelevant. I am suggesting that Israel and the Palestinian territories can be merged into a dynamic, multiethnic, culturally rich nation, with new forms of coexistence between its different constituents. It's not going to be easy, but that is not a reason for desisting. The establishment of the state of Israel, despite all the obstacles, was a miracle. The survival of the Palestinian dream over the past five decades has been remarkable. Let us now embark on another daring project. Both of us, Israelis and Palestinians, must repudiate our phobias and prejudices and make a quantum jump—a leap into a different dimension—vaulting beyond despair to a new time of hope. The state of Jerusalem is surely the best solution that we can manage right now, and it could turn out to be a fascinating and exciting adventure.

GLOSSARY

Al-Haq (Arabic)	The Law; a Palestinian human rights group
Aliya Bet (Hebrew)	Illegal immigration of Jews to Palestine during the British Mandate
beit midrash (Hebrew)	Jewish house of religious study
Bey (Arabic)	Ottoman title of honor
din rodef (Hebrew)	Excommunication verdict (strong Jewish religious denunciation—a virtual death sentence)
Druze, sing. and pl. (Arabic)	Minority Muslim community, living in the hill regions of Israel, Syria, and Lebanon. Israeli Druze serve in the IDF.
Fatah (Arabic)	Largest Palestinian military group
galut (Hebrew)	Jewish exile from the Land of Israel
ghaffir (Arabic)	Jewish police officer of the British Mandate period
Gush Emunim (Hebrew)	Movement of Believers; a Nationalist Religious movement, promoting Jewish settlement in the West Bank and Gaza
Haaretz (Hebrew)	*The Land*, Israel's most prestigious daily newspaper
Hagana (Hebrew)	Jewish self-defense force
haj (Arabic)	Pilgrimage to Mecca (after completing the pilgrimage, the pilgrim may place *Haj* before his name, as in Haj Amin Husseini)
Hamas (Arabic)	Militant Palestinian Islamic movement
Haram al-Sharif (Arabic)	Muslim holy sanctuary on Jerusalem's Temple Mount

"Hatikva" (Hebrew)	The Hope; Zionist anthem that became the Israeli national anthem
Hizbolla (Arabic)	Militant Lebanese Islamic movement
hudna (Arabic)	Truce
IDF	Israel Defense Forces (Israeli army)
Intifada (Arabic)	Palestinian uprising
Irgun Zvai Leumi (Hebrew)	Jewish military group (breakaway from the Hagana)
Isfalur	Confederation of Israel, Palestine, and Jordan (envisioned by Israeli peace campaigner Lova Eliav)
Islamic Jihad (Arabic)	Small militant Palestinian Islamic movement
kavass (Arabic)	Major-domo of the Ottoman and British periods
keffiye (Arabic)	Arab headscarf
kibbutz, pl. kibbutzim (Hebrew)	Jewish communal village
kibbutznik (Hebrew)	Kibbutz member
Knesset (Hebrew)	Israel's parliament
la-onf (Arabic)	Nonviolence
Midrash (Hebrew)	Collection of sermons
Milhemet Hashihrur (Hebrew)	1948 War of Liberation (or War of Independence in English)
moshav, pl. moshavim (Hebrew)	Jewish cooperative village
Mukkata (Arabic)	The Palestinian government offices in Ramalla
Nahal (Hebrew)	Kibbutz-affiliated unit of the IDF
nakba (Arabic)	Disaster (Arabic term for the war of 1948)
Netivot Shalom (Hebrew)	Paths of Peace; Israeli religious peace movement
Noar Oved (Hebrew)	Israeli youth movement
Pikuah nefesh (Hebrew)	Sanctity of life
PLO	Palestine Liberation Organization (includes Fatah and other groups)

pogrom	Deliberate murder, attacks, looting, and destruction directed toward helpless people; specifically used to describe an attack on Jews
Ramadan (Arabic)	The ninth month of the Islamic calendar, when Muslims fast between dawn and dusk
samid (Arabic)	Steadfast person
Sephardi (Hebrew)	Jew from North Africa or the Middle East
shaheed (Arabic)	Muslim martyr (applied by many Palestinians to suicide bombers)
Shin Bet (Hebrew)	Israel's internal security service
shiva (Hebrew)	Jewish seven-day period of mourning
Taayush (Hebrew)	Jewish–Arab coexistence movement
Talmud (Hebrew)	Rabbinical commentary on the Bible
Tanzim (Arabic)	Palestinian fighting units (members of Fatah)
tarboosh (Arabic)	Cylindrical crimson hat (associated with Ottoman Empire officials, also called a fez)
Torah (Hebrew)	The first five books of the Bible; the Old Testament
tzinok (Hebrew)	Tiny prison cell, for solitary confinement
waqf (Arabic)	Muslim charitable foundation
Yediot Aharonot (Hebrew)	*Latest News*, Israel's largest daily newspaper
yeshiva (Hebrew)	Jewish religious seminary
Yeshivat Hesder	(Hebrew) Religious seminary, integrating service in the IDF
Yom Kippur	(Hebrew) Jewish Day of Atonement
Zionism	Jewish movement, dating from the nineteenth century, for national renewal through return to the Land of Israel and the establishment of a Jewish state

SELECTED BIBLIOGRAPHY

Books

Armstrong, Karen. *Islam: A Short History*. London: Weidenfeld & Nicholson, 2000.

Ben-Gurion, David. *My Talks with Arab Leaders*. Jerusalem: Keter, 1973.

Bergman, Ronen. *Authority Given* (in Hebrew). Tel Aviv: Miskal, 2002.

Bethel, Nicholas. *The Palestine Triangle*. London: Andre Deutsch, 1979.

Carey, Roane, ed. *The New Intifada*. London: Verso, 2001.

Carter, Jimmy. *The Blood of Abraham*. Boston: Houghton Mifflin, 1985.

Collins, Larry, and Dominique Lapierre. *O, Jerusalem!* London: History Book Club, 1972.

Crossman, Richard. *A Nation Reborn*. London: Hamish Hamilton, 1960.

Crum, Bartley C. *Behind the Silken Curtain*. New York: Simon & Shuster, 1947.

Eliav, Arie Lova. *Land of the Hart*. Philadelphia: Jewish Publication Society of America, 1976.

———. *The Voyage of the Ulua*. New York: Funk & Wagnalls, 1969.

Elon, Amos. *The Israelis*. New York: Holt, Rinehart & Winston, 1971.

Frankenthal, Yitzhak. *The Peace Process—Guide to the Perplexed*. Tel Aviv: Parents' Circle, 2001.

Grose, Peter. *Israel in the Mind of America*. New York: Knopf, 1984.

Herzog, Chaim. *The Arab-Israeli Wars*. New York: Random House, 1982.

Hirst, David. *The Gun and the Olive Branch*. London: Faber & Faber, 1977.

Huleileh, Samir, with Simcha Bahiri and Daniel Gavron. *Peace Pays*. Jerusalem: Israel/Palestine Center for Research and Information, 1993.

Israeli, Raphael. *PLO in Lebanon*. London: Weidenfeld & Nicholson, 1983.

Kashu, Sayed. *Arabs Dancing* (in Hebrew). Tel Aviv: Modan, 2002.

Morris, Benny. *Righteous Victims*. New York: Knopf, 1999.

Nashashibi, Nasser Eddin. *Jerusalem's Other Voice*. Exeter: Ithaca, 1990.

Said, Edward. *The Question of Palestine*. New York: Random House, 1980.

Schiff, Zeev, and Ehud Yaari. *Intifada*. New York: Simon & Shuster, 1990.

Segal, Haggai. *Dear Brothers*. New York, Beit Shamai, 1988.

Segev, Tom, *Elvis in Jerusalem*. New York: Holt, 2001.

Shehada, Raja. *Strangers in the House*. South Royalton, Vt.: Steerforth, 2002.
Shepherd, Naomi. *The Zealous Intruders*. London: Collins, 1987.
Shlaim, Avi. *Collusion across the Jordan*. Oxford: Clarendon, 1988.
Solomon, Zehava. *Combat Stress Reaction*. New York: Plenum, 1993.
Storrs, Ronald. *Orientations*. London: Nicholson & Watson, 1939.
Vester, Bertha Spafford. *Our Jerusalem*. Jerusalem: Ariel, 1988.
Wallace, John, and Janet Wallace. *Still Small Voices*. New York: Harcourt Brace Jovanovich, 1989.

Newspapers, Journals, and Websites

Bitterlemons.org
Challenge, Tel Aviv
Haaretz (Hebrew and English), Tel Aviv
International Herald Tribune
Kol Ha'ir (Hebrew), Jerusalem
openDemocracy.net
Palestine-Israel Journal, Jerusalem
Windows (Hebrew and Arabic), Tel Aviv
Yediot Aharonot (Hebrew), Tel Aviv

INDEX

ABOUT THE AUTHOR

Daniel Gavron was born in London in 1935 and immigrated to Israel in 1961, living in a kibbutz, a moshav, and the desert town of Arad before moving to the Jerusalem area in 1971. He worked as a reporter for Israel Radio and became the head of English News. He subsequently joined the *Jerusalem Post* as a feature writer.

Gavron has written pieces for the *New York Times*, the *Wall Street Journal*, *Commentary*, *National Jewish Monthly*, and *Ariel*. His broadcasts have been heard on the British Broadcasting Corporation, the Canadian Broadcasting Corporation, National Public Radio, Radio Telefis Eirrean, and others.

A member of the team that founded *Palestine-Israel Journal*, Gavron is also the author of several books.

The father of three grown children, he currently lives near Jerusalem with his wife of forty-six years and his dog.